English Result

Elementary   Student's Book

Mark Hancock & Annie McDonald

OXFORD
UNIVERSITY PRESS

2   **Contents**

4 **Contents**

Say hello!

2 How are you? ☐ I'm fine, thanks. ☐ Sorry? ☐ Good morning. ☐ Good afternoon.
☐ Nice to meet you. ☐ What's your name? ☐ My name's Bill. ☐ See you later!

1

2

3

4

5

6

7

8

9

Jim and Satomi

Day one

Jim Hi, my name's Jim. What's your name?
Satomi Hello, Jim. I'm Satomi.
J Sorry?
S Sa-to-mi. Satomi.
J Oh, OK. Nice to meet you, Satomi.
S Nice to meet you!

Day two

S Good morning, Jim. How are you?
J I'm fine thanks, Satomi. And you?
S I'm fine. See you later.
J See you later. Bye!

Day three

J Good morning, Satomi.
S Good afternoon, Jim!
J What? Oh yes, it's afternoon. Oops!

How to **say hello**

v greeting phrases **P** rhythm and stress

A Vocabulary greeting phrases

1 Look at **Say hello!** opposite. Work with a partner. Match the phrases with pictures 1–9.
Example How are you? = 2

2 **1A.1▶** Listen and repeat.

3 Work with a partner. Make conversations with phrases from **Say hello!**.
Examples A Good morning.
  B Good morning.
  A How are you?
  B I'm fine, thanks.

B Have conversations

4 Complete the conversations with words / phrases from **Say hello!**.

Day one
J Hi, my name's Jim.
  ¹ *What's your name?*
S Hello, Jim. I'm Satomi.
J ² _____?
S Sa-to-mi. Satomi.
J Oh, OK. Nice to meet you, Satomi.
S ³ _____ you!

Jim

Satomi

Day two
S Good morning, Jim.
  ⁴ _____?
J I'm ⁵ _____,
  Satomi. And you?
S I'm fine. ⁶ _____.
J See you later. Bye!

Day three
J ⁷ _____, Satomi.
S Good afternoon, Jim!
J What? Oh yes, it's ⁸ _____. Oops!

5 Now use **Jim and Satomi** opposite to help you.

6 **1A.2▶** Listen and check. Now check with the audio script on ≫ p.150.

7 Say the conversations with a partner.

8 Say the conversations with another partner. Use your real name!

C Pronunciation rhythm and stress

9 **1A.3▶** Wayne or Jane? Sue or Lou? Listen and <u>underline</u> the names you hear.

A Hi, hello. What's your name?

B Hi, hello. My name's Wayne / Jane.

A Nice to meet you. My name's Lou / Sue.

B Hello Sue / Lou. Nice to meet you!

B Morning, good morning! Hello again Lou / Sue.

A Morning, good morning! Hi, how are you?

B Fine thanks! Fine thanks! Fine, and you?

A Fine thanks! Fine thanks! I'm fine too.

10 Listen again and repeat.

11 Say the conversations with a partner.

12 Say it again. Half the class is A and half is B.

ABC Put it all together

13 Read **Jim and Satomi** again. Write two similar conversations with a partner. Practise saying them. Then try to say them without reading!
Example A Hello, my name's Sonia.
  B Hi. I'm Alex …

14 Have conversations with other students in your class. Write their names.

I can say hello.
I can ask people's names.
Tick ✓ the lines. with a lot of help   with some help   on my own   very easily

7

Walk & talk!

Contacts

Name:	Jacky Smith
Telephone:	082 929 8039
Mobile:	607 483 6652
Email:	smithj@coolmail.com
Website:	www.jaysmith.uk

options — Exit

Blue Phone™

Numbers 1–20

1 = one
2 = two
3 = three
4 = four
5 = five
6 = six
7 = seven
8 = eight
9 = nine
10 = ten
11 = eleven
12 = twelve
13 = thirteen
14 = fourteen
15 = fifteen
16 = sixteen
17 = seventeen
18 = eighteen
19 = nineteen
20 = twenty
0 = oh
@ = at
. = dot
/ = slash

How to say phone numbers & email addresses

G possessives *my, your, his, her*   **V** letters and numbers   **P** letters and numbers

A Vocabulary letters and numbers

1 Work with a partner. Count in English.
Example   One, two, three ...

2 Match the words with the numbers.

☐ two	☐ four	☐ eight	1	2	3
☐ six	☑ one	☐ three	4	5	6
☐ nine	☐ seven	☐ five	7	8	9

3 **1B.1▶** Listen and repeat the numbers.

4 **1B.2▶** Look at the mobile phone opposite. Listen and repeat.

5 **1B.3▶** Listen and say the next letter.
Example   **Audio** A, B ...   **You** C!

6 Test a partner.
Example   **A** M, N ...   **B** O!

7 **1B.4▶** Look at **Numbers 1–20** opposite. Listen and repeat the numbers from 10 to 20.

8 Continue the lists. Say the next three numbers.
1 two, four, six, eight, ...
2 three, six, nine, ...
3 four, eight, ...
4 twenty, nineteen, eighteen, ...
5 eighteen, sixteen, fourteen, ...

B Pronunciation letters and numbers

9 **1B.5▶** Look at the table below. Listen and say *dot, slash,* or *at.*
Example   **Audio** H ...   **You** Slash!

.	J	M	K	E	P	D	R	C
/	H	G	N	Q	A	B	T	U
@	8	L	X	I	V	3	O	2

10 Test a partner.
Example   **A** M ...   **B** Dot!

C Listen for phone numbers and email addresses

11 **1B.6▶** Listen. Correct the information on the screen of the mobile phone opposite.

12 Read the audio script on >> p.150 and check your answers.

13 **1B.7▶** Listen and say *phone number, email,* or *website.*
Example   **Audio** minerva@teleten.com
   You Email!

D Grammar possessives *my, your, his, her*

14 Write these words in the conversations.
her   his   ~~my~~   your
1 **A** What's your name?
  B *My* name's Jacky.
2 **A** What's Jacky's phone number?
  B *Her* phone number is 925 8049.
3 **A** What's Jim's email address?
  B *His* email address is jim@teleline.uk.
4 **A** What's *your* phone number?
  B My phone number is 91 456 2110.

15 Ask your partner's phone number and email address.

What's	your	name?
		phone number?
		email address?

16 Work with a partner.
Student A Look at **Names and numbers** on >> p.128.
Student B Look at **Names and numbers** on >> p.132.

Ask questions and complete the information. Check the spelling!
Example   **A** Number 2. What's his name?
   B Craig.
   A How do you spell it?
   B C-R-A-I-G.

More practice? **Grammar Bank** >> p.136.

ABCD Put it all together

17 Make a phone book. Ask five other students in the class for their names, phone numbers, and email addresses.
Example   **A** What's your name?
   B Pablo.
   A What's your phone number?

18 Ask your partner about people in your class.
Example   **A** What's his name?
   B Pablo.
   A What's his ... ?

I can say phone numbers and email addresses. ▓▓▓▓▓▓▓

Tick ✓ the line.   with a lot of help   with some help   on my own   very easily

Address puzzle

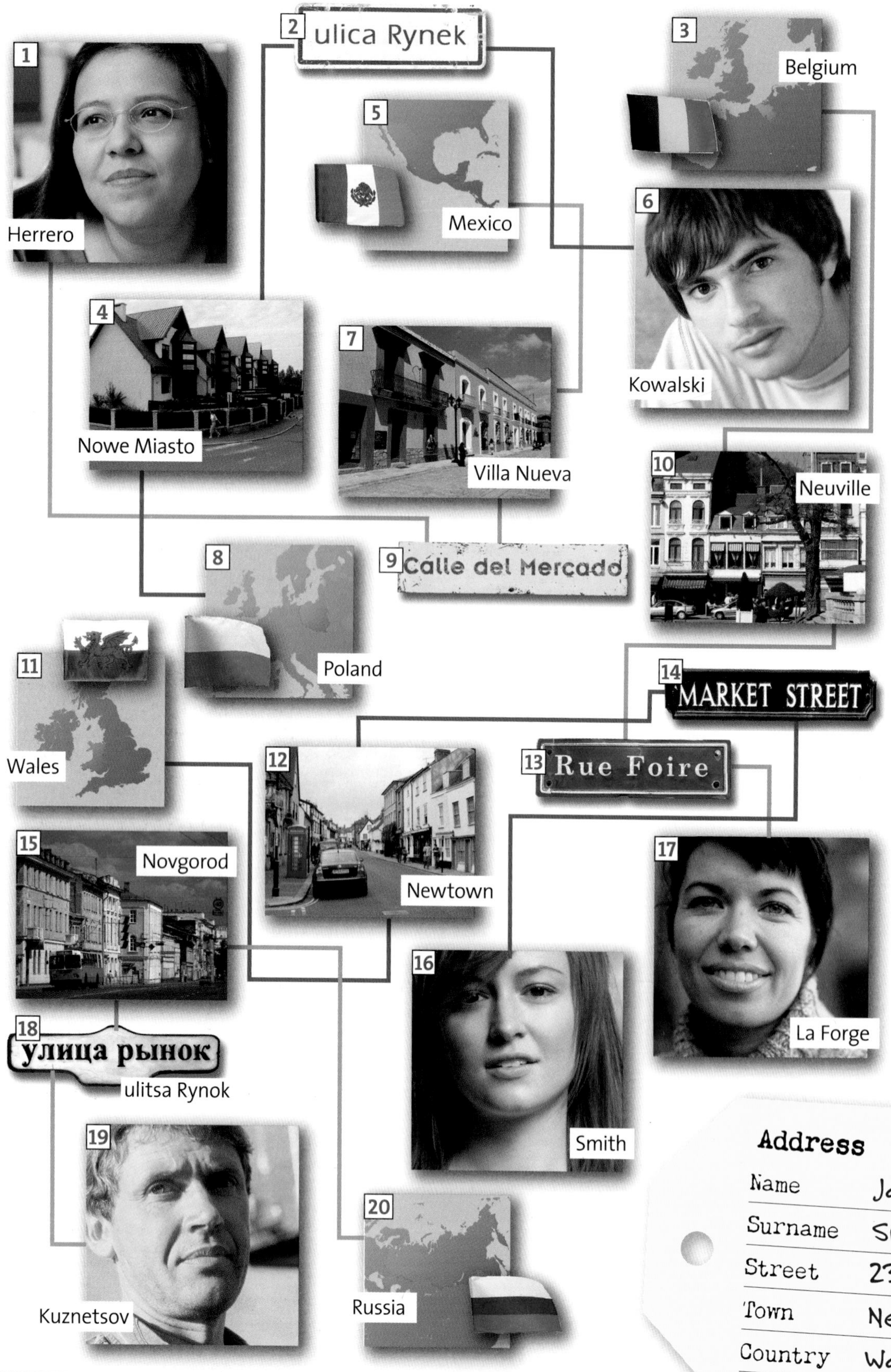

**Numbers
20 +**

21 twenty-one
22 twenty-two
23 twenty-three
30 thirty
40 forty
50 fifty
60 sixty
70 seventy
80 eighty
90 ninety
100 a hundred
101 a hundred
and one

1 Herrero

2 ulica Rynek

3 Belgium

5 Mexico

6 Kowalski

4 Nowe Miasto

7 Villa Nueva

10 Neuville

8 Poland

9 Calle del Mercado

11 Wales

14 MARKET STREET

13 Rue Foire

12 Newtown

15 Novgorod

17 La Forge

16 Smith

18 улица рынок
ulitsa Rynok

19 Kuznetsov

20 Russia

Address

Name	Jacky
Surname	Smith
Street	23 Market Street
Town	Newtown
Country	Wales

How to give your name and address

G pronouns and possessives; present simple of *be* ⊞ V parts of an address; numbers 20+ P stress in questions

A Vocabulary parts of an address; numbers 20+

1 Look at the **Address puzzle** opposite. Find:
1 five surnames *1, 6, 16, 17, 19*
2 five countries
3 five street names
4 five towns

2 Complete the table with a partner.

first name	surname	country	street	town
Jacky	Smith	Wales	Market Street	Newtown
Jan	Kowalski	Poland	Nowe Miasto	
Ivan	Kuznetsov	Russia	ulitsa Rynok	Novgorod
Juanita	Herrero	Mexico	Villa Vieja	Villa Nueva
Jeanette	La Forge	Belgium	Rue Foire	Neuville

3 **1C.1▶** Listen and check.

4 Write the words and numbers.
twenty-two *22*
thirty-three ___
forty-four ___
fifty-five ___
_____-six 66
_____-seven 77
_____-eight 88
_____-nine 99
a hundred and ten ___

5 **1C.2▶** Listen and repeat.

B Pronunciation stress in questions

6 **1C.3▶** Listen and repeat the questions.
Example **first** name ...
your **first** name ...
What's your **first** name?

7 Work with a partner. Write the questions.
A *Where are you from?*
B Wales.
A _____?
B 23 Market Street, Newtown.
A _____?
B Jacky.
A _____?
B Smith.

8 Read the audio script on ≫ p.150 and check your answers.

9 Say the conversation in exercise 7 with a partner.

10 Ask and answer with three other students. Give true answers.
Example A Where are you from?
B Italy.

C Grammar pronouns and possessives; present simple of *be* ⊞

11 Read the grammar box and complete the sentences.

pronouns	I	you	he	she	we	they
possessives	my	your	his	her	our	their

1 I'm from Wales. *My* name's Jacky.
2 They're from France. _____ names are Jean and Yves.
3 ____'m from Belgium. My name's Jeanette.
4 ____'s from Mexico. _____ name's Juanita.
5 A Where are _____ from? B I'm from Mexico.
6 A What's _____ surname? B Gonzalez.
7 ____'re from Europe. Our names are Jan and Jacky.
8 ____'s from Poland. _____ name's Jan.
9 We're from Spain. _____ names are Isabel and Juan.
10 ____'re from Turkey. Their names are Bülent and Nur.

12 Complete the grammar box.

I'm / am	you / we / they 're / are	she / he / it 's / is
I'___ from Wales.	You'___ from Belgium.	She'___ from Mexico.
	They'___ from France.	He'___ from Russia.
	We'___ from Europe.	My address ___ 23 Market Street.

13 Complete the text.
[1] I'*m* Juanita. [2] I___ a student of English. [3] I___ from Mexico. The other students in my class [4] ___ all from Europe. [5] They___ from Russia, Poland, and Belgium. My partner in the class [6] ___ Jan. His [7] surname___ Kowalski. [8] He___ from Poland. Our [9] teacher___ Jacky. [10] She___ from Wales.

14 Write a similar text about your class. Read it to your partner.
More practice? **Grammar Bank** ≫ p.136.

ABC Put it all together

15 Work with one or two partners. Look at **Smith and Jones** on ≫ p.126. Take turns to be student A.

Student A You are one of the people in the photos. You choose.

Students B and C Ask these questions. Guess Student A's first name.
What's your address?
What's your phone number?
What's your surname?
Where are you from?

Example A Where are you from?
B Scotland.
A What's your phone number?
B 995 5599.
A I know! You're Liz Jones!

I can give my name and address.

Tick ✓ the line. with a lot of help with some help on my own very easily

On the bus

Jeff Excuse me, are you a medical student?

Anita Yes, I am.

J Yeah, me too. What's your name?

A Anita. And you?

J I'm Jeff. Where are you from?

A I'm from London, but my mum and dad aren't British. They're from China. Are you from London?

J No, I'm not. I'm from Nottingham. My mum's English but my dad isn't. He's from Trinidad.

A Oh really?

J Yeah. Oh, this is my stop. OK, bye. Nice to meet you ... Sorry, what's your name again?

A Anita.

J Nice to meet you, Anita.

A Bye Jeff. See you!

In the street

Natalia Excuse me! Are you Eddy Martínez?

Eddy Yes, that's right.

N How do you do, Mr Martínez? I love your books.

E Oh really? Thank you. Erm ... What's your name?

N Natalia Dubois.

E Nice to meet you, Miss Dubois – or is it Mrs Dubois? Or Ms Dubois?

N Please just call me Natalia!

E OK. Where are you from Natalia? You aren't French ...

N No. I'm from Australia, but my father's Belgian.

E Really? Are you here on holiday?

N No, I'm not. I'm here for work. I'm a teacher.

E Oh, here's my taxi. Sorry, I'm late for a meeting ...

N No problem. Goodbye, Mr Martínez.

E Bye. Nice to meet you!

How to start a conversation

G present simple of be ⊞⊟? **v** *Mr, Mrs, Ms, Miss*; polite words and phrases

A Listen for information

1 **1D.1▶** Look at **On the bus** opposite but cover the text. Listen and tick ✓ the names, places, and nationalities that you hear.

Anita ✓ Jackie ☐ Jeff ☐ John ☐
London ☐ Paris ☐ China ☐ Japan ☐
British ☐ English ☐ German ☐

2 Read the **On the bus** text and check your answers.

3 **1D.2▶** Look at **In the street** opposite but cover the text. Listen and underline the correct information about Natalia Dubois.
   1 She's from Austria / Australia.
   2 Her father's Belgian / British.
   3 She's a writer / teacher.

4 Read the **In the street** text and check your answers.

5 Match the sentences with the names.

Anita Jeff Natalia Eddy

   1 She isn't a student. *Natalia*
   2 He isn't a student.
   3 They aren't in the street.
   4 She isn't from London.
   5 Her mum and dad aren't from China.
   6 They aren't on the bus.

B Grammar present simple of *be* ⊞⊟?

6 Complete the grammar box.

+	–	?
I'm from London. He ____ from Trinidad. She's single. We'____ late. You're a student. They'____ on a bus.	I'm not from China. He isn't from Britain. She ____ married. We aren't late. You ____ a student. They aren't in the street.	Are you from London? Is he from Britain? ____ she married? Are we late? ____ you a student? ____ they on a bus?
short answers	Yes, I am. Yes, he / she / it is. Yes, you / we / they are.	No, I'm not. No, he / she / it isn't. No, you / we / they aren't.

7 Underline examples of ⊟ and ? verbs in the **On the bus** and **In the street** texts opposite.

8 Complete the questions and write true answers.
   1 *Are* ____ you a teacher? *No, I'm not. I'm a student.*
   2 ____ you from London?
   3 ____ your mum from China?
   4 ____ your teacher British?
   5 ____ your surname Martínez?
   6 ____ you married?

9 Ask your partner questions from this box.

Are	you	French / Spanish / married ... ?
Is	your friend	from Belgium / London ...?
	your mum	a teacher / student ...?
	Jeff	
	Anita	
	other	

Example **A** Is your mum a teacher?
          B No, she isn't. She's a writer.

More practice? **Grammar Bank** >> p.136.

C Vocabulary *Mr, Mrs, Ms, Miss*; polite words and phrases

10 Underline the correct words in the rules.
   1 Use *Mr* /ˈmɪstə/ before a man's first name / surname.
   2 Use *Mrs* /ˈmɪsɪz/ or *Ms* /məz/ before a single / married woman's first name / surname.
   3 Use *Miss* /mɪs/ or *Ms* before a single / married woman's first name / surname.

11 Complete the sentences with one of these polite words and phrases.

Please Thank you Excuse me Sorry

   1 _____, are you Dan Brown?
   2 **A** I love your books. **B** Oh really? _____.
   3 _____ just call me Dan.
   4 _____, what's your name again?

12 **1D.3▶** Listen and repeat phrases from **On the bus** and **In the street**. Copy the pronunciation.

13 Say this conversation with a partner, but make it polite. Use the words from exercises 10 and 11.
   A Brad Pitt?
   B Yes.
   A Hello, Pitt. I love your films.
   B Oh. What's your name?
   A Jackie Smith.
   B Nice to meet you, Smith.
   A Call me Jackie.
   B I'm late for a meeting. Bye.

   Example **A** Excuse me! Are you Brad Pitt?

ABC Put it all together

14 Look at the photos on >> p.126. Work with a partner. Choose one of the situations and write a conversation similar to **On the bus** or **In the street**.
   Example **A** Excuse me, are you ... ? **B** Yes, I am ...

15 Practise saying your conversation.

16 Close your book. Act your conversation for another pair. Listen to the other conversation and guess which photo.

I can start a conversation.

Tick ✓ the lines.   with a lot of help   with some help   on my own   very easily

Writing Personal information

A Read and give information

1 Complete the questions with these words.

Are   How   What's   Where

1 _What's_ your name?
2 _____ are you from?
3 _____ you married?
4 _____ your phone number?
5 _____ your passport number?
6 _____ your address?
7 _____ old are you?
8 _____ your email address?

2 Match the questions in exercise 1 with words on the form.

Application Form

1 **Full name**	
☐ **Age**	
☐ **Marital status**	
☐ **Country of origin**	
☐ **Home address**	
☐ **Telephone**	
☐ **Email**	
☐ **Passport number**	

3 Read the conversation and fill in the first four answers on the form in exercise 2.

A Full name?
B Satomi Sakamoto.
A How do you spell that, please?
B S-A-T-O-M-I S-A-K-A-M-O-T-O.
A Age?
B Can you repeat that, please?
A Age. How old are you?
B Oh. I'm 22.
A Marital status?
B Sorry, I don't understand.
A Are you married or single?
B Oh. I'm single.
A Country of origin?
B Japan.

4 **1E.1▶** Listen and fill in the other answers on the form.

B Ask for language help

5 Order the words to make sentences. Write them in the conversations.

Can   please?   repeat   you   that,
Sorry,   understand.   don't   I
How   you   that,   do   please?   spell

1 A Age?
  B _____
  A How old are you?

2 A Full name?
  B _____
  A Full name?

3 A My surname's Gleason.
  B _____
  A G-L-E-A-S-O-N.

6 Work with a partner. Say the conversations in exercise 5. Write similar conversations. Practise saying them.

C Write and check capital letters

7 Correct the text.

ᴹ
m̶y name's john evans. i'm from york in england. england is in britain, in europe. i'm british. i speak english. my address is 18 park street. my phone number's 837 7382.

8 Work with a partner. Put ✓ or ✗ next to the rules.
Use capital letters for:
☑ names
☒ numbers (e.g. *one, two*)
☐ the start of a sentence
☐ the pronoun *I*
☐ towns and countries
☐ nationalities and languages
☐ short words (e.g. *in*)
☐ street names
☐ 'people' words (e.g. *Mr*)

ABC Put it all together

9 Copy the application form in exercise 2. Ask another student the questions from exercise 1 (and ask for help if you don't understand). Write their answers on the form. Remember to use capital letters.

I can give personal information.
I can ask for help when I don't understand.

Tick ✓ the lines.   with a lot of help   with some help   on my own   very easily

A Grammar

1 Questions Find eight questions and write your answers.

¹ What's	² Where	are	you	³ How
your	⁴ What's	your	from?	old
first	name?	phone	number?	are
⁵ Are	you	⁶ What's	your	you?
⁷ What's	married?	⁸ Are	email	address?
your	surname?	you	from	China?

1 _____
2 _____
3 _____
4 _____
5 _____
6 _____
7 _____
8 _____

2 Present simple of *be* ⊞ Complete the text.

¹I'm___ Ivan. ²I___ a student of English. ³I___ from Russia. Two other students in my class ⁴___ from Europe and ⁵one___ from Mexico. My partner in the class ⁶___ Jeanette. Her ⁷surname___ La Forge. ⁸She___ from Belgium. Our ⁹teacher___ Jacky. ¹⁰She___ from Wales.

3 Pronouns and possessives Underline the correct word.

1 I/My name's Jim and I/my'm from England.
2 Satomi's from Japan. She/Her isn't married. She/Her email address is sato1@dinj.ja.
3 Jan's from Poland. He/His surname's Kowalski. He/His's single.
4 Jeanette and Olivier are from Belgium. They/Their're married. They/Their home is in Brussels.
5 What's you/your name and where do you/your come from?
6 We're married. We/Our names are Tom and Jen. We/Our aren't from England, we/our're from Scotland.

B Vocabulary

4 Greetings Put the conversation in order.

☐ I'm from England. Well, nice to meet you.
☐ I'm from Poland. And you?
☐¹ Hello. What's your name?
☐ Jan. J-A-N.
☐ My name's Jan.
☐ Nice to meet you!
☐ Oh, OK. Where are you from, Jan?
☐ Sorry?
☐² I'm Jim. And you?

5 Addresses Label the card with these words and phrases.

at   country   dot   email address   ~~first name~~
phone number   slash   street   surname   town   website

1 *first name*		2
	Marcela Cardoso	
3		
	Rua Alvaro Ramos, 23	
	Campo Grande, MS	
5	BRASIL	4
6	607 892 8465	
7	cardmar@rapidfire.br	8
9	http://www.cardosis.com	10
		11

6 Numbers Continue the lists.

1 one, two, three, *four*, *five*
2 two, four, six, _____, _____
3 nine, ten, eleven, _____, _____
4 five, ten, fifteen, _____, _____
5 thirty, forty, fifty, _____, _____
6 eleven, twenty-two, thirty-three, _____, _____
7 thirteen, thirty, fourteen, forty, fifteen, _____, _____, _____

7 Can you read the text messages? Write the sentences.

1 How R U? *How are you?* _____
2 Where R U from? _____
3 R U @ school? _____
4 C U L8R! _____

Things in the classroom

bag board CD chair desk door pen pencil phone picture student teacher window

A. What's that in English?
B. Can you repeat that, please?
C. How do you spell that?
D. Can you say that slowly, please?
E. Can you write that, please?

Actions in the classroom

close listen /ˈlɪsn/ look open read say write /raɪt/

How to use English in the classroom

G imperatives   **V** English in the classroom; days of the week   **P** counting syllables

A   Vocabulary   English in the classroom

1   Look at **Things in the classroom** opposite. Work with a partner. Match the words with things a–m in the photo.
Example   a = board

2   **2A.1▶** Listen and repeat.

3   Look at **Things in the classroom**. Test a partner.
Example   **A** b ...   **B** Picture!

4   Work with a partner. Ask and answer.
Example   **A** What's that in English?
            B Window.
            A How do you spell it?

5   Pronunciation Write words from **Things in the classroom** in the table.

one-syllable words ●	two-syllable words ●●
bag	pencil

B   Ask questions about English

6   **2A.2▶** Read questions A–E opposite. Listen to the conversations and say which question.
Example   1 = question A

7   Look at the audio script on ≫ p.150. <u>Underline</u> the questions.

8   **2A.3▶** Pronunciation Listen and repeat the questions.
Example   in**Eng**lish
            that in **Eng**lish
            What's that in **Eng**lish?

9   Ask the teacher about three more things in the classroom.
Example   What's that in English?

C   Grammar   imperatives

10   Look at **Actions in the classroom** opposite. Match the verbs with photos 1–7.
Example   1 = write

11   Write the verbs in these sentences.
   1   <u>*Close*</u>   the door.
   2   _____ the conversation with a partner.
   3   _____ at the picture.
   4   _____ the timetable.
   5   _____ to the CD.
   6   _____ your books at page 20.
   7   _____ your name on the board.

More practice? **Grammar Bank** ≫ p.137.

D   Read a timetable

12   **2A.4▶** Pronunciation Listen. Which day has three syllables?
Monday, **Tues**day
Wednesday, **Thurs**day
Friday, **Sat**urday
Sunday, **Mon**day

13   Listen again and repeat.

14   Read the timetable and answer the questions.

MERIDIAN SCHOOL OF LANGUAGES

Basic English	Mon & Wed or Tue & Thu morning
Intensive English	Wed–Fri afternoon & Sat morning
Basic French	Mon & Wed evening
Basic Italian	Tue & Thu evening

Multi-media centre Mon–Sat, all day (closed Sun)

   1   When's Basic Italian? *On Tuesday and Thursday evening.*
   2   When's Basic French?
   3   When's Intensive English?
   4   When's the multi-media centre closed?
   5   When's Basic English?

15   **2A.5▶** Listen and complete the conversation.
Jim   OK, that's all for today. See ¹_____.
Pablo   No, ² _____ Saturday!
J   Oh yes. ³ _____ on Monday!
P   ⁴_____ 'fin de semana' in English?
J   ⁵ _____.
P   ⁶_____ a good weekend!
J   Oh ⁷ _____. You too!

16   Compare with a partner. Practise saying the conversation.

ABCD   Put it all together

17   Work with a partner.
Student A Look at the classroom on ≫ p.128.
Student B Look at the classroom on ≫ p.132.

Ask the names of the things in the picture.
Examples   **A** Number 1: What's that in English?
            B Map.
            A Can you repeat that, please?
            B Yes. Map.
            B Number 2: What's that in English?
            A Clock.
            B How do you spell it?
            A C-L-O-C-K.

I can use English in the classroom.

Tick ✓ the line.   with a lot of help   with some help   on my own   very easily

The family

mother
father
daughter
son
sister
brother
wife
husband

This is Bob Marley.

This is Bob's wife, Rita.

This is Bob's son, Steve.

This is Bob's daughter, Stephanie.

Celebrity Quiz

Who are these people?

1

This is the English singer, John Lennon.

2

This is the Brazilian singer, Maria Bethania.

3

This is the Spanish singer, Enrique Iglesias.

4

This is the Mexican artist, Frida Kahlo.

5

This is the American actor, Humphrey Bogart.

6

This is the American actress, Goldie Hawn.

7

This is the German actor, Klaus Kinski.

Who are those people? →

8 9 10 11 12 13 14

Want a clue?
Here are their names!
- Yoko Ono
- Natasha Kinski
- Diego Rivera
- Kate Hudson
- Caetano Veloso
- Lauren Bacall
- Julio Iglesias

How to introduce your family

G possessive *'s*; demonstratives *this, that, these, those*   V family

A Vocabulary family

1 Work with a partner. Look at **The family** opposite. Write the names.

1 Bob's wife = *Rita*
2 Rita's husband =
3 Stephanie's mother =
4 Steve's father =
5 Steve's sister =
6 Stephanie's brother =
7 Bob's daughter =
8 Rita's son =

2 **2B.1▶** Listen and repeat.
Father, **mo**ther,
Sister, **bro**ther,
Wife and **hus**band,
Daughter, **son**

3 Write the possessives in these phrases.
her   his   my   our   their   your

1 me and __my__ brother
2 my class and _____ teacher
3 you and _____ sister
4 Mr Simpson and _____ son, Bart
5 Mrs Einstein and _____ son, Albert
6 me and _____ sister, and _____ mother
7 Mr and Mrs Presley and _____ son, Elvis

B Grammar possessive *'s*; demonstratives

4 Add *'s* to the sentences in the grammar box.

possessive *'s*	
Example The wife of Bob. ✗ Bob's wife. ✓	
1 Rita's Bob wife. ✗	*Rita's Bob's wife. ✓*
2 Steve's Rita son. ✗	
3 Stephanie's Bob daughter. ✗	
4 Steve's Stephanie brother. ✗	

5 What is the *'s* – is it possessive or *is*? Write *P* or *is*.

1 Bob's married.   *is*
2 Rita's Bob's wife.   __ __
3 Bob's from Jamaica.   __
4 Rita's a singer.   __
5 Stephanie's brother's Steve.   __ __

6 Tell your partner the names of three people in your family.
Example   My mother's name's Maria.

7 Write these sentences in the grammar box.
Those are my children.   ~~This is my sister.~~
That's my brother.   These are my children.

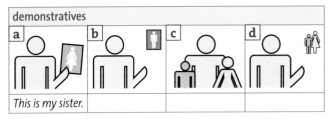

demonstratives			
a	**b**	**c**	**d**
This is my sister.			

8 Look at **Celebrity Quiz** opposite. Match people in the photos with these sentences.

1 These people are singers.   *John Lennon ...*
2 Those people are singers.
3 These people are actors/actresses.
4 Those people are actors/actresses.

9 Work with a partner. Say sentences with *this* or *that*.
Example   A This is Enrique Iglesias.
        B Yes, and that's his father, Julio Iglesias.
        A And who's that?
        B I don't know.

More practice? **Grammar Bank** >> p.137.

C Listen for key words

10 Two people are doing the quiz. Read and complete.
A OK, so this is the English singer, John Lennon ...
B Yeah, John Lennon, yeah, and number _____ –
   that's his wife, _____ _____.

11 **2B.2▶** Listen and check.

12 **2B.3▶** Listen to the people doing the quiz. Check your answers to exercise 9.

13 Read the audio script on >> p.151 to check again.

D Ask questions to show interest

14 Your teacher draws their family on the board. Look at your teacher's family and ask questions.
Examples   Is that your mother? What's her name?
        Who's that?

15 What do you remember? Tell your partner.

ABCD Put it all together

16 Draw your family. Ask about your partner's family.
Example   A Who's this?
        B My sister.
        A What's her name?
Then tell another student about your partner's family.

I can introduce my family.
Tick ✓ *the line.*   with a lot of help   with some help   on my own   very easily

People

a baby
a child
a boy
a girl
a married couple
grandparents
a grandmother
a grandfather
an old man
a woman
a man
a teenager
a boyfriend
a girlfriend

Jobs

a designer
a doctor
an engineer
a factory worker
a farmer
a housewife
an office worker
a shop assistant
a vet

Who's the driver?

Drivers of red cars aren't all young men! Who are the drivers of these red cars?

Here are some descriptions from our readers. Can you match them with the cars?!

The Family of Five
The driver is a woman. She's 35 years old and she's married. She's a housewife and a mother of three young children. Her husband is an office worker.

The Grandparents
The drivers are an old couple. The man is a retired factory worker. The woman is a shop assistant. They're grandparents.

The Footballer
The driver is a young man. He's a footballer and he's rich. He isn't married. His girlfriend is a model.

The Doctors
The drivers are a married couple. She's a doctor and he's a vet. They aren't young. Their children are teenagers.

The English Teacher
The driver is an English teacher. She's 28. She's married and her son is five. He's at primary school. Her husband is a taxi driver.

The Student
The driver is a woman. She's 20. Her parents are divorced. She isn't married. She's a student.

The Farmer
The driver is a man. He's a farmer. He's a husband and a father of four children. He isn't rich. He's 50.

The Young Couple
The driver is an engineer. He's 30 and he's married. His wife's a designer. They aren't parents.

How to describe people

G adjectives; articles *a, an*   V people; jobs   P linking words together

A Vocabulary people; jobs

1 Look at **People** and **Jobs** opposite. Work with a partner. Match the words with the people in photos a–o.
   Example   a= a child, a boy

2 **2C.1▶** Listen and check. Listen again and repeat.

3 Write these words in the table.
   boyfriend   ~~girl~~   grandmother   man   parent   wife

	baby	boy	¹ *girl*
	child		
	teenager		
	adult	² _____	woman
	couple	³ _____	girlfriend
		husband	⁴ _____
	⁵ _____	father	mother
	grandparent	grandfather	⁶ _____

B Read for detail

4 Look at **Who's the driver?** opposite. Choose a car you like. Tell your partner.

5 Read and match photos 1–8 with the texts. More than one answer is possible

6 Compare your answers with other students.
   Example   I think the driver of car 7 is the woman in 'The Family of Five'.

C Grammar adjectives; articles *a, an*

7 Read the grammar box. Then put the words in order to make sentences.

A *be* + article + adjective + noun	B *be* + adjective
She's a rich woman.	She's rich.

1 old he's man an   *He's an old man.*
2 woman she's a young
3 young that 's woman
4 rich a footballer he's
5 that 's footballer rich
6 grandparents old are my

8 Underline the adjectives *old, young,* and *rich* in **Who's the driver?** Are they A or B in the grammar box above?

9 Complete the grammar box with these words.
   teacher   English teacher   old man   man

a before a consonant sound	*an* before a vowel sound
a doctor	an engineer
a farmer	an office worker

10 Complete with *a* or *an*.
   1 She's *an* old woman.
   2 He's _____ rich man.
   3 You're _____ adult.
   4 He's _____ married man.
   5 I'm _____ English teacher.
   6 She's _____ young girl.
   7 He's _____ office worker.

   More practice? **Grammar Bank** >> p.137.

D Pronunciation linking words together

11 **2C.2▶** Listen.

   ┌consonant sound   ))
   'an‿old woman'   sounds like   'a nold woman'
      └vowel sound

12 **2C.3▶** Listen and draw the ‿.
   1 You aren't‿old.
   2 He isn't an adult.
   3 My son isn't an engineer.

13 **2C.4▶** Listen again and repeat.

14 What's your job? And your family and friends? Write four sentences. Use a dictionary.
   Examples   I'm a designer.
                My mother's a dentist.
                My boyfriend's an engineer.

15 Compare with a partner.

ABCD Put it all together

16 Work with a partner. Look at the photos of houses on >> p.126 and imagine the people. Write notes about them. Answer these questions.

   Are they old?   Are they young?   Are they married?
   Are they parents?   Doctors?   Students?   Engineers?

17 Work with a different partner. Take turns to be A and B.
   Student A Describe the people in one of the houses.
   Student B Guess which house it is.

   Example **A** I think the person in this house is young.
              She ...

I can describe people. ▬▬▬▬▬▬▬▬▬▬▬
Tick ✓ the line.   with a lot of help   with some help   on my own   very easily   21

Anila & Paul

What's the time?

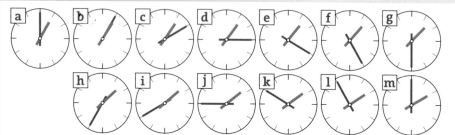

five past one	two o'clock
five to two	one o'clock
half past one	quarter past one
ten past one	quarter to two
ten to two	twenty-five past one
twenty past one	twenty-five to two
twenty to two	

How to talk about the time

G prepositions of time *at, on*   V numbers and time   P stress in corrections

A Read and complete the conversation

1 Read Anila and Paul opposite. <u>Underline</u> the times.
2 Read the story again. Complete it with these sentences.
   Ten to nine?   My watch says ten to five!
   And what time is it now?   Four fifteen?
3 **2D.1▶** Listen and check. Listen again and repeat.
4 Say the conversation with a partner.

B Pronunciation stress in corrections

5 **2D.2▶** Listen and repeat.

A	thirteen	fourteen	fifteen	sixteen	seventeen	eighteen	nineteen
B	thirty	forty	fifty	sixty	seventy	eighty	ninety

6 **2D.3▶** Listen and say A or B.
7 **2D.4▶** Listen and <u>underline</u> the stressed syllable.
   1 **A** Thirteen.   **P** Thirty?   **A** No, thir<u>teen</u>!
   2 **A** Forty.   **P** Fourteen? **A** No, forty!
   3 **A** Fifty.   **P** Fifteen?   **A** No, fifty!
8 Say the conversations in exercise 7 with a partner. Continue to 19 and 90.

C Listen for detail

9 **2D.5▶** Look at What's the time? opposite. Listen and say which clock.
   Example   **Audio** Five past one.   **You** b!
10 Listen again and repeat.
11 **2D.6▶** Listen and follow the times from start to end.

START	1.05	3.30	5.45	9.10
7.20	8.55	2.40	5.30	10.00
11.15	12.00	4.25	6.35	7.20
8.55	1.30	3.45	9.15	2.40
5.20	8.05	12.45	11.00	**END**

12 Work with a partner. Say another way from start to end.
   Example   Start – five past one – five to nine ...

13 Use a different way to tell the time.
   1 ten to five = *four fifty*
   2 half past ten
   3 quarter past nine
   4 quarter to one
   5 twenty to twelve

14 Play a memory game with a partner.
   1 Take 12 pieces of paper. Write a different time on each one.
   2 Put them on the desk and look at them for a minute.
   3 Turn them over.
   4 Point at a piece of paper and ask your partner.
      Example **A** What time is it?
              B It's half past three ...
              A Yes that's right.

D Grammar prepositions of time *at, on*

15 Read the grammar box.

at + time	*on* + day	no preposition
at five thirty	on Wednesday	tomorrow morning
at ten to ten	on Friday morning	this evening

   Complete the phrases with *at, on,* or –.
   _____ Tuesday _____ six o'clock _____ 10.30
   _____ this morning _____ today _____ Wednesday

16 Complete the conversation.
   Paul When's *Celebrity Quiz* on TV?
   Anila It's ¹_____ Friday ²_____ seven o'clock.
   P And when's the tennis?
   A This evening.
   P And what time's the football?
   A It's ³_____ 9.30 ⁴_____ Thursday.
   More practice? **Grammar Bank** » p.137.

ABCD Put it all together

17 Have conversations with a partner. Take turns to be A or B.

   Student A | What time's | the news on TV? |
                  | When's | the end of the lesson? |
                  | | the next lesson? |

   Student B | It's | at six o'clock | this evening. |
                  | | at half past seven | tomorrow morning. |
                  | | at eight fifteen | on Thursday. |
                  | | | on Monday. |

   Example **A** What time's the end of the lesson?
           B It's at half past seven.

I can talk about the time.
Tick ✓ the line.   with a lot of help   with some help   on my own   very easily   23

Writing A message of introduction

A Punctuation the apostrophe (')

1 Read the box. Write A or B.

A	's = short for *is*	My name's Claire.
B	's = possessive	Bob's wife.

1. ☐A He's an engineer.
2. ☐ Our son's five years old.
3. ☐ Our son's name is Ben.
4. ☐ London's in Britain.
5. ☐ My wife's from London.
6. ☐ This is our teacher's bag.

2 Put eight more apostrophes in this letter.

Hi! My name's Max. Im from Canada. Im eighteen years old and I live with my parents. My mothers names Sara and shes a doctor. My fathers names Jed and hes a driver.

B Read for detail

3 Are these right ✓ or wrong ✗?

1. I'm ⟨single⟩ My ⟨wife's⟩ a factory worker. ✗
2. I'm a grandmother. My son's baby's one year old.
3. It's seven o'clock. It's nearly midnight.
4. It's Tuesday today. Tomorrow's Wednesday.
5. My grandfather's young. He's nearly ninety-five.
6. This is my mother. Her son's my sister.

4 Correct the wrong ✗ sentences in exercise 3.
Example 1 I'm **married**. My wife's a factory worker.

5 Read the message. Which words are wrong? <u>Underline</u> one wrong word in lines 1–5 and write the correct word.

Welcome to the club!
Please write a message of introduction to our members.

Hi! My name's Claire. I'm from France.
1. I'm a teacher. I'm twenty-five <u>days</u> old ____ *years*
2. and I'm married. I live with my wife _____
3. and daughter. His husband's name is Stefan. _____
4. He's an office worker. Our son's _____
5. name is Sandra. He's five years old. _____
I can speak a little English. This is me
and my husband in London.

Preview | Submit

AB Put it all together

6 Write a message of introduction to the club. Begin like this:

Hi! My name's _____. I'm from _____.
I'm a _____. I'm _____ years old and
I'm _____. I live ...

Include one wrong word.

7 Give your message to your partner. Check your partner's writing and find the wrong word.

I can write a message of introduction. ▬▬▬▬▬

Tick ✓ the line.   with a lot of help   with some help   on my own   very easily

Unit 2 Review

A Grammar

1 Imperatives Find six classroom instructions.

1 Close	**2** Listen	to	the	**3** Write
your	books,	**4** Look	conversation.	your
5 Read	please.	at	and	name
the	questions.	the	address.	thirty.
text	the	picture	on	page
and	answer	**6** Open	the	window.

2 Possessive 's Write sentences about the people in Marta's family.

```
            Dorota
        Agata─Henryk
Aleksander─Marta
    Adam    Sylwia
```

1 _Marta's husband's name is_ _____ Aleksander.
2 _____ Agata.
3 _____ Henryk.
4 _____ Dorota.
5 _____ Adam.
6 _____ Sylwia.

3 Demonstratives Write about Marta's family with *this / that / these / those*.

1 _Those are my parents._   2 _____

3 _____   4 _____

4 Articles Correct the text. Add *a* or *an*.

Marta and Aleksander are married couple. Marta is office worker and Aleksander is engineer. Marta's grandmother is old and she's retired. Her father's taxi driver and her mother's English teacher. Marta's children are young – Adam's six and Sylwia's eight.

B Vocabulary

5 Classroom English Complete the conversation with these words.

repeat slowly spell ~~What's~~ write

A ¹ _What's_ that in English?
B Umbrella.
A Sorry, can you ² _____ that, please?
B Yes, sure. Umbrella.
A Can you say that ³ _____, please?
B U m b r e l l a.
A How do you ⁴ _____ it?
B U-M-B-R-E-L-L-A.
A Oh, OK. Thanks. Can you ⁵ _____ it on the board, please?

6 Time Write the times in full.

1 MON 6.45 _At quarter to seven on Monday._
           On Monday at six forty-five.
2 TUE 20.30 _____
3 WED 11.15 _____
4 THU 12.10 _____
5 FRI 22.15 _____
6 SAT 13.20 _____
7 SUN 17.25 _____

7 People and jobs Find 16 more words.

```
L  H O U S E W I F E  X  A  T
E  N X W O M E N O S  I  D  A
N  D F O P V B A B Y  M  A  C
G  O A B M E G I R L  U  D  T
I  C R O A T C H I L  D  M  R
N  T M Y N C O U P L  E  E  E
E  O E R D X U B T E  D  H  S
E  R R T E E N A G E  R  S  S
R  S R D E S I G N E  R  S  E
N  D A E D O P K I A  L  U  S
O  G R A N D M O T H  E  R  O
O  F F I C E W O R K  E  R  S
```

25

Places

bookshop bus café car park cash machine chemist's music shop platform pub
restaurant station taxi telephones ticket office toilets train

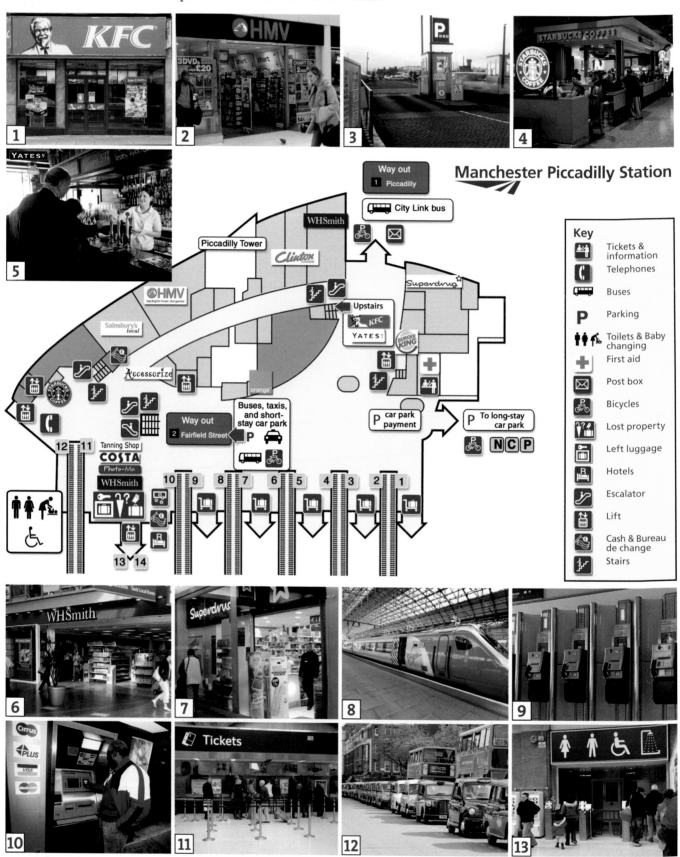

How to ask for information

v places   P word stress

A Vocabulary places

1 Look at **Places** opposite. Work with a partner. Match the words with the places in photos 1–13.
Example   1 = restaurant

2 **3A.1▶** Listen and say the photo number.
Example **Audio** Bookshop.   **You** 6!

3 Listen again and repeat.

4 **Pronunciation** Listen again and write the words in the correct column.

●	●●	●●●	●●●●
bus	bookshop	cash machine	ticket office
	café		
	car park		

5 Find the places in photos 1–13 on the map opposite.

B Read and find information on a map

6 Look at the map opposite. Match the questions and answers.
1 [d] Where are the toilets?
2 ☐ Where's the pub?
3 ☐ Where are the taxis?
4 ☐ Where's the chemist's?
5 ☐ Where's the long-stay car park exit?

a They're near the Fairfield Street exit.
b It's near the Piccadilly exit.
c It's near platform 1.
d ~~They're near platform 12.~~
e It's upstairs.

7 **3A.2▶** Listen and check.

C Listen for detail

8 Look at the photo of the woman. Where is she?

9 What does she do? Guess. Put these things in order.

a ☐   b ☐   c ☐

10 **3A.3▶** Listen and check.

11 Listen again and look at the map. Which three places does the woman go to?

12 Read the audio script on ≫ p.151 and check your answers.

D Practise asking and answering

13 Write four or more questions.

Excuse me,	where's	the station, please?
	where are	the toilets, please?
	is this	platform 5?
		the train to London?
		the telephones, please?
		your ideas

14 Work with a partner. Ask your questions from exercise 13 and give answers. Remember to say *thank you*!

It's	over there.	Yes, it is.
They're	near platform 1.	Yes, they are.
	near the exit.	No, it isn't. It's …
	upstairs.	No, they aren't. They're …
	your ideas	Sorry, I don't know.

Example   **A** Excuse me, where are the toilets, please?
        B They're near platform 12.
        A Platform 12? OK, thanks.

15 Do exercise 14 again from memory.

ABCD Put it all together

16 Work with a partner.
Student A Look at the map on ≫ p.128.
Student B Look at the map on ≫ p.132.
Ask your partner questions to complete the map.

Example   **A** Excuse me, where are the telephones, please?
        B They're near platform 1.
        A OK, thanks.

I can ask for information about places.

Tick ✓ the line.   with a lot of help   with some help   on my own   very easily

27

Countries

Aust**ral**ia and **Germ**any
India, **J**apan
Egypt and **It**aly
Spain, Greece, and France

Russia and South **Af**rica
Canada, Bra**zil**
The US**A** and **Chi**na
Turkey and Pe**ru**

Nationalities

American Australian Brazilian Canadian
Chinese Egyptian French German Greek
Indian Italian Japanese Peruvian Russian
South African Spanish Turkish

People and places

My name's Isabel. I'm Peruvian. I'm from Arequipa, in the south of Peru. It isn't the capital. The capital is Lima. The currency of Peru is the nuevo sol, and the main language is Spanish.

How to **talk about countries**

A Vocabulary countries, nationalities, languages

1 Look at **Countries** opposite. Work with a partner. Match photos 1–16 with the countries.
Example   1 = Egypt

2 **3B.1▶** Listen and repeat.
Example   Aus**tra**lia and **Ger**many …

3 **3B.2▶** Look at **Nationalities** opposite. Listen to the nationality. Say the country.
Example   **Audio** American.   **You** The USA!

4 Test a partner.
Example   **A** Australian.   **B** Australia!

5 Complete this table and add three more examples. Use your dictionary.

> **Japón** *nm* ⟨Japan⟩
> **japonés, -esa** ▶ *adj, nm*⟨Japanese⟩ *hablar ~* to speak Japanese
> ▶ *nm-nf* Japanese man/woman [*pl* men/women]: *los japoneses* the Japanese

Diccionario Oxford Pocket para estudiantes de inglés

country	nationality	language
the USA	*American*	*English*
	Brazilian	Portuguese
	Egyptian	Arabic
Greece		Greek
Japan	Japanese	Japanese
	Peruvian	Spanish

B Read for detail

6 Read **People and places** opposite. Is Isabel from Lima?

7 Complete this table about Isabel's country.

country	*Peru*
capital	
nationality	
language	
currency	

8 Write the answers to these questions.
1 Where are you from?
2 What's the capital of your country?
3 What's your nationality?
4 What's the language of your country?
5 What's the currency of your country?

9 **3B.3▶** Listen and answer the questions.
Example   **Audio** Where are you from?   **You** Hungary.

10 Ask your partner the questions.

C Listen for questions

11 Read and <u>underline</u> the question. What's the answer?
Picture number eight is in Germany. The currency of Germany is the euro. The language and nationality is German. But what's the capital of Germany?
a Bonn   b Frankfurt   c Berlin

12 **3B.4▶** Listen and play a quiz game. Choose the correct answer.

1	a Sydney	b Canberra	c Auckland
2	a Portuguese	b Spanish	c French
3	a Ankara	b Istanbul	c Damascus
4	a the euro	b the lira	c the rouble
5	a Egyptian	b Arabic	c English

D Grammar articles *a, an, the*

13 Complete the grammar box with these places.
Germany   Britain   Rome

The only one (*the*)	Not the only one (*a / an*)
_____ is the capital of Italy.	Next word starts with a consonant sound: Frankfurt is a city in _____.
	Next word starts with a vowel sound: _____ is an island.

14 Complete with *a, an,* or *the*.
1 Chicago is *a* city in the USA.
2 Washington is ____ capital of the USA.
3 Swahili is ____ African language.
4 ____ currency of Germany is ____ euro.
5 Cuba is ____ island.
6 Kenya is ____ country in Africa and ____ capital of Kenya is Nairobi.
7 Paris is ____ capital city in Europe. It's ____ capital of France.

More practice? **Grammar Bank** » p.138.

ABCD Put it all together

15 Work with a partner. Read audio script 3B.4 on » p.151. Write three more quiz questions.

16 Ask your questions to other pairs of students.

I can talk about countries.

Tick ✓ the line.   with a lot of help   with some help   on my own   very easily

Find the people

People

People on **bikes**
People on **bu**ses
Workers in their **off**ices
Workers in their **fac**tories

Drivers in their **lo**rries
Cars in the **car** park
Waiters in the **res**taurant
Glasses on the **ta**bles

Children at **school**
Children in their **class**es
People in the **mar**ket
People in their **hou**ses

How to say where you are in town

G plurals; prepositions of place *in, on* V things and places in town P plural endings

A Vocabulary things and places in town

1 Ask your partner the names of things in **Find the people** opposite.
   Example **A** What's this in English?
             B A school./I don't know.

2 **3C.1▶** Listen to **People** opposite. Match each line with numbers 1–11 in **Find the people**.
   Example People on bikes = 5

3 Pronunciation Listen again and repeat.
   Example People on bikes, people on buses …

B Grammar plurals

4 Complete the grammar box with words from **People**.

How to spell plurals			
+ s	**+ es**	**y + ies**	**irregular**
boy – boys	church – churches	city – cities	this – these
girl – girls	watch – watches	country – countries	that – those
place – places	address – addresses	lorry – _____	woman – women
page – pages	bus – _____	factory – _____	man – men
bike – bikes	glass – _____		child – _____
tree – trees	class – _____		person – _____
car – _____			
office – _____			
table – _____			
house – _____			
waiter – _____			

5 Write these phrases next to the pictures.
   that person   those people
   these people   ~~this person~~

 1   2   3   4

   this person _____   _____   _____

6 Complete with *in* or *on*. Write the plurals.
   1 a man _on_ a bike   *men on bikes*
   2 a woman ____ a bus
   3 a child ____ a class
   4 a glass ____ a table
   5 a city ____ a country
   6 a person ____ a church
   7 a car ____ a car park
   8 a worker ____ an office

   More practice? **Grammar Bank** >> p.138.

C Pronunciation plural endings

7 **3C.2▶** Listen and say A or B.

A	girl	bike	shop	phone
B	girls	bikes	shops	phones

8 Say words from exercise 7. Your partner says A or B.
   Example **A** Girls **B** B!

9 **3C.3▶** Listen. Do the plurals have one or two syllables?
   bus buses [2]   car cars [1]   school schools [ ]
   class classes [ ]   place places [ ]   bike bikes [ ]
   church churches [ ] page pages [ ]   boy boys [ ]

10 Look at the blue letters in the words in exercise 9. Complete this pronunciation rule.
   If the noun ends with one of these spellings, plural = extra syllable:
                -s   -ss   -_____ -_____ -_____
   Examples bus   class   _____   _____   _____

D Listen for detail

11 Look at people a–f opposite. Find them in the big picture. Then match questions a–f below with answers 1–6.
   [a] [3] Where are these children?
   [b] [ ] Where are these women?
   [c] [ ] Where's this boy?
   [d] [ ] Where are these men?
   [e] [ ] Where's this woman?
   [f] [ ] Where's this man?

   1 She's in the car park. She's near that car.
   2 They're in the street. They're near those bikes.
   3 ~~They're in the park. They're near those trees.~~
   4 He's in the market. He's near the chemist's.
   5 He's on the bus. He's near those children.
   6 They're in the restaurant. They're near the door.

12 **3C.4▶** Listen to this conversation. Find Tony in **Find the people** opposite.

13 **3C.5▶** Listen to two more conversations. Find Alice and Wendy.

ABCD Put it all together

14 Draw yourself in the picture opposite. Ask other students in the class where they are. Write their names on the picture.
   Example **A**   Where are you?
             Lena I'm in the street, near the cinema.

15 Tell your partner where other students in your class are.
   Example **A** Lena's in the street, near the cinema.

I can say where I am in town. ▬▬▬▬▬▬▬
Tick ✓ the line. with a lot of help with some help on my own very easily

How well?

I don't speak German.   I speak a little German.   I speak German quite well.   I speak German very well.

How to talk about language skills

G present simple ⊞⊡? *do, don't*   V phrases describing language ability   P *Sue* /s/ or *shoe* /ʃ/

A Read a conversation

1 Look at Sue and Iris opposite. Find seven languages.
2 **3D.1▶** Listen to the conversation and find five differences with Sue and Iris.
3 Say the Sue and Iris conversation with a partner.

B Pronunciation *Sue* /s/ or *shoe* /ʃ/

4 **3D.2▶** Listen and say A or B.

A /s/	Iris	Sue
B /ʃ/	Irish Éire	shoe

5 Test a partner.
Example   A Iris.   B A!

6 **3D.3▶** Listen and repeat.
Example   Are you Irish, Iris?   Is this your shoe, Sue?

C Grammar present simple ⊞⊡? *do, don't*

7 Complete the grammar box.

+	I speak French.	We _____ English.	They speak German.
–	I _____ French.	We don't speak English.	They _____ German.
?	Do you speak French?	Do you speak English?	_____ they _____ German?

short answers	Yes, I / we / they do.	No, I / we / they don't.

8 Order the words to make sentences.
1 French I speak don't   *I don't speak French.*
2 speak you German do ?
3 understand I Russian
4 don't I Italian speak
5 any languages speak other you do ?
6 speak I Portuguese
7 don't understand they English

9 Write true sentences. Compare with a partner.
1 In my country, we ...   *speak French.*
2 I don't speak ...
3 I speak ...
4 I like ...
5 I understand ...
6 I don't ...

More practice? **Grammar Bank** >> p.138.

D Listen for detail

10 Look at How well? opposite. Complete sentences 1–4 for you. Compare with a partner.
Example   I don't speak Italian.
1 I don't speak _____.
2 I speak a little _____.
3 I speak _____ quite well.
4 I speak _____ very well.

11 **3D.4▶** Listen to Philippe. Which five languages do you hear? Write them in the first column.

language	very well	quite well	a little	no
German				

12 Listen again. Tick ✓ the correct columns: *very well*, *quite well*, *a little*, or *no*.

13 Play a guessing game with a partner. Choose a person.

	Maria	David	Olga	Keiko	Marc
English	a little	very well	a little	very well	very well
French	no	quite well	quite well	no	quite well
Italian	very well	very well	no	no	no
German	no	very well	no	a little	very well

Example   A Do you speak English?
   B Yes, I speak English very well.
   A Do you speak German?
   B Yes, I speak a little German.
   A You're Keiko!

More practice? **Grammar Bank** >> p.138.

ABCD Put it all together

14 Make questions and ask other students in the class.

Do you	speak	English?
	understand	German?
	like	French?
		any other languages?
		your ideas

Example   A Do you speak Italian?   B Yes, a little.

I can talk about language skills.
Tick ✓ the line.   with a lot of help   with some help   on my own   very easily

Writing My country and languages

A Read for detail

1 Read the text. Find one false 'fact'.

Where I'm from

I'm Polish and I live in Poland. The capital city is Warsaw but I live in a town called Nowe Miasto. It's near Warsaw. Warsaw is in France. In Poland, the currency is the złoty. The main language is Polish but I speak Russian very well too. My mother's from Russia. I also speak a little English and a little French.

Jan Kowalski

2 Complete the column for Jan.

	Jan	Me
nationality		
country		
town	Nowe Miasto	
capital		
currency		
first language	Polish	
second language	Russian	
other languages		

3 Complete the column for you. Tell your partner.

B Build sentences

4 <u>Underline</u> the words *and* and *but* in Jan Kowalski's text.

5 Complete with *and* or *but*.
  1 I'm French _____ I live in France.
  2 I'm French _____ I live in Italy.

6 Join these sentences about Jan with *and* or *but*.
  1 I'm Polish. I live in Poland.
     I'm Polish and I live in Poland.
  2 Warsaw is the capital. I don't live there.
  3 The currency is the złoty. The main language is Polish.
  4 I speak a little English. I speak a little French.
  5 I speak Russian. I don't speak Spanish.

7 Write sentences with *and* and *but* about you.
  More practice? **Grammar Bank** >> p.138.

C Review your writing

8 Correct the text. Add full stops and capital letters.

I'm from turkey the capital of turkey is ankara but I live in trabzon our currency is the turkish lira my first language is turkish but I speak german very well I speak a little english and I understand a little russian

Bülent Demirci

ABC Put it all together

9 Write about your country and languages. Use your notes from exercise 3. Use *and* and *but*.

10 Check the full stops and capital letters, or ask your partner to check.

11 Find one thing in your partner's writing that's the same for you.

I can write about my country and languages.

Tick ✓ the line.   with a lot of help   with some help   on my own   very easily

Unit 3 Review

A Grammar

1 Articles Complete with *a*, *an*, or *the*.

||||||||| **Three Island People** |||||||||

 I'm from Manila. Manila is ¹ *the* capital of the Philippines. It's ² _____ big city and it's on ³ _____ island. The island's called Luzon.

 I'm from Surabaya. Surabaya is ⁴ _____ city in Indonesia and it's on ⁵ _____ island. The island's called Java. ⁶ _____ capital of Java is Jakarta.

 I'm from St John's in Canada. St John's is ⁷ _____ small city in Newfoundland. It's ⁸ _____ capital of Newfoundland.

2 Plurals Write the plurals.

1 a boy on a bike – *boys on bikes*
2 a woman on a bus – _____
3 a child in a class – _____
4 a man in a lorry – _____
5 a shop in a street – _____
6 a person in a supermarket – _____
7 a waiter in a restaurant – _____
8 a worker in a factory – _____

3 Present simple Find eight sentences.

¹ I	² I	speak	a	little
don't	speak	Gaelic.	³ I	German.
⁴ Do	very	French	speak	⁵ I
you	well.	Portuguese.	speak	don't
speak	⁶ Do	you	speak	Italian?
any	⁷ I	don't	⁸ I	understand
other	languages?	speak	Polish.	Russian.

B Vocabulary

4 Places Order the letters to make words for these things.

1 usb
  bus
2 artin
  _____
3 sach himance
  _____
4 afcé
  _____
5 sttoile
  _____
6 **P** arc krap
  _____
7 pobhooks
  _____
8 cumis posh
  _____
9 his'stemc
  _____
10 bup
  _____
11 leehnotep
  _____

5 Countries and nationalities Complete the table.

	capital	country	nationality
1	London	Eng*land*	*British*
2	Moscow	Russ_____	
3	Tokyo	Jap_____	
4	Washington	The _____	Am_____
5	Beijing	Ch_____	
6	Rome	It_____	
7	Paris	Fr_____	
8	Athens	Gr_____	
9	Madrid	Sp_____	
10	Berlin	Ger_____	

6 In town Underline the best word.

1 a country / tree / city in the park
2 a page / platform / house in a street
3 a house / watch / train in the station
4 a waiter / car / class in the car park
5 a chemist's / market / table in the restaurant
6 a church / driver / bus in a lorry
7 a worker / capital / language in a factory

Signs

a — PRIVATE NO ENTRY

b — Landed / Confirmed / Cancelled / Confirmed / Cancelled

c — FREE ENTRY

d — OUT OF ORDER

e — SORRY WE'RE CLOSED

f — SALE SALE EVERYTHING HALF PRICE

g — SOLD OUT

h — OPEN

i — FULL

j — Please help yourself

k — SORRY NO VACANCIES

Good news, bad news

1 Hi Ana. How are you? So-so.

2 What's wrong? Well, the good news is my boyfriend's here in England.

3 Oh really? That's great! And the bad news? He's with his new girlfriend!

4 Oh, I see. I'm sorry! Thanks. Anyway, how are you?

5 Not bad. The good news is I'm in a play. Oh really? Well done! And the bad news?

6 Tonight's the first night and I don't know my lines. Oh no! Good luck!

How to respond to news

G prepositions of place *at*   V signs; responses to news   P responses to news

A Vocabulary signs

1 Look at **Signs** opposite. Where can you see signs a–k? Work with a partner and match them with these places.

airport   beach   car park   cash machine   cinema   garden   hotel   house   museum   restaurant   shop   station   supermarket   telephone   theatre   toilets

Example   'Private' – a garden, a car park, a beach, a house

2 Read the signs. Are they good or bad news? Say *Oh good!* or *Oh no!*

3 Work with a partner. Match 1–8 with a–h below.
   1 [h] I'm at the cinema but
   2 [ ] I'm at the airport but
   3 [ ] I'm at my favourite restaurant but
   4 [ ] CDs are half-price today but
   5 [ ] I'm at the ticket machine but
   6 [ ] It's free entry at the theatre today but
   7 [ ] The beach is great but
   8 [ ] The hotel's cheap but

   a the play's cancelled.
   b there are no vacancies.
   c it's out of order.
   d a sign says 'private, no entry'.
   e all the tables are full.
   f the flight's cancelled.
   g they're sold out.
   h ~~it's closed today.~~

B Listen for detail

4 **4A.1▶** Listen to Jim and Ana and answer the questions.
   1 What's Ana's good news?   *Her boyfriend's in England.*
   2 What's Ana's bad news?
   3 What's Jim's good news?
   4 What's Jim's bad news?

5 Read **Good news, bad news** opposite and check.

6 Read **Good news, bad news** again. Who says:
   1 What's wrong?
   2 Oh really? That's great!
   3 Oh, I see. I'm sorry!
   4 Oh really? Well done!
   5 Oh no! Good luck!

7 Read **Good news, bad news** for one minute. Write three important words from the conversation.

8 Close your book and listen again to 4A.1. Tick ✓ your words when you hear them.

C Pronunciation responses to news

9 **4A.2▶** Listen and copy the pronunciation.

   Oh **no!** Good **luck!**

   Oh **real**ly! That's **great!**

   What's **wrong?**

   Oh **real**ly! Well **done!**

   Oh I see. I'm sorry!

10 Work with a partner.
   Student A Read out one of the sentences below.
   Student B Respond with one of the phrases in exercise 9.

   1 My English exam's tomorrow.
   2 My exam result's very good.
   3 These books are half-price today.
   4 My exam result isn't very good.
   5 Oh no!

11 Say the **Good news, bad news** conversation with a partner.

ABC Put it all together

12 Think of good and bad news to tell your partner and write notes. Look at exercise 3 or use your own ideas.
   Example   Hotel: ✓cheap   ✗no vacancies

13 Work with a partner. Use your notes to complete the conversation with your good and bad news.
   A Hi. How are you?
   B So-so.
   A What's wrong?
   B Well, the good news is _____.
   A Oh really? That's great! And the bad news?
   B _____.
   A Oh, I see. I'm sorry.

14 Close your book. Act your conversations for another pair.

I can respond to good and bad news.
Tick ✓ the line.   with a lot of help   with some help   on my own   very easily

Find the differences

38 4B

Months

January
February
March
April
May
June
July
August
September
October
November
December

Ordinal numbers

1st	first
2nd	second
3rd	third
4th	fourth
5th	fifth
6th	sixth
7th	seventh
8th	eighth
9th	ninth
10th	tenth
11th	eleventh
12th	twelfth
13th	thirteenth
14th	fourteenth
15th	fifteenth
16th	sixteenth
17th	seventeenth
18th	eighteenth
19th	nineteenth
20th	twentieth
21st	twenty-first
30th	thirtieth
31st	thirty-first
	etc.

Say *January the first*
or   *the first of January*

Write January 1st
or   1st January

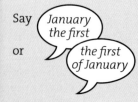

How to say dates

G prepositions of time *at, in, on*   V months and ordinal numbers   P word stress; /θ/

A Vocabulary months and ordinal numbers

1 Look at the pictures opposite. This is the desk of a language student in Britain. Answer the questions.
  1 What's her name?
  2 Where's she from?
  3 How old is she?

2 Look at **Find the differences** opposite. Compare with your partner.
  Example   In picture A, the book is *The Third Man*.
  In picture B, it's *The Tenth Man*.

3 Find the names of the twelve months in the pictures. Cover **Months** opposite and put the months in order.

4 Complete the text on >> p.126.

5 **4B.1▶** Listen and check. Listen again and repeat.

6 Write the months under the correct stress pattern.

●	●●	●●	●●●	●●●
March			January	

7 **4B.2▶** Listen, check, and repeat.

B Pronunciation /θ/

8 **4B.3▶** Listen and say A or B.

A	/θ/ three	/θ/ eighth	/θ/ three	/θ/ thing	/θ/ eighth	/θ/ sixth
B	/t/ tree	/t/ eight	/f/ free	/s/ sing	/s/ eights	/s/ six

Example   **Audio** Tree.   **You** B!

9 Test a partner.
  Example   **A** Three.   **B** A!

C Read puzzles

10 Can you do these puzzles? Work with a partner.
  1 March is the third month and April is the fourth, so March is before April in the calendar. But where is April before March?
  2 It starts at the end of August and finishes before October. What is it?
  3 You don't see it in June, but you see it at the end of July. What is it?
  4 People say 'Good morning' more in January, March, May, July, August, October, and December. Why?

11 Read the answers on >> p.126.

D Grammar prepositions of time *at, in, on*

12 Complete the grammar box with more examples.

at	in	on
a time ...	a month ...	a date ...
at half past three	in June	on March 19th
other ...	a part of the day ...	a day ...
at the weekend	in the morning	on Tuesday (morning)
at the end of August		
at night		

13 Complete with *at*, *in*, or *on*.
  1 *on* February 14th   6 ___ the afternoon
  2 ___ March   7 ___ half past six
  3 ___ Friday   8 ___ January 1st
  4 ___ the end of May   9 ___ Friday morning
  5 ___ July 4th   10 ___ December 31st

14 Ask and answer the questions. Clue: the answers to questions 1–5 are in exercise 13.
  1 When's New Year's Day?   *On January the first.*
  2 When's New Year's Eve?
  3 When's Valentine's Day?
  4 When's Mother's Day in Britain?
  5 When's American Independence Day?
  6 What's the date today?
  7 When's Mother's Day in your country?

15 Work with a partner.
  Student A   Look at the birthday list on >> p.128.
  Student B   Look at the birthday list on >> p.132.

  More practice? **Grammar Bank** >> p.139.

ABCD Put it all together

16 Ask and answer. Make an 'important dates' page for students in your class. Here are some ideas:
  birthday   exam   end of term   your next holiday
  your favourite day   your favourite month
  important dates in your country

  Example Magda, when's your birthday?

Person	Event	Month	Date
Magda	birthday	January	18th
Simone	next holiday	April	
Toby	Maths exam		

17 Put your events in order and tell the class.
  Example   Magda's birthday's on January the eighteenth.

I can say dates.
Tick ✓ the line.   with a lot of help   with some help   on my own   very easily

Lily's morning

brush (her) teeth
check (her) email
get dressed
get up
have a shower
have breakfast
leave the house
wake up

a b c d e f g h

Personality Test

Are you a morning flower or a morning monster?

1 **You hear the alarm clock. What do you do?**

A I get up.
B I wake up before the alarm clock.
C I press 'snooze' five times.

2 **You get up. What do you do first?**

A I sit on the bed and think.
B I have a shower and then get dressed.
C I get dressed and then have a shower.

3 **You go to the bathroom. Somebody is there before you. What do you do?**

A I go back to bed.
B I say 'Good morning!' and go to the kitchen for an orange juice.
C I walk into the door.

4 **What do you have for breakfast?**

A I have a healthy breakfast, for example fruit and yogurt.
B I have tea or coffee first, then I have a big breakfast later.
C No time for breakfast. I'm always late for work (or school, or university).

5 **What do you do first, brush your teeth, get dressed, or have breakfast?**

A I get dressed.
B I have breakfast.
C I do all three together.

6 **You leave the house. What do you do next?**

A I go to work (or school, or university).
B I go for a run.
C I run to the bus and then phone to say I'm late.

7 **You read a newspaper. Where do you read it?**

A On the bus (or train).
B At breakfast.
C At home in the evening.

8 **You wake up. It's a holiday. What do you do?**

A I sleep another hour.
B I get up, check my email, and go for a run.
C I get up at lunchtime.

Key **Do you have more A, B, or C answers? Count them.**

More As You're normal. Mornings are OK … if you don't live with a morning flower or a morning monster!

More Bs You're a morning flower. Morning is your favourite time. But don't say 'Good morning!' to a morning monster. They hate morning flowers!

More Cs You're a morning monster. Morning is not a good time for you. Don't go near other people before ten o'clock!

newspaper
walk into a door
go for a run
snooze (sleep 10 more minutes)
alarm clock
bread
orange juice
fruit

How to describe habits

G present simple with *he / she / it*   V morning habits   P final *-s*

4C

A Vocabulary morning habits

1 Look at **Lily's morning** opposite. Match pictures a–h with the phrases.
Example   a = get up

2 What do you do in the morning? Tell your partner.
Example   I get up, then I …

B Listen for key words

3 Look at pictures a–h of Lily again. Guess the order of her actions.

☑ first   ☐ second   ☐ third   ☐ fourth
☐ fifth   ☐ sixth   ☐ seventh   ☐ eighth

4 **4C.1▶** Listen and check.

5 When you listen, you don't need to understand all the words. Look at the audio script on » p.152 and <u>underline</u> important words you need to understand.
Example   <u>What</u> do you <u>do</u> in the <u>morning</u>, Lily?

6 Read the audio script again. What does *ehm* mean?

C Read and respond

7 Do the **Personality test** opposite and count your score.

8 **4C.2▶** Listen and write Jim's answers. Is he a morning flower or a morning monster? Count his score.

1 ☐c   2 ☐   3 ☐   4 ☐   5 ☐   6 ☐   7 ☐   8 ☐
Total A ☐   B ☐   C ☐

9 Interview a partner using the personality test.

D Grammar present simple with *he / she / it*

10 Complete the grammar box.

	I / you / we / they	*he / she / it*
+	I _____ in an office.	He works in an office.
–	I _____ at weekends.	He doesn't work at weekends.
?	Do you _____ in a bank?	Does he work in a bank?

short answers	Yes, I do. No, I don't.	Yes, he _____. No, he doesn't.

Is this rule true or false?
Use the present simple to talk about habits.

11 Write these examples in the table.

~~brushes~~   ~~checks~~   does   finishes   gets   goes
~~has~~   is   leaves   phones   plays   studies   watches

After *he, she,* and *it* …			
+ *-s*	+ *-es*	change *y* to *i* + *-es*	irregular
checks	brushes		has

12 Complete the sentences about Lily's morning.
1 She _wakes_ up.
2 She _doesn't_ go for a run.
3 She _____ breakfast and _____ her email.
4 She _____ read the newspaper.
5 She _____ her teeth and _____ dressed.
6 She _____ watch TV.

13 Look at the personality test again. Ask another partner about the person they interviewed in exercise 9.

Does	she	wake up before the alarm clock?
	he	press 'snooze' five times?
		sit on the bed and think?

More practice? **Grammar Bank** » p.139.

E Pronunciation final *-s*

14 **4C.3▶** Listen and say A or B.

A	B
My brothers get up early.	My brother gets up early.
My sisters like morning.	My sister likes mornings.
My friends study in the morning.	My friend studies in the morning.

15 Test a partner.
Example   **A** My brothers get up early.   **B** A!

16 Work with a partner.
Student A Look at the pictures of Eric's morning on » p.129.
Student B Look at the pictures of Erica's morning on » p.133.

ABCDE Put it all together

17 Work with two or three partners. Think of a person in your family (or a friend) and tell your partners their name.
Example   My sister's name is Elizabeth.
Write ten questions about your partners' family members.
Example   Does Elizabeth get up early?

18 Ask the questions to your partners. Decide if the people are morning flowers or morning monsters.

I can describe morning habits.
Tick ✓ the line.   with a lot of help   with some help   on my own   very easily

How often?

 always   usually   often   sometimes   never

Office Life

Episode one

1

Boss We usually work nine to five here, Justin. You're always late.
Justin Not always, Mr Minnit.

2

Boss Yes, you always arrive late!
Justin But I never leave late!

3

Boss Hmm. And how often do you have coffee breaks?
Justin Not very often, Mr Minnit.

4

Boss But you're always at the coffee machine with Holly.
Justin That's not true. I'm often at the coffee machine without Holly.

5

Boss And another thing. The lunch break is one hour. But you sometimes leave at twelve o'clock and come back to the office at two! Explain that please!

6

Justin Well, I sometimes go for lunch with Holly, and we add our lunch hours together. One and one make two!

7

Boss Justin, it's 9.35. Start work now!
Justin 9.35? Oh no – I'm late for my coffee break!

How to describe a typical day

G adverbs of frequency   P *leave* /iː/ or *live* /ɪ/

A Read a conversation

1 Read **Office Life** opposite and answer these questions.
  1 What are the names of the three people?
  2 Is Justin a good worker?

2 Read again and answer the questions with a partner.
  1 What time do they start work? *Nine o'clock*
  2 Does Justin arrive at nine?
  3 What time do they finish work?
  4 Does Justin leave after five?
  5 Does Justin have a lot of coffee breaks?
  6 How long is the lunch break?
  7 Does Justin always have a one-hour lunch break?
  8 Why does Justin say 'Oh no' at the end?

3 **Office Life** is a TV show. Guess four places where people laugh.

4 4D.1▶ Listen and check.

5 Say the **Office Life** conversation with a partner.

B Pronunciation *leave* /iː/ or *live* /ɪ/

6 4D.2▶ Listen and say A or B.

A /iː/	B /ɪ/
Justin doesn't leave with Holly.	Justin doesn't live with Holly.
He leaves alone.	He lives alone.
Justin's seat's near Holly.	Justin sits near Holly.

7 Test a partner.
Example   A Justin doesn't live with Holly.   B B!

C Grammar adverbs of frequency

8 Look at **How often?** opposite and the examples below. Underline *before* or *after* in the grammar box.
Examples   You're always late.
             You always arrive late.
             They don't always have a one-hour lunch break.

Rule	*Always* goes before / after *be* and *do*.
	Always goes before / after a main verb.
be	am / am not, is / isn't, are / aren't
do	do / don't, does / doesn't
main verb	arrive, leave, go, etc.

9 Order the words to make sentences. The first word is always *Justin*.
  1 is late Justin always   *Justin is always late.*
  2 at Justin o'clock usually five leaves
  3 late the Justin office leaves never
  4 has sometimes Justin with lunch Holly
  5 are Holly and machine coffee the at Justin often
  6 always lunch go with Holly for Justin doesn't

10 Use one of these words to complete the sentences. Make the sentences true for you.

always   usually   often   sometimes   never
  1 I _____ get up early.
  2 I _____ leave the house before 7.30.
  3 I _____ have a big lunch.
  4 I _____ read a newspaper on the bus or train.
  5 I _____ write letters to my friends.
  6 I _____ watch TV in the evening.

11 Close your book and ask questions. Find other students with the same answers as you.
Example   A Do you get up early?
             B Yes, usually. / No, never. / Yes, sometimes.

More practice? **Grammar Bank** ≫ p.139.

D Listen for key words

12 4D.3▶ Listen to this writer. Tick ✓ the words you hear.
  ✓ writer   ☐ home   ☐ late   ☐ news   ☐ email
  ☐ bus   ☐ coffee ☐ lunch ☐ bed   ☐ evening

13 Read these sentences. Are they true or false? Listen again.
  1 He doesn't work in an office.
  2 He has a cup of tea before work.
  3 He goes to bed after lunch.
  4 He always works in the evening.

14 Read the audio script on ≫ p.153 and check your answers.

ABCD Put it all together

15 Write five or more sentences about your daily routines. You can use some of these phrases.
  … get up at …
  … have … for breakfast
  … leave the house at …
  … go to work / school / university by …
  … go for lunch with …
  … leave work / school / university at …
  … have a coffee break at …
  … in the evening
  … go to bed at …

16 Take another student's sentences. Read them out to the class. The other students guess who it is.

I can describe a typical day.
Tick ✓ the lines.   with a lot of help   with some help   on my own   very easily

Writing Everyday life in my country

A Vocabulary review

1 Make questions and test a partner.

What's the	first	month of the year?
	second	day of the week?
	third	

Example **A** What's the eighth month of the year?
B August.
A How do you spell that, please?
B A-U-G-U-S-T.

2 **4E.1▶** Listen and repeat. The audio starts from the end:
... Wednesdays.
... work on Wednesdays.
... walks to work on Wednesdays.

Wendy **al**ways **walks** to **work** on **Wednes**days.
Fiona **al**ways **phones Phil** on **Feb**ruary the **first**.
Simon's **son starts school** on Sep**tem**ber the **sev**enth.

3 Don't look at the sentences in exercise 2. Ask and answer these questions with a partner. When does ...
1 Wendy walk to work?
2 Fiona phone Phil?
3 Simon's son start school?

B Read and complete

4 Read the text. When is New Year in Ethiopia?

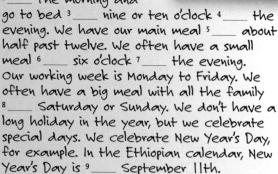

Ethiopia: Fact File

In Ethiopia, we usually get up ¹____ six o'clock ²____ the morning and go to bed ³____ nine or ten o'clock ⁴____ the evening. We have our main meal ⁵____ about half past twelve. We often have a small meal ⁶____ six o'clock ⁷____ the evening. Our working week is Monday to Friday. We often have a big meal with all the family ⁸____ Saturday or Sunday. We don't have a long holiday in the year, but we celebrate special days. We celebrate New Year's Day, for example. In the Ethiopian calendar, New Year's Day is ⁹____ September 11th.

Yohannis Kidanu

5 Complete the text with *in*, *on*, and *at*.

C Make notes

6 Complete the notes about Ethiopia.

In your country ...	Ethiopia	My country
When do you get up?	6.00	
When do you go to bed?		
When do you have your main meal?		
When do you have other meals?		
When is your working week?	Mon-Fri	
What do you do on your free days?		
Do you have a long holiday in the year?		
Do you celebrate special days? (give an example)		

7 Write notes about your country.

ABC Put it all together

8 Work with a partner. Ask and answer about everyday life in your country.
Examples *If your partner is from a different country ...*
A In _____, we usually get up at seven o'clock. When do you get up in your country?
B We usually get up at six o'clock. When do you ... ?

If your partner is from the same country ...
A I think we usually get up at seven o'clock. What do you think?
B Yes, I agree. / No, I think we usually get up at eight o'clock.
A OK. What about ... ?

9 Write about everyday life in your country, like in exercise 4. Use your notes from exercise 7.

10 Give your writing to a different partner. Are you the same or different? Tell your partner.

11 Check your partner's writing:
Are the prepositions *in*, *on*, and *at* correct?
Is the spelling correct?
Is all the information included?

I can write about everyday life in my country.

Tick ✓ the line. with a lot of help   with some help   on my own   very easily

Unit 4 Review

A Grammar

1 Present simple Complete the text with the correct form of these verbs.

~~arrive~~ come do finish go have leave phone play write

Complaint memo

To: Tim Eismoney
Managing Director
From: Arnold Minnit *Manager*
Subject: Justin Tyme

Justin always [1] *arrives* late at the office. He [2] _____ a lot of coffee breaks. He often [3] _____ for lunch at 12 o'clock and [4] _____ back to the office at two.

Justin [5] _____ the office at five o'clock, but he [6] _____ work at four. In the last hour, he [7] _____ his friends, [8] _____ personal emails, [9] _____ computer games, and [10] _____ crosswords.

Mr Arnold Minnit
Manager

2 Frequency adverbs Find and copy eight sentences beginning with 'Ana'.

[1] Ana	usually	gets	[2] Ana	sometimes	goes	for
[3] Ana	never	up	o'clock.	always	[4] Ana	a
[5] Ana	goes	at	eight	has	coffee	run
is	to	work	by	train.	for	in
sometimes	late	for	work.	[6] Ana	breakfast.	the
[7] Ana	at	lunch	has	usually	[8] Ana	morning.
often	half	past	one.	weekends.	never	watches
goes	to	the	cinema	at	news.	the

Example 1 = Ana usually gets up at eight o'clock.

3 Change the sentences in exercise 2. Make them true for you.

Example I never get up at eight o'clock.

4 Prepositions of time Complete the sentences with *at*, *in*, or *on*. Are they true or false for you?

1 We don't have a class _on_ Wednesday.
2 My birthday isn't ____ May or June.
3 I always get up early ____ the morning.
4 I get up late ____ the weekend.
5 We have a holiday ____ May 1st.
6 I go to bed ____ eleven o'clock.
7 The shops are closed ____ Sunday.
8 I always watch TV ____ the evening.
9 School finishes ____ the end of June.
10 I sometimes sleep for an hour ____ the afternoon.

B Vocabulary

5 Dates Order these dates.

- [ ] December 8th
- [ ] September 9th
- [ ] October 15th
- [ ] January 15th
- [ ] November 25th
- [ ] May 3rd
- [ ] March 12th
- [ ] June 2nd
- [ ] October 2nd
- [ ] July 10th
- [1] January 5th
- [ ] February 1st
- [ ] August 4th
- [ ] April 20th

6 Dates Say the complete dates.

Example 1 = January the fifth

7 Responses Complete the phrases.

1 I've got an exam this afternoon.
   Oh, *good luck*!
2 My exam result is A+!
   W____ d____!
3 My holiday's cancelled.
   Oh, I____ s____!
4 W____ w____?
   The phone's out of order.
5 My son's in the Christmas play!
   Oh, t____'____ gr____!
6 I'm late and all the taxis are full.
   O____ n____!

8 Habits and routines Complete the text.

I get up at 7.30 and [1] *have* a shower. Then I [2] _____ dressed and [3] _____ breakfast. I [4] _____ the house and [5] _____ to school on the bus. On the bus, I [6] _____ to music on my mini-disc player. My first class [7] _____ at 8.45. I [8] _____ lunch at 12.30. After school, I [9] _____ football with my friends. Then I [10] _____ home and [11] _____ TV. I [12] _____ to bed at 10.30. And then I remember my homework ...

PARTY PUZZLE

JANE · **PETE** · **ROSE** · **MIKE**

JUDE · **JOE** · **KATE** · **STEVE**

These are your friends. You invite them for dinner. At dinner, you don't want all the men to sit together and all the women to sit together, so you make a plan of the table like this:

table plan

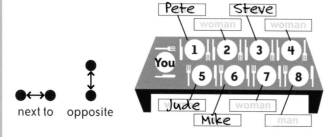

next to · opposite

Also, you don't want people to sit near (next to or opposite) people they know. You want to introduce them to new people! Jude is your best friend, so you put her near you in place number 5. But where do you put your other friends? These are the people they know:

WHO KNOWS WHO?

Joe knows **Kate** very well, and she knows him – they're a couple and they live together. **Joe** also knows **Jude** because he works with her. Jude likes him a lot.

Jane knows **Mike**. She thinks Mike's great – in fact, she loves him. Unfortunately for Jane, Mike doesn't like her.

Pete's an Erasmus student from Holland. He knows **Jane** and **Rose**. They're his neighbours and he sees them every day. He likes them, especially Rose. Rose helps him with his English sometimes.

Steve knows **Jude**. She's his ex-girlfriend, but now he hates her.

At the party

a Do you know my girlfriend Kate? Come and meet her.
b Jude. It's short for Judith.
c Kate, this is Steve.
d Sorry, what's your name again?
e Who are they? Do you know them?
f Who's he? Do you know him?
g Hi Mike. Do you remember me?
h Yeah, that's Mike, but I don't know the other one. Let's go and meet them.
i Yeah, that's Pete. He's from Amsterdam. Come and meet him.

1 | a

2

3

4

5

6

7

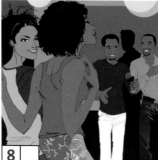

8

9

How to introduce people

G object pronouns; prepositions of place *next to, opposite* **V** phrases to introduce people **P** vowels

A Read for detail

1 Look at **Party puzzle** opposite. How many people are at the dinner party?

2 Look at **Party puzzle** opposite. Who says this? Read and find the names.
1 'Kate's my girlfriend.' *Joe*
2 'Steve hates me.'
3 'I think Jane loves me!'
4 'Pete's my neighbour.'
5 'My boyfriend works with Jude.'
6 'I like Rose and Jane.'

3 Prepare to do the puzzle. Put ✓ and ✗ in this table.
✓ = She knows him or he knows her.
✗ = She doesn't know him or he doesn't know her.

	Jane	Jude	Kate	Rose
Steve		✓	✗	
Joe				
Mike				
Pete				

4 Do the puzzle with your partner. Write the names on the table plan in **Party puzzle**.

B Grammar object pronouns

5 Write the object pronouns in the box.
her him it me them us you

subject	verb	object
Joe	knows	Kate.

subject pronoun	verb	object pronoun
He	knows	her.

subject pronouns	I	you	he	she	it	we	they
object pronouns							

6 Find object pronouns in **Who knows who?** opposite.

7 Complete the sentences.
1 **Jane**   Pete knows Rose and Rose knows _him_.
2 **Pete / Mike** We know Jane and she knows _____.
3 **Mike**   I don't like Jane but she loves _____.
4 **Steve**   I know Jude but I don't like _____.
5 **Pete**   I know Jane and Rose and I like _____.
6 **Joe to Kate** You know me and I know _____.
7 **Jude**   My name's Judith, but I don't like _____.

8 **5A.1▶** Listen and complete the sentences.
Example I know you ... *and you know me.*

More practice? **Grammar Bank** ≫ p.140.

C Pronunciation vowels *a, e, i, o, u*

9 **5A.2▶** The green vowels in these names are pronounced like the letters in the alphabet. Listen and repeat.

a /eɪ/	**e** /iː/	**i** /aɪ/	**o** /əʊ/	**u** /juː/
Kate	Pete	Mike	Rose	Jude

10 **5A.3▶** Listen to the difference between the green and blue vowel letters. Can you see a spelling rule? (Clue: *Pete* and *pet* – what is the difference in spelling?)
This is Kate's cat and that's Pete's pet.
Mike and Mick are short for Michael.
Rose Ross knows Jude Judd.

11 Listen again and repeat.

D Vocabulary phrases to introduce people

12 Look at **At the party** opposite. Who can you see in pictures 1–9?
Example picture 1 = Rose, Joe, Kate

13 Match pictures 1–9 with sentences a–i in **At the party**.

14 **5A.4▶** Listen and check. Listen again and repeat.

15 Work with two partners. Write a conversation like this, but change the words in *italics* for true information.
Juan *Bülent*, do you know my friend *Gosia*? She's from *Warsaw*. Come and meet her. *Gosia*, this is *Bülent*.
Bülent Nice to meet you. Sorry, what's your name again?
Gosia *Gosia*. It's short for *Małgorzata*. Where are you from?
Bülent I'm from *Turkey*.

16 Practise saying your conversation.

ABCD Put it all together

17 You are a famous actor or actress. Choose a name from this list, or choose another one you know.
Audrey Tatou (France)
Ewan McGregor (Scotland)
Halle Berry (the USA)
Javier Bardem (Spain)
Jennifer Lopez (the USA)
Pierce Brosnan (Ireland)

You are at the Oscars party. Stand up and meet the other actors and actresses.
Example **A** Hi, I'm Robert de Niro. What's your name?
        B I'm Jane Fonda and this is my friend Jodie Foster – do you know her?

I can introduce people.
Tick ✓ the line.   with a lot of help   with some help   on my own   very easily

Colours

black grey brown
red blue green yellow
blond white

Adjectives

tall short **big small** new OLD **fat** thin long

	A	E	I	O	U
1					
2					
3					
4					
5					
6					

How to describe people and objects

G order of adjectives   V adjectives   P *man* /æ/ or *men* /e/

A Vocabulary adjectives

1 **5B.1▶** Look at the photos opposite. Listen and say which photos.
Example   **Audio** A red car.   **You** 3E and 5O!

2 Test a partner.
Example   **A** A green bag.   **B** 6A and 4U.

B Pronunciation *man* /æ/ or *men* /e/

3 **5B.2▶** Listen and say A or B.

A /æ/	the man	the tall man	the tall blond man
B /e/	the men	the tall men	the tall blond men

4 Test a partner.
Example   **A** The men.   **B** B!

5 **5B.3▶** Listen. How many /æ/ and /e/ sounds are there?
/æ/ My flatmate Matt's got a fat black cat.
/e/ My best friend Jen's got ten red pens.

C Grammar order of adjectives

6 Look at the examples in the grammar box.

noun	adjective + noun	2 adjectives + noun
a car	a new car	a new red car
eyes	brown eyes (*not* ~~browns~~ eyes!)	big brown eyes

Put ✓ or ✗ next to these rules.
☐ Put -*s* at the end of adjectives to make plurals.
☐ Put the adjective before the noun.
☐ Put colour adjectives after other adjectives.

7 Correct the mistakes.
1 a dog fat white   *a fat white dog*
2 a grey big dog
3 smalls blues eyes
4 blond long hair
5 hair short black
6 a bag green small
7 olds reds cars
8 a big cat black

8 Work with a partner. Make a sentence about one of the photos opposite, but only say one adjective. Your partner asks a question.
Example   **A** I like the red car.
            B The **new** red car or the **old** red car?
            A The **old** red car.

More practice? **Grammar Bank** ≫ p.140.

D Listen for detail

9 **5B.4▶** Play a game of bingo.
1 Choose nine photos opposite, in a 3x3 square.
2 Listen and tick ✓.
3 Say 'Bingo' when all nine have got a tick ✓.

10 **5B.5▶** Listen to a man speaking about his best friend and his neighbour. Complete the notes.

	best friend	neighbour
hair	short black hair	
eyes		
car		
pet		big brown dog

11 Read the audio script on ≫ p.153 and check your answers.

ABCD Put it all together

12 Work with a partner.
Student A Look at the pictures of your best friend and your neighbour on ≫ p.129.
Student B Look at the pictures of your best friend and your neighbour on ≫ p.133.

Make sentences about the people. How many differences can you find?

My best friend's	got	long brown hair.
My neighbour's		short brown hair.
He's		blue eyes.
She's		brown eyes.
		your ideas

13 Make notes about two people you know. Tell your partner about the people.

My brother:
long brown hair
blue eyes
white car

I can describe people and objects.

Office supplies

batteries   pencils
CDs   pens
a computer   a printer
files   printer ink
notebooks   rubbers
paper   rulers

At the shops

Customer Excuse me, can you help me?
Assistant Yes, of course.
C Have you got any printer ink?
A Yes, what printer have you got?
C It's an Epson. I don't know the model.
A Is it this one?
C Yes, that's it.
A OK. Black and colour?
C Just black, thanks. I've got lots of colour ink.
A OK. Here you are.
C Thanks. Oh, and I haven't got any paper ...
A OK, the paper's over there.

a | office supplies shop

I haven't got any other ...

b | news-stand

We've got these two bottles ...

c | delicatessen

We've got this book ...

d | bookshop

I'm sorry, we haven't got any ...

e | greengrocer's

How to ask for things in shops

G *have got* V office supplies; shopping phrases

A Vocabulary office supplies

1 Look at **Office supplies** opposite. Work with a partner. Match the words and pictures.
Example   1 = rulers

2 **5C.1▶** Listen, check, and repeat.

3 What else can you find in an office supplies shop? Think of three more things or find them in your dictionary. Compare with a partner.

B Read a shop conversation

4 **5C.2▶** Read and listen to **At the shops** opposite. What's the man saying in photo a? Choose one sentence from **At the shops** and write it in the photo.

5 Read the **At the shops** conversation again. Answer the questions with *Yes, she has* or *No, she hasn't*.
Has the woman got ...
1 a printer? *Yes, she has.*
2 any black printer ink?
3 any colour printer ink?
4 any paper?

6 **5C.3▶** Listen and repeat sentences from **At the shops**. Copy the pronunciation.

7 Say the **At the shops** conversation with a partner.

C Grammar *I / you / we / they have got*

8 Complete the grammar box.

+	I've got a pen.	We've got a printer.	They've _____ a computer.
−	I haven't got a pen.	We _____ _____ a printer.	They haven't got a computer.
?	Have you got a pen?	Have you got a printer?	_____ they _____ a computer?

short answers			
+	Yes, I have.	Yes, we _____.	Yes, they have.
−	No, I haven't.	No, we haven't.	No, they _____.

9 Work with a partner. Ask and answer.
Student A You are a customer in a shop. Ask for office supplies.
Student B You work in the shop. You haven't got the things A wants, so offer other similar things.

Example   **A** Have you got any red pens?
            B No, I'm sorry. We haven't got any red pens, but we've got some blue pens.
            A Oh, OK. And have you got any small notebooks?

10 Write true answers. Have you got ...
1 any brothers or sisters?
   Yes, I have. / No, I haven't.
2 a dog or a cat?
3 a car?
4 a computer?
5 any children?
6 any CDs?
7 a garden?
8 a mobile phone?

11 After *Yes, I have*, write more information.
Example   1 Have you got any brothers or sisters?
                Yes, I have. I've got two brothers.

12 Ask and answer questions from exercise 10 with a partner.
Example   **A** Have you got any brothers or sisters?
            B Yes, I have. I've got two brothers. And you?

More practice? **Grammar Bank** ≫ p.140.

D Listen for detail

13 **5C.4▶** Listen to four shop conversations. Match the conversations with photos b–e in **At the shops** opposite.
Example   Conversation 1 = bookshop

14 Listen again and complete the information in the table. Compare with a partner.

	The customer wants ...	The shop has got ...
bookshop	books about _____ and baby care	the books
delicatessen	English _____	English _____ wine German _____ wine
greengrocer's	_____ and a bag of _____	tomatoes (but not green) and _____
news-stand	_____ and chewing gum	Le Monde

15 Read the audio script on ≫ p.153 and check your answers.

ABCD Put it all together

16 Work with a partner. Choose:
1 a kind of shop
2 three things you want

Write a conversation in the shop. You can use a dictionary.

17 Practise saying your conversation with your partner. Then close your book and act your conversation for another pair.

 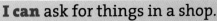

✈ In-flight offers

1

Flight simulator CD-ROM
€19.99

new

2

Alpine adventure watch
with GPS & altimeter!
€119.99

3

Travel alarm clock
€9.99

new Chinese Cookbook

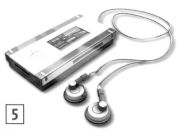

4

Electric travel wok
€59.99

with free Chinese cook book

5

iPop MP3 player
€149.99

with free carrying case

6

The world of animals
Picture calendar
€10.99

7

French wine collection
Box of six mini bottles of French wine
€29.99

new

8

Pocket-size mini keyboard
for mobile phones
€49.99

9

Fine Belgian chocolates
Box of chocolates
€15.99

10

Perfume gift box
Fine fragrances from around the world
€29.99

Your friends

Jane

Pete

Mike

Rose

Jude

Joe

Kate

Steve

How to **ask about people's interests**

G *has got*   V gifts   P stress timing

A Read and guess meanings

1 Read **In-flight offers** opposite. Work with a partner and choose a gift for the people in **Your friends** opposite.

Example   I think the chocolate is a good present for Pete.

2 Are any words the same (or similar) in your language?

Examples   'CD' is the same in Spanish.
We use the word 'mini' in French.

3 Two things in **In-flight offers** are not real. Find them!

4 Which gift would you like? Tell your partner.

B Grammar *he / she / it has got*

5 Complete the grammar box.

+	She's got a watch.	He's got a phone.	It's got an alarm.
–	She hasn't got a watch.	He _____ a phone.	It _____ an alarm?
?	Has she got a watch?	_____ a phone?	_____ an alarm?

short answers			
+	Yes, she has.	Yes, he _____.	Yes, it has.
–	No, she hasn't.	No, he hasn't.	No, it _____.

6 Complete the questions with *Has* or *Does*.

Examples   _Has_ he got a calendar?
Does he like films?

1 _____ she got a car?
2 _____ he drink wine?
3 _____ she like perfume?
4 _____ she got a computer?
5 _____ he cook?
6 _____ he got a mobile phone?
7 _____ she like chocolate?
8 _____ she ski?

7 Write answers to the questions in exercise 6 about two people in your family. Use *Yes, ... has / No ... hasn't / Yes, ... does / No, ... doesn't*.

8 Tell your partner the names of the two people in your family. Then ask and answer with a partner.

Example   **A** My sister's name's Maria.
B Has she got a car?
A No, she hasn't.
B Does she like ... ?

More practice? **Grammar Bank** ≫ p.140.

9 **5D.1▶** Listen and complete the conversation.
A I need a gift for my friend Jane. Have you ¹_got_ any ideas?
B ² _____ she like wine?
A No, she ³ _____.

B Has she got a DVD player?
A No, she ⁴ _____.
B OK, give her a DVD player.
A They're very expensive.
B Oh, OK. Does she ⁵ _____ animals?
A Yes, she ⁶ likes them.
B OK, give her an animal calendar.
A Good idea. Thanks.

10 Read the audio script on ≫ p.153 and check your answers.

11 Work with a partner.

Student A Jude and Mike are your friends. Look at the information on ≫ p.129.

Student B Rose and Pete are your friends. Look at the information on ≫ p.133.

Have conversations like the one in exercise 9. You can use the questions in exercise 6 to help you.

C Listen for detail

12 **5D.2▶** Listen. What are the differences with the conversation in exercise 9? Now <u>underline</u> the differences in the audio script on ≫ p.153.

13 **5D.3▶** Listen to another conversation and answer the questions.
1 Does Rose ski?
2 Has Rose got a car?
3 Has Rose got a mobile phone?

14 Listen again. Choose a gift from **In-flight offers** for Rose.

D Pronunciation stress timing

15 **5D.4▶** Listen to these sentences. Notice the number of unstressed syllables ● between the stressed syllables ●.

She's **got** a gui**tar** but she **has**n't got a **car**.

He's **got** a **car** but he **has**n't got a gui**tar**.

16 Listen again and repeat.

17 Work with a partner. Say similar sentences about people you know. Use other words, for example *car, bike, watch, alarm clock, CD player*.

Example   My brother's got a bike but he hasn't got a car.

ABCD Put it all together

18 Have conversations, like the one in exercise 9, about your real friends and family.

Example   **A** I need a gift for my brother. Have you got any ideas?
B Does he like ... ? / Has he got ... ?

I can ask about people's interests.

Tick ✓ the line.   with a lot of help   with some help   on my own   very easily

Writing A self-portrait

A Vocabulary review

1 Which one is not correct? ~~Cross~~ it out.

1. a black hair
   b ~~green hair~~
   c blond hair
2. a a blue cat
   b an old cat
   c a small cat
3. a white wine
   b red wine
   c blue wine
4. a my favourite Rome
   b my favourite place
   c my favourite food
5. a the nine o'clock news
   b the nine o'clock gift
   c the nine o'clock train
6. a white eyes
   b blue eyes
   c green eyes

2 Complete the sentences about you. Use adjectives.

1. I've got _____ eyes.
2. I've got _____ hair.
3. In my bag, I've got …
4. At home, I've got …
5. I haven't got …

B Read and check spelling

3 Read **A Self-portrait**. Correct the spelling mistakes – add 16 more letter 'e's.

4 **5E.1▶** Listen and repeat.

C Make notes

5 Complete the notes about Mike.

	Mike	me
eyes	brown	
hair		
live	in a _____	
work	in a supermarket	
food	Chinese	
drink		
car	no	
bike		
pet		
don't like	_____, ties	
watch	nine o'clock news	
listen to	_____ ✓ blues ✗	
favourite place	flat	

6 Write notes about you. You can use your dictionary.

ABC Put it all together

7 Write a self-portrait from your notes.
   Example   I've got blond hair and I've got blue eyes …

8 Check your spelling and adjective order, or ask your partner to check your writing.

A Self-portrait
by Mike Campbell

I've got black hair,
I'v got brown eyes

I don't lik hats and
I don't lik ties

I'v got an old bik but I havn't got a car

I liv in a flat and I work in a 'Spar'*

I drink whit win but never Champagne

My favourit food's chicken chow mein

I listen to jazz but I don't lik blues

I always watch the nin o'clock news

I havn't got a dog but I'v got a small cat

My favourit plac is my little flat

tie

* Spar = the name of a supermarket

I can write a self-portrait.

Tick ✓ the line.   with a lot of help   with some help   on my own   very easily

Unit 5 Review

A Grammar

1 **Pronouns** Complete the text with *me, him, her, it, us,* or *them*.

Who knows who?

I know Jim very well – we're teachers and we work together. We also know Jude because she works with ¹ _us_ . I like ² _her_ a lot. She always talks to ³ _me/us_ in the coffee break. Micky's an Erasmus student from Germany. He knows Ana and Satomi. They're his neighbours and he sees ⁴ _them_ every day. He likes ⁵ _them_, especially Satomi. ⁶ _She_ helps ⁷ _him_ with his English sometimes. Micky's got a red car and I often see ⁸ _it_ in the school car park.

2 *Have got* Order the words to make questions.

1 brothers   got   sisters   you   any   or   Have
   Have you got any brothers or sisters ?

2 you   children   got   any   Have
   _____ ?

3 you   got   dog   Have   a   or   cat   a
   _____ ?

4 Have   car   a   parents   got   your
   _____ ?

5 Has   your   hair   mother   red   got
   _____ ?

6 teacher   your   Has   brown   got   eyes
   _____ ?

3 Write your answers for the questions in exercise 2.
   Example   1 Yes, I have. I've got one sister.
   1 _____
   2 _____
   3 _____
   4 _____
   5 _____
   6 _____

4 **Order of adjectives** Complete the sentences with the words in (brackets).

1 I haven't got a _____ (small cat black) but I've got a _____ (dog black big).

2 My best friend's got _____ (brown long hair) and _____ (blue big eyes). She's got a _____ (yellow car small) and a _____ (cat fat brown).

3 My neighbour's a _____ (man tall) with _____ (hair short blond) and _____ (eyes brown). He's got a _____ (car big green) and a _____ (black cat thin).

B Vocabulary

5 **Phrases for introducing** Match 1–8 with a–h.

1 [h] Do you know my ...   a you know them?
2 [ ] Come and ...   b Rose.
3 [ ] Mike, this is ...   c remember me?
4 [ ] Hi Mike. Do you ...   d name again?
5 [ ] Sorry, what's your ...   e meet him.
6 [ ] Mike. It's short ...   f from Amsterdam.
7 [ ] That's Pete. He's ...   g for Michael.
8 [ ] Who are they? Do ...   h ~~brother Mike?~~

6 **Colours** Find eight more colours.

B	Y	E	L	L	O	W
R	W	H	I	T	E	B
O	G	R	E	E	N	L
W	B	L	U	E	R	O
N	G	R	E	Y	E	N
B	L	A	C	K	D	D

1 *brown* _____
2 _____
3 _____
4 _____
5 _____
6 _____
7 _____
8 _____
9 _____

7 **Adjectives** Match the opposites.

1 [ ] old   a tall
2 [ ] short   b thin
3 [ ] fat   c new
4 [ ] small   d big

8 **Office supplies** Write the names of these things.

1	2	3
4	5	6
7	8	9
10	11	12

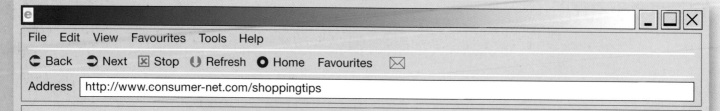

Six tips for shoppers

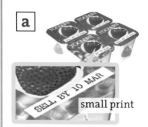

a

small print

b   batteries

1   Watch out for the number 99!
The price is 5.99. You see the 5 and you think it's cheap. But it's really 6 – is that cheap?

2   Don't buy food for the bin!
You want one bag of oranges. The shop offers three bags for the price of two. But can you really use three bags of oranges?

3   Watch out for the extras!
It's a cheap printer. But how much is the ink? It's a cheap watch. But how much are the batteries?

4   Never buy cheap things!
Cheap things are always bad. Expensive things are always good.

5   Read the small print!
There's a special offer on the yogurt. But the sell-by date is today!

6   Don't buy it if you don't want it!
Three DVDs for 9.99 – that's cheap if you want the DVDs. But it's expensive if you don't!

c

d   DVD   9.99

e   0.99   2.99   3.99   1.99 price

Food and drink

apples
biscuits
coffee
crisps
sandwiches
soup
tea
water

Tea and a sandwich

Waitress Can I help you?
Jim How much are the sandwiches, please?
W Three pounds fifty.
J OK, a sandwich, please.
W Here you are. Would you like anything to drink?
J How much is the tea?
W Ninety p.
J OK, I'd like a cup of tea, please.
W That's four pounds forty, please.
J Here you are.
W And here's your change. Thank you.

How to **ask about prices**

G countable and uncountable   V food and drink; prices   P sentence stress

A   Read tips on a web page

1   Work with a partner. Are these good offers? Write ✓ or ✗.
1   ✓ Two for the price of one.
2   ☐ One for the price of two.
3   ☐ Fly from Paris to New York for only 50 euros!
4   ☐ Laptop computer, only 5000 dollars!
5   ☐ Today only – everything half-price!
6   ☐ Cup of coffee – 20 euros!
7   ☐ Buy two, get one free!
8   ☐ Usual price, twenty pounds. Today, nineteen ninety-nine!

2   Look at **Six tips for shoppers** opposite. Find one bad tip.

3   Match the five good tips with photos a–e.
Example   a = tip 5

B   Listen for prices

4   **6A.1▶** Listen and find the way from start to end.

START ↓	€5.15	€7.13	€3.14	€9.16	€6.40
€5.50 →	€7.30	€3.40	€9.60	€6.14	€2.15
€7.13	€3.14	€9.16	€6.40	€2.50	€13.17
€3.40	€9.60	€8.90	€2.15	€13.70	€15.15
€9.16	€8.19	€2.50	€30.17	€15.50	€50.15
€8.90	€2.15	€30.70	€50.50	€15.15	END

5   Choose a new way from start to end. Tell a partner.
Example   Five euros fifty – seven euros thirteen ...

6   Work with a partner.
Student A Say prices for these things.
Student B Say *That's cheap!* or *That's expensive!*

a computer	a car	a blank CD
a mobile phone	a pen	a cinema ticket
a cup of coffee	a TV	a ticket to Australia
a newspaper	a lunch	

Example   A This pen costs 15 euros.
            B That's expensive!

C   Grammar   countable and uncountable

7   Look at **Food and drink** opposite. Match the words with food and drink 1–8 in the photo.
Example   1 = soup

8   Write words from **Food and drink** in the grammar box.

singular and plural (countable)	examples
sandwich – sandwiches	How much is a sandwich? How much are the sandwiches?
–	
–	
–	

no singular or plural (uncountable)	example
tea	How much is the tea?

Complete this rule with *is* and *are*.
Write _____ before a singular noun, _____ before a plural noun, and _____ before an uncountable noun.

9   Complete the sentences.
1   How much _____ the apples?
2   How much _____ the water?
3   How much _____ the crisps?
4   How much _____ the sandwiches?
5   How much _____ the coffee?

10   Ask a partner the price of the things in **Food and drink**. Invent the answers.
Example   A How much is the water?
            B Fifty-nine cents.

11   **6A.2▶** Pronunciation Listen and repeat the rhyme.
How **much** are the **bis**cuits?
How **much** is the **tea**?
The **tea's** one pound **fif**ty.
The **bis**cuits are **free**.

More practice? **Grammar Bank** >> p.141.

D   Listen to a conversation

12   **6A.3▶** Close your book and listen. What does Jim want to eat and drink?

13   Complete **Tea and a sandwich** opposite.

14   Listen again and check. Say the conversation with a partner.

ABCD   Put it all together

15   Work with a partner. Have a conversation in a café.
Student A look at >> p.129.   **Student B** look at >> p.133.

The GREASY SPOON

Bread and jam £1.00

Morning, night and afternoon Here at The GREASY SPOON

Sausages with chips and eggs £5.50

A piece of pizza (extra cheese!) £2.20

Tea or coffee £1.20

Apple pie or chocolate cake £2.50

Fish and chips with beans or peas £7.80

Chicken legs £3.00

Potatoes, onions, carrots, and steak £10.00

Tomato salad £1.50

Toasted sandwich (cheese or ham) £2.50

Breakfast in the afternoon Here at The GREASY SPOON

Ordering food

Waitress Can I help you?

Jim Yes. I'd like some sausages with chips and eggs, please.

W Sorry, we haven't got any eggs today.

J OK, then can I have sausages with chips, please?

W Sorry, we haven't got any chips.

J Have you got any sausages?

W No, sorry.

J OK. I'd like a toasted sandwich …

How to order food in a café

G *some, any*   V food   P spellings *ee* and *ea*

A Vocabulary food

1 Complete this table with words from **The Greasy Spoon** opposite.

meat and fish	fruit and vegetables	other
sausages	a*pples*	e*ggs*
st_____	*potatoes*	che_____
h_____	on_____	pi_____
ch_____	ca_____	br_____
f_____	to_____	j_____
	b_____	apple p_____
	p_____	chocolate c_____

2 Don't look at the page opposite. Complete the menu from memory.

The Greasy Spoon

Sausages with chips and ¹_____
Tomato salad
²_____ legs
Tea or ³_____
Bread and jam
Toasted sandwich
Cheese or ⁴_____

Breakfast in the afternoon
Here at 'The Greasy Spoon'

A piece of pizza (extra ⁵_____!)
Fish and ⁶_____ with beans or peas
⁷_____, onions, carrots, and steak
Apple pie or chocolate ⁸_____

Morning, night, and afternoon
Here at 'The Greasy Spoon'!

3 **6B.1▶** Listen and check. Practise saying the rhyme.

B Grammar *some, any*

4 Add words from exercise 1 to these lists.
countable – onions, carrots, ...
uncountable – fish, meat, ...

5 Underline one word to make a correct sentence.
1 I'd like two milks / eggs / breads, please.
2 I'd like some cheese / pea / chip, please.
3 Have you got any eggs / sausage / apple?
4 I'd like a ham / jam / sausage, please.
5 Have you got any apples / breads / waters, please?
6 Can I have some pea / tomato / meat, please?

6 Complete the grammar box. Use *some* or *any*.

	countable singular	countable plural
+	We've got an onion.	We've got _____ onions.
–	We haven't got an onion.	We haven't got _____ onions.
?	Have you got an onion?	Have you got _____ onions?

	uncountable
+	We've got _____ cheese.
–	We haven't got _____ cheese.
?	Have you got _____ cheese?

7 Have you got the food in photos a–j at home? Write five sentences.
Examples We've got some ham. We haven't got any eggs.

8 Ask a partner.
Example A Have you got any apples at home?
B Yes, we have. (*or* I don't know!)

More practice? **Grammar Bank** ≫ p.141.

C Pronunciation spellings *ee* and *ea*

9 Match the rhyming words.
cake   green   ~~peas~~   red   street   tree   week
1 cheese *peas*   3 bread   5 bean   7 speak
2 tea   4 meat   6 steak

10 Usually, *ee* and *ea* = /iː/. Find four words in exercise 9 which <u>don't</u> have this vowel sound.

D Listen for differences

11 **6B.2▶** Read **Ordering food** opposite. Listen and <u>underline</u> the differences.
Example On the audio, they say 'beans', not 'chips'.

12 Say the **Ordering food** conversation with a partner.

ABCD Put it all together

13 Work with a partner. Say the conversation in **Ordering food** again, but order different food.

14 Change roles and do it again. Then close your book and act the conversation for another pair.

I can order food in a café.
Tick ✓ the line.   with a lot of help   with some help   on my own   very easily

SUPERMARKET TRIVIA!

RULES

1 Put a ⬤ on A.
2 Listen to the question and write your answer.
3 Listen to the answer:
   Is your answer correct? Go to the next square.
   Is your answer wrong? Read the PENALTY!
4 The first person to pass the checkout wins.

PENALTY!

A There aren't any trolleys. Don't go to B.
B There are some trolleys in the way. Don't go to C.
C Your mobile rings – it's your mum! Don't go to D.
D Oops! You want a bag of sugar. Go back to C.
E You want some meat, and there are five people before you. Don't go to F.
F There's some bread in the oven. You like hot bread. Wait. Go back to E.
G You want a pizza. Go back to F.
H There aren't any oranges. Go back to B and get a bottle of orange juice.
I There's a woman with two trolleys. She's in the way. Don't go to J.
J Some of the milk is old – read the dates carefully! Don't go to K.
K Oops! There aren't any tomatoes in your trolley. Go back to H.
L There are ten people before you at the checkout. Don't go out.

Labels on board: chicken, sausages, bread, pizzas, D, E, F, steak, jam, sugar, salt, apples, C, G, soup, oranges, bananas, pasta, juice, B, H, tomatoes, trolley, carrots, A, water, I, milk, yogurt, cheese, L, K, J, checkout, butter, eggs

How to **talk about food**

G *there is, there are*   V food; supermarkets   P *-er* = /ə/

A Vocabulary food

1 Look at the supermarket opposite. Find examples of *meat, fruit and vegetables*, and *other food*.

2 Test a partner.
Example   **A** Oranges?   **B** Fruit and vegetables!

B Grammar *there is, there are*

3 **6C.1▶** Look at the supermarket opposite. Listen and say *true* or *false*.

4 Complete the grammar box.

+	There's some jam.	There _____ some apples.
–	There _____ any jam.	There _____ any apples.
?	_____ there any jam?	Are there any apples?

short answers	Yes, there _____. Yes, there are.	No, there isn't. No, there _____.

5 Answer the questions. Use these phrases.

Yes, there is.   No, there isn't.   I don't know.
Yes, there are.   No, there aren't.

1 Is there any yogurt in a Greek salad? *No, there isn't.*
2 Is there any cheese in a Greek salad?
3 Are there any potatoes in a Russian salad?
4 Are there any peas in a fruit salad?

6 **6C.2▶** Listen and check.

7 Ask a partner five questions.

Is there any	meat	in	Spanish paella?
Are there any	sugar		Mexican chilli con carne?
	vegetables		a hamburger?
	milk		French onion soup?
	onions		curry?
			spaghetti bolognese?

Example   **A** Is there any meat in Spanish paella?
            B Yes, there is./No, there isn't./I don't know.

8 Work with a partner. How are these things different? Choose two and write sentences.
Example   There isn't any cheese in a hamburger, but there's some cheese in a cheeseburger.

a cappuccino – an espresso
an English breakfast – a continental breakfast
a cup of tea in England – a cup of tea in Turkey
a Spanish omelette – a French omelette
a Greek salad – a Russian salad

More practice? **Grammar Bank** >> p.141.

C Read for detail

9 Read **Rules** opposite. Write *true* or *false*.
1 First, listen to the question. Then write your answer. *True*
2 Don't write the answer to the question.
3 The answer is on the audio.
4 When you pass the checkout, you win.

10 Read **Penalty!** opposite. Match pictures a–d with a penalty.

D Listen and respond

11 **6C.3▶** Listen to the questions. Tick ✓ the key words.

1 ☐ potatoes ☐ apples   ☐ Greek   ☐ Russian
2 ☐ yellow   ☐ green   ☐ red   ☐ blue
   ☐ apples   ☐ bananas
3 ☐ meat   ☐ sugar   ☐ paella ☐ vegetables
   ☐ salad

12 **6C.4▶** Read **Rules** opposite again. Then listen and play the **Supermarket Trivia!** game. Start at square A.

E Pronunciation *-er* = /ə/

13 **6C.5▶** Listen. Note the red syllables are all pronounced /ə/. Listen again and repeat.

   Waiter,   **wai**ter!
There's **bu**tter in my **wat**er
   And **sug**ar on my **pi**zza
   And **pa**sta on my **daugh**ter!

14 Think of more words ending with *-er* = /ə/. Say your words.

Clues   **family**   **jobs**   **months**
          father ...   designer ...   December ...

ABCDE Put it all together

15 Work with a partner. Find six differences.
   Student A Look at the picture on >> p.129.
   Student B Look at the picture on >> p.133.
   Example   **A** Are there any apples in your picture?
               B Yes, there are.
               A OK, that's the same. Are there any carrots?
               B No, there aren't.
               A OK, that's different.

I can talk about food.
Tick ✓ the line.   with a lot of help   with some help   on my own   very easily

Offers

Help yourself!   Do you take sugar?   Would you like another one?
Would you like a crisp?   Try this. It's delicious!   How much do you want?

How to offer things

A Vocabulary offering phrases

1 Look at **Offers** opposite. Work with a partner. Match pictures a–f with the phrases.
Example a = Would you like a crisp?

2 **6D.1▶** Listen and check.

3 **6D.2▶** Listen and repeat the phrases.
Example self ... yourself ... Help yourself!

B Read for general meaning

4 Read **Sue and Iris** and choose the best title for the story.
a Best Friends   b In the Kitchen   c Going Shopping

5 **6D.3▶** Read again and listen to the story. Answer the questions.

	Who offers ...	
a	a biscuit?	*Sue*
b	some tea bags?	
c	a cup of tea?	
d	some milk?	
e	some sugar?	

	Who asks for ...	
f	a biscuit?	
g	some tea bags?	

6 Match these sentences with the offers and requests in exercise 5. Write the letter.
1 [c] Would you like a cup of tea? *Iris offers Sue a cup of tea.*
2 ☐ Would you like another one?
3 ☐ Help yourself!
4 ☐ How much sugar do you want?
5 ☐ How many do you need?
6 ☐ I'd like a biscuit.
7 ☐ Have you got any?

7 Say the **Sue and Iris** conversation with a partner.

C Grammar *much, many, a lot of*

8 Work with a partner. Look at **Sue and Iris**. Complete these sentences with *many, much,* or *a lot of*.
1 There isn't ____ milk.
2 How ____ tea bags are there?
3 There are ____ ____ ____ biscuits.
4 There's ____ ____ ____ coffee.

9 Complete the grammar box. Use *is* or *are*.

	countable	uncountable
+	There ____ **a lot of** biscuits.	There'____ **a lot of** milk.
–	There ____n't **many** biscuits.	There ____n't **much** milk.
?	How **many** biscuits ____ there?	How **much** milk ____ there?

10 Work with a partner and write sentences about these things in **Sue and Iris**.
books bread butter carrots eggs fruit milk orange juice potatoes water yogurt
Examples There isn't much milk. There are a lot of books.

11 Look at the table on >> p.127. Ask other students questions.
Example A How much fruit do you eat? B A lot.

More practice? **Grammar Bank** >> p.141.

D Pronunciation unstressed words *a, of, some, and, with, or*

12 **6D.4▶** Listen to the rhyme. Notice all the lines have the pattern ●●●.

•	●	•	●
a	**cup**	of	**tea**
some	**bread**	and	**ham**
a	**lot**	of	**cake**
with	**cream**	or	**jam**

13 Say the rhyme. Stress the words in **bold**. These words are unstressed: *a, of, some, and, with, or.*

14 Work with a partner.
Student A Offer things from this table.
Student B Say *Yes, please* or *No, thanks.*

Would you like	a cup	with milk?	of cheese?
	some tea	of coffee?	of biscuits?
	some bread	of oranges?	with sugar?
	a piece	of pizza?	and butter?
	a bag	and jam?	and cheese?
	a packet		

E Listen for key words

15 **6D.5▶** Listen. What time of day is it?
a morning   b afternoon   c evening

16 Listen again. What does the woman want to eat and drink for breakfast? Tick ✓ the food and drink.

☐ tea   ✓ coffee   ☐ orange juice   ☐ an apple
☐ cheese   ☐ yogurt   ☐ toast   ☐ an egg
☐ two eggs   ☐ ham   ☐ sausages

ABCDE Put it all together

17 Write notes about what you like for breakfast.
My favourite breakfast is ... I also like ... I don't like ...

18 **Student A** You are a visitor in B's home. Answer B's questions about what you'd like for breakfast.
Student B Look at **Food in the Kitchen 1** on >> p.129. Offer Student A something for breakfast.
Change roles. Student B look at **Food in the Kitchen 2** on >> p.134.

I can offer food and drink.
Tick ✓ the lines. with a lot of help with some help on my own very easily

Writing Food in my country

A Read for detail

1 Work with a partner. What do you know about food in Spain?
- types of food?
- places to eat?
- meal times?

2 Read the text and answer the questions.
1 What do people eat for breakfast in Madrid?
2 What time is lunch?
3 What are 'tapas'?

Food facts for visitors to Madrid

In Madrid, there are a lot of bars. For breakfast, a lot of people go to the bars to drink ¹_____, and eat small cakes. They don't drink much tea, and they never drink it with milk.

Don't go for lunch before two o'clock – you can't get the 'menu of the day' before that. The menu of the day is a three-course meal. The first course is ²_____, the second course is ³_____, and the third course is ⁴_____. After all that, you need a siesta!

The evening meal is at ⁵_____. The restaurants aren't open before that. But a lot of people don't have a big meal in the evening – they just go to a bar for 'tapas'. Tapas are small snacks with a drink. Don't worry about the time – a lot of the bars are open long after midnight.

3 Complete the text with these phrases.
a dessert, for example ice cream or a small black coffee
b orange juice or coffee with milk
c nine or ten o'clock
d meat, chicken, or fish
e soup, salad, or vegetables

B Build phrases

4 Complete with *or* or *with*.
1 tea *or* coffee
2 an apple _____ a banana
3 coffee _____ sugar
4 soup _____ bread
5 potatoes _____ rice
6 a hamburger _____ chips
7 chicken _____ fish
8 pizza _____ pasta
9 soup _____ salad
10 potato _____ butter

5 **6E.1▶** Listen, check, and repeat.
More practice? **Grammar Bank** ≫ p.141.

6 Write typical food for you, your country, or your town. Use your dictionary.
Example   typical breakfast food = cereal with milk
                                or toast and jam

1 breakfast   food   =
                        drink =
2 lunch   food   =
                        drink =
3 evening meal food   =
                        drink =

7 Tell your partner.

8 Correct the spelling mistakes.
1 In Germany, peaple eat a lot of sausages.   *people*
2 They sometimes have biscuits and chease for dessert.
3 A typical second course is stek and cheaps.
4 They eat bred and jam for brekfast.

AB Put it all together

9 Look at the text about Madrid in exercise 2. Write food facts for a visitor to a different place you know. Include phrases with *or* and *with*. Start like this:
Food facts for visitors to ...
In _____, there are lots of places to eat. For breakfast ...

10 Check your spelling or ask your partner to check it.

11 Read your partner's text. Does it give you a lot of information?

I can write about food in my country.

Tick ✓ the line.   with a lot of help   with some help   on my own   very easily

Unit 6 Review

A Grammar

1 Countable and uncountable Put these words in the correct column. Write the plurals of countable words.

~~apple~~ biscuit carrot ~~coffee~~ crisp meat onion sandwich soup tea water yogurt

singular and plural (countable)	no singular or plural (uncountable)
apple – apples	coffee

2 *Some, any, much, many* Find eight sentences.

1 I've	got	**2** We've	got	some	biscuits.
3 Have	an	onion.	**4** There	rice.	**5** There
you	eggs.	many	aren't	much	isn't
got	any	onions?	got	any	carrots.
you	got	**6** I	haven't	apples.	any
7 Have	an	apple?	**8** We	haven't	got

3 *There is …/There are …* Write sentences like the examples.

Remember [?] = use *any*
          [+] = use *some* or *a lot of*
          [–] = use *any*

Examples [?] yogurt Greek salad
            Is there any yogurt in a Greek salad?
            [+] potatoes Russian salad
            There are a lot of potatoes in a Russian salad.
            [–] peas fruit salad
            There aren't any peas in a fruit salad.

1 [?] cheese Greek salad
2 [+] potatoes a Spanish omelette
3 [–] milk Turkish coffee
4 [+] vegetables paella
5 [–] eggs and bacon continental breakfast
6 [–] ham hamburger
7 [–] tomatoes fruit salad
8 [?] jam ham sandwich

Write three more questions to ask your partner.

B Vocabulary

4 Phrases for asking, offering, and answering Match 1–9 with a–i.

1 [d] I'd like a cup of coffee, please.
2 [ ] Would you like a cup of tea?
3 [ ] How much is a cup of tea?
4 [ ] Help yourself!
5 [ ] How much are the biscuits?
6 [ ] Can I have sausages with beans, please?
7 [ ] Is there any cheese in a Greek salad?
8 [ ] Are there any peas in a fruit salad?
9 [ ] Can I help you?

a They're free.
b Yes, how much are the sandwiches, please?
c Yes, there is.
d ~~Do you take sugar?~~
e No thanks. Have you got any coffee?
f It's 95p.
g Thank you.
h Sorry, we haven't got any beans.
i No, there aren't.

5 Food and drink Do the crossword with a partner.

Student A Look at the clues on ≫ p.130.
Student B Look at the clues on ≫ p.134.

Leisure activities

go fishing
go for a run
go for a swim
go roller-skating
go sailing
play basketball
play cards
play the guitar
play table tennis
read the newspaper
ride a bike

Life at Villa Clooney

George Clooney, actor and movie director, has a busy life. He works very hard but he plays hard too. So what does he do in his free time?

George spends a lot of his leisure time at his 17-room Italian villa on Lake Como. He describes the start of his typical day at the villa: 'I wake up at 7.30. I read the newspapers for an hour and a half.'

Then the morning really starts. He feeds his ducks and then he goes to the gym. He goes sailing in his boat and rides his motorbike.

After that, it's time to think about lunch – what to eat, what wine to drink. At two o'clock, everybody comes in and they have lunch. 'There are usually about 15 to 25 people here,' he says.

In the afternoon he often reads film scripts and phones Los Angeles. Then he goes for a swim in his pool. He usually has a lot of friends over from the States. In the evening they have big dinner parties and enjoy the view of the lake.

Why does George spend his summers in Italy? 'It's not hard for me to live there,' he says. 'I love riding my motorbike in the area. I love listening to Italians, the way they speak, the way they live – it's great.'

How to talk about free-time activities

v leisure activities

A Vocabulary leisure activities

1 Look at **Leisure activities** opposite. Find the leisure activities in the picture.

Example   1 = go sailing

2 7A.1▶ Listen and check. Listen again and repeat.

3 How often do you do the activities? Tell a partner. Use these words.

never   sometimes   often

Example   **A** I sometimes go sailing. What about you?
            B I never go sailing.

4 What other leisure activities do you do? Write three more activities. Use your dictionary. Tell your partner.

B Listen for detail

Jim

5 7A.2▶ Listen to Jim. Which leisure activities does he do? Make notes.

6 Check your answers in the audio script on ≫ p.154.

C Read a magazine article

7 Look at the photos in **Life at Villa Clooney** opposite. What do you know about George Clooney?

Examples   He's American.
            He rides a motorbike.

8 Read the article and choose the best alternative title.
a All Work and No Play
b Summer in Italy
c A Life of Leisure

9 Order the words to make questions. Find the answers in the article.
1 George's villa where's ?
2 he does what time wake up ?
3 in the morning does he what do ?
4 have lunch does what time he ?
5 are how many people there at lunch ?
6 in the afternoon he do what does ?
7 he in do the does what evening ?
8 does George to Italy go when ?

10 Compare with your partner.

D Talk about free time

11 Complete the conversation.
A On a day off, what ¹ _time___ do you get up?
B Oh, ten or eleven o'clock. What about ² _____?
A I get ³ _____ early, about eight o'clock.
B What do you do ⁴ _____ the morning?
A I ⁵ _____ a book or go on the Internet. And you?
B I ⁶ _____ for a walk.
A Do you ever go ⁷ _____ a run?
B No, but I sometimes ⁸ _____ for a swim. And in the evening?
A I often ⁹ _____ cards.

12 Say the conversation with a partner.

13 Work with a partner. Think of questions to ask George Clooney about his free time.

14 Work with a partner.
Student A You work for a newspaper. Interview George Clooney about his free time.
Student B You are George Clooney. Answer the questions.

15 Change roles. Choose a different famous person if you want.

ABCD Put it all together

16 Make notes about four things you do in your free time.

17 Ask your partner about his or her free time. Make questions from the table below.

Example   **A** On your days off, what time do you get up?
            B At ten o'clock. What time do you go to bed?
            A I go to bed at …

On your days off,	what do you do	in the morning?
		in the afternoon?
		in the evening?
	what time do you	get up?
		have lunch?
		have dinner?
		go to bed?
	do you ever	go to the gym?
		go to the park?
		go for a run?
		play cards?
		your ideas

1 *Bathers at Asnières*, Georges-Pierre Seurat, 1884

2 *Boar Lane, Leeds*, John Atkinson Grimshaw, 1881

3 *Wheatfield with Cypresses*, Vincent Van Gogh, 1889

4 *Blotter*, Peter Doig, 1993

Weather

nouns	adjectives
the sun	sunny
clouds	cloudy
rain	rainy
snow	snowy
ice	icy
wind	windy
	wet
	dry
	hot
	warm
	cool
	cold

hot
warm
cool
cold

sun   cloud   rain   snow

ice   wind   wet   dry

How to talk about the weather

G *Let's ..., How about ...* V weather P /w/

A Vocabulary weather

1   Work with a partner. Make sentences about pictures 1–4 opposite.

There is / There are ...
boats on a river
clouds
a field and mountains
ice on a lake
lights in the windows
snow in a park
a wet street

Example   **A** There are boats on a river.
            B Picture 1.

2   Work with a partner. Look at **Weather** opposite. Then describe the weather in pictures 1–4. Use these adjectives.

cloudy   cold   rainy   snowy
sunny   warm   wet   windy

Example   Picture 1   It's warm and sunny.

3   Join these pairs with *and* or *but*.
Examples   warm *and* sunny (normal)
             cold *but* sunny (not normal)

1   snowy _____ cold; snowy _____ warm
2   cloudy _____ wet; cloudy _____ dry
3   windy _____ hot; windy _____ cold

4   **7B.1▶** Pronunciation of /w/ Listen and repeat.
This **w**eek's **w**eather's **w**arm, **w**indy, and **w**et.

B Listen for key words

5   **7B.2▶** Listen. Say which picture.

6   Listen again and check. Listen and read the audio script on ≫ p.154.

7   How do you know the answer to exercise 5? Underline the key words in the audio script.
Example   ... shows a <u>street</u> in a <u>town</u> in England ...

8   **7B.3▶** Listen and say which picture.

9   Listen again and write the key words with a partner. Then find your key words in the audio script on ≫ p.154.

C Make suggestions

10   **7B.4▶** Listen and follow the conversations in the conversation map. Write the numbers.
Conversation 1   [1] [2] [4] [ ] [ ] [ ] [13]
Conversation 2   [1] [ ] [ ] [ ] [ ] [ ] [13]

¹What shall we do?

²I don't know. What's the weather like?

³It's warm and sunny. | ⁴It's cold and wet.

⁵Let's go out. | ⁶How about going to the shops?

⁷OK. Where shall we go? | ⁸I haven't got any money.

⁹How about the park? | ¹⁰How about going for a swim? | ¹¹OK. How about a game of cards? | ¹²OK. Let's watch a DVD.

¹³Yes, all right.

11   Work with a partner. Say two more conversations from the conversation map.

D Grammar *Let's ..., How about ...*

12   Write more examples from the conversation map in this grammar box.

Let's ... (+ verb)	How about ... (+ noun or -ing form)
go out	the park
	going for a swim

13   Write six suggestions with *Let's ...* and *How about ...* .
Examples   Let's go fishing.   How about going for a run?

14   Work with a partner. Write another conversation similar to the ones in exercise 10. Change the weather and the suggestions.

15   Practise saying your conversation. Then close your book and act your conversation for another pair.
More practice? **Grammar Bank** ≫ p.142.

ABCD Put it all together

16   Work with two partners. Suggest things to do.
Student A Go to ≫ p.127.
Student B Go to ≫ p.130.
Student C Go to ≫ p.134.

I can talk about the weather.
I can make suggestions.
Tick ✓ the lines.   with a lot of help   with some help   on my own   very easily

Abilities

I can **play** the gui**tar**
Ride a **bike**, drive a **car**
I can **climb** up a **wall**
I can **run**, kick a **ball**
I can **jump**, I can **ski**
I can **climb** up a **tree**
I'm the **star** of the **gym**
But I **caaaan't swim!**

I can **skate**, I can **cook**
I can **read** a long **book**
I can **sit**, I can **stand**
I can **walk** on my **hands**
I can **write**, I can **draw**
I can **do** a lot **more**
I'm the **star** of the **gym**
But I **caaaan't swim!**

a
b
c
d
e
f
g
h
i

Can you do this?

1

2

3

4

5 Are you having fun?

6 red river, yellow river, red river, yellow river, red river, yellow river ...

7 /wɒts ðə taɪm/

8

9

10

11

12

Jim and Ana

Jim Can you do that, in picture 1?

Ana Yes, I can do it easily. No problem. Look. But number 2, that's difficult. I can't do that. Can you?

J Ehm ... yes, I can, but it's difficult. I can do it very slowly. Can you do that, in picture 3?

A Yes, I can, but not very well.

How to describe abilities

G *can, can't*; adverbs   V abilities   P unstressed *can*, stressed *can't*

A Vocabulary abilities

1 7C.1▶ Read and listen to **Abilities** opposite. Find phrases for the activities in pictures a–i.
Example a = kick a ball

2 Don't look at **Abilities**. Listen again. Write the rhyming words.
guitar – *car*
wall –
ski –
cook –
stand –
draw –

3 Practise saying **Abilities**.

B Grammar can, can't

4 Complete the grammar box.

+	I can swim.	He _____ drive.	She _____.
–	I _____.	He can't drive.	She can't draw.
?	Can you swim?	_____ he _____?	_____ she _____?
short answers		Yes, I / he / she can.	No, I / he / she can't.

Use *can* for abilities.
Example I can ride a bike.

5 What can <u>you</u> do in **Abilities**? Put a tick ✓ next to the activities you can do.

6 Write two sentences with *can* that are true for you, and two with *can't*.

7 Ask other students about what they can do.
Example **A** Can you play the guitar?
           B No, I can't. What about you?

More practice? **Grammar Bank** ›› p.142.

C Pronunciation can, can't

8 7C.2▶ Listen. Do you hear A or B?

A I can swim.	B I can't swim.
•• ●	• ● ●
I can **swim**.	I ca**aaaaan't** swim.

9 Test a partner.
Example **A** I can't swim.
           B B!

D Grammar adverbs

10 Write these adjectives in the grammar box.
bad   easy   quick   slow

adjective	regular adverb	irregular adverb
good	—	well
	easily	
	quickly	
	badly	
	slowly	

Use adverbs to describe how you do something.

11 7C.3▶ Look at pictures 1, 2, and 3 in **Can you do this?** opposite. Listen and complete the sentences.
Picture 1 Ana can do it _easily_.
           (She can do it, no problem.)
Picture 2 Jim can do it very _____.
           (He can do it, but not quickly.)
Picture 3 Ana can do it, but not _____ _____.
           (She can do it, but badly.)

12 Now check with **Jim and Ana** opposite.
More practice? **Grammar Bank** ›› p.142.

E Talk about abilities

13 Talk with a partner about the things in **Can you do this?**. Use adverbs in your answers. How many can you and your partner do?

Questions				Answers	
Can you	do	that?		Yes,	easily.
	read				but not very easily.
	understand				but not very well.
	say				but badly.
					but very slowly.
					but not quickly.
				No, I can't.	

ABCDE Put it all together

14 Look at the 'can do' sentences at the end of the lessons in units 1–6. Write questions to ask other students. Answer the questions for you. Then ask three other students.

✓✓✓ = easily   ✓✓ = yes, I can   ✓ = yes, but not very well   ✗ = no, I can't

Ability Can you ...	Me	1	2	3
say dates?				
_____?				
_____?				
_____?				

I can describe abilities.

Tick ✓ the line.   with a lot of help   with some help   on my own   very easily   71

HARRY PIMM

1 You're here for a haircut, I see! Me too. I hate having my hair over my eyes and ears!

Poodle

FISHING

2 Would you like a magazine? There's one about fishing here ... do you like fishing?

FISHING

No, you don't like fishing – you like meeting friends and dancing, right?

3

4 Young people today haven't got hobbies. They just like talking on their mobile phones.

I haven't got a mobile phone, but I've got lots of hobbies.

5

I enjoy taking photos. I like listening to the radio. And I love watching Formula 1 on TV.

6

7 What about you? Do you like Formula 1?

The vet can see your dog now, Mrs Blanche. Please go in.

8

Vet? Isn't this the hairdresser's?

Likes and dislikes

like / enjoy   love   don't like   hate

 a   b   c   d

How to invite and reply

G *I'd like … , Would you like … ?* V social phrases P *for* and *to*

A Read and respond

1 Look at **Personality test** opposite. Match photos 1–10 with actions a–j.
   Example 1 = c (go for a run)

2 **8A.1▶** Listen, check, and repeat.

3 Do the test with a partner. What's your score?

4 Compare your answers with another partner.

5 Read this text and count Satomi's score. Compare with a partner.

In my free time …

In the morning, we have a ten-minute break and I go for a coffee with my friends. I sometimes go for a sandwich with them at lunchtime or we go to the shops. When I have a free lesson, I often go for walks and I usually go alone. I never go for a run. After class, I sometimes go for a drink with my friends. At the weekend, I usually go out with my family to the park, the cinema, or the pool. I always go to the gym on Saturdays, but never with my friends.

B Vocabulary social phrases

6 Complete the conversations with these questions.

What are you reading?   Would you like to come?
~~Where are you going?~~   Would you like to come?
Are you enjoying it?

Pablo Hi Jim!
Jim Hello. ¹ *Where are you going?*
P We're going to the park. ² _____
J Sorry, I can't. I haven't got time. See you later. Have fun!

Jim Hi Ana. ³ _____
Ana It's a book by Dan Brown.
J ⁴ _____
A Yes, it's very good.
J I'm going for a walk. ⁵ _____
A Yes, sure. I'd love to.

7 **8A.2▶** Listen and check.

8 Say the conversations with a partner.

C Pronunciation *for* and *to*

9 **8A.3▶** Don't pronounce *for* and *to* like *four* and *two*. Listen to the difference.
   for = /fə(r)/
   four = /fɔː(r)/
   going for a walk ✓
   going 4 a walk ✗

   to = /tə/
   two = /tuː/
   going to the park ✓
   going 2 the park ✗

10 **8A.4▶** Listen and say *right* or *wrong*.

11 **8A.5▶** Listen and read **Would you like to come?** opposite.

12 Listen again and repeat.

D Grammar *I'd like … , Would you like … ?*

13 Complete the grammar box.

+	I'd like a drink.	I'd _____ out.
?	Would _____ a drink?	Would you like to go out?

14 Work with a partner. Invite and answer.
   Student A

I'm going	for a …	Would you like to come?
	to the …	

   Student B

Yes, sure. I'd love to.
Sorry, I can't. I haven't got time. See you later. Have fun!

   More practice? **Grammar Bank** ›› p.143.

ABCD Put it all together

15 Close your books and act your conversation from exercise 14.
   Example **A** I'm going for a coffee. Would you like to come?
            B Yes, I'd love to.

16 Now invite your classmates. How many friends are going with you?

I can invite and reply. ▬▬▬▬▬▬▬
Tick ✓ the line.   with a lot of help   with some help   on my own   very easily   77

The Wedding

Clothes
a baseball cap   boots   a coat   a dress   a hat
a jacket   jeans   sandals   a shirt   shoes
shorts   a long skirt   a short skirt   a suit
a sweater   a tie   trousers   a T-shirt

A

What to wear

B

*What **not** to wear*

How to say what to wear

G imperatives V family; clothes P *shirt* /ɜː/ or *short* /ɔː/

A Vocabulary family; clothes

1 Work with a partner. Do you remember words for people in a family? Make a list.

2 Look at **The Wedding** picture A opposite. Find words with these meanings. Use your dictionary to check.
   1 your mum's or dad's brother   *uncle*
   2 your mum's or dad's sister
   3 your brother's or sister's son
   4 your brother's or sister's daughter
   5 your sister's husband

3 Look at **Clothes** opposite. Find the clothes in **The Wedding** picture B.
   Example baseball cap = 5

4 Complete the words.

   What shall I wear?

   J*eans* or tr*ousers*?
   A dr_____ or a sk_____?
   A co_____ or a sw_____?
   A ja_____ and a sh_____?
   A ha_____ or a ca_____?
   A ti_____ and a su_____?
   Sh_____s and a T-sh_____?
   Sh_____s or b_____s?

5 **8B.1▶** Listen and check. Listen again and repeat.

B Pronunciation *shirt* /ɜː/ or *short* /ɔː/

6 **8B.2▶** Listen to the difference.

A /ɜː/ /ɔː/	B /ɔː/ /ɜː/
There's a bird on the board.	There's a board on the bird.

Don't wear shirts to walk.	Don't wear shorts to work.
I hate Earl's four coats.	I hate all fur coats.

7 **8B.3▶** Listen and say A or B.

8 Test a partner.
   Example **A** There's a bird on the board. **B** A!

C Grammar imperatives

9 Work with a partner. Look at **The Wedding** pictures A and B. How many differences can you find?

10 Look at picture B with a partner. Who are these tips for?
   1 Don't climb the tree!   *Laura's nephew*
   2 Look at the camera!
   3 Wear a long skirt!
   4 Don't wear sandals!

11 Add the tips from exercise 10 to this grammar box.

+ what to do	− what not to do
Wear a hat.	Don't wear a cap.

12 Say what to do / not to do for these people in picture B.
   1 Earl   *Don't wear jeans. / Wear trousers.*
   2 Earl's mum   6 Laura's nephew
   3 Earl's uncle   7 Earl's aunt
   4 Laura's niece   8 Laura's mum
   5 Laura's other niece   9 Laura's brother-in-law

   More practice? **Grammar Bank** ≫ p.143.

D Listen for key words

13 Match the activities and the tips.
   1 [c] I'm going to a wedding.
   2 [ ] I'm going for a run.
   3 [ ] I'm going to the mountains.
   4 [ ] I'm going to the Sahara.
   a Wear good boots and a warm coat.
   b Take lots of water and a hat.
   c ~~Wear a long dress. Don't wear jeans.~~
   d Don't wear sandals.

14 **8B.4▶** Listen. Tick ✓ the clothes words you hear.
   ☐ skirt   ☐ suit   ☐ tie   ☐ dress
   ☐ jacket ☐ jeans ☐ trousers

15 Put the conversation in order.
   ☐ **A** No, I haven't.
   [1] **A** I'm going to a wedding. What shall I wear?
   ☐ **A** Yes, I've got a jacket for work.
   ☐ **B** OK, so wear a jacket and trousers.
   ☐ **B** Wear a suit and tie. Have you got a suit?
   ☐ **B** Hmm ... Have you got a jacket?

16 Listen to 8B.4 again and check.

17 Say the conversation with a partner.

ABCD Put it all together

18 Work with a partner. Ask for clothes tips.
   Student A Go to ≫ p.130.   **Student B** Go to ≫ p.134.

I can say what to wear.
Tick ✓ the line. with a lot of help with some help on my own very easily

National Navy Day on the Arbat in Moscow 1991
Photographer: David Turnley

Moscow Madness

She's **smil**ing, she's **laugh**ing
She's **danc**ing in the **street**
She's **hav**ing **fun** out in the **sun**
In the **Mos**cow **summ**er **heat**

One man's **play**ing the **sax**ophone
An**oth**er man's **play**ing the guitar
Everybody's **watch**ing her
She's **feel**ing like a **star**

She's **danc**ing with a **sail**or
What's he doing **here**?
Call it **Mos**cow **mad**ness
It's that **time** of **year**

How to say what's happening

G present continuous ⊞☐❓ **V** action verbs **P** -ing /ɪŋ/

A Read and guess meanings

1 Look at the photo opposite. Choose the best title.
   a Having Fun with Friends
   b Dancing in the Street
   c Everybody's Laughing

2 Look at the photo for one minute! Then cover the photo and answer the questions.
   1 Is the girl wearing a red skirt?
   2 Is the sailor wearing a watch?
   3 Are the girl's friends wearing blue jeans?
   4 Is the guitar player wearing glasses?
   5 Are the musicians wearing jackets?
   6 Is the girl looking at the sailor?

3 Look at the photo and check your answers.

4 8C.1▶ Read and listen to **Moscow Madness** opposite. What isn't it about?
   a summer in Moscow
   b a sailor and a girl
   c a concert

5 Read again and complete the glossary opposite.

B Grammar present continuous ⊞☐❓

6 Complete the grammar box.

+	I'm dancing.	She _____.	They're watching.
–	I'm not dancing.	She isn't smiling.	They _____.
?	Are you dancing?	_____ she _____?	_____ they _____?

short answers			
+	Yes, I am.	Yes, you are.	Yes, she is.	Yes, they are.
–	No, I'm not.	No, you aren't.	No, she isn't.	No, they aren't.

Use the present continuous to describe actions **now**.
To spell the -ing form of verbs:
1 Usually just add -ing (wear – wearing).
2 Usually remove final -e (smile – smiling).
3 Double final consonant after a short vowel sound (shop – shopping).

7 Complete with the -ing form of the verbs.
   1 She's _____. laugh
   2 They're _____ music. play
   3 He's _____. dance
   4 They aren't _____ sandals. wear
   5 They aren't _____. smile

8 Look at the photo again. Who is doing the actions in exercise 7?

9 What are you doing now? Write two true positive ⊞ sentences and two true negative ☐ sentences. Choose from the phrases below, or use your own ideas.
   dance   drink a cup of coffee   listen to the radio
   send an email   sit on a chair   think about grammar
   use a black pen   use a dictionary   wear a sweater
   wear something blue   write in my book
   Examples   I'm wearing a sweater.   I'm not dancing.

10 Ask your partner questions. Use the phrases in exercise 9 or your own ideas.
   Example   Are you thinking about the weekend?

   More practice? **Grammar Bank** ≫ p.143.

C Pronunciation -ing /ɪŋ/

11 8C.2▶ Listen and say A, B, or C.

A	thing	B	thin	C	think

   Verbs ending -ing rhyme with *thing*.

12 Practise saying the **Moscow Madness** poem. Pronounce the -ing verbs carefully.

D Listen for general meaning

13 8C.3▶ Listen. Is this:
   a a phone call?
   b a TV programme?
   c a radio news programme?
   d a conversation?

14 Listen to 8C.3 again. Fill some gaps in the text below with words from the photo opposite. Then ask your teacher questions to complete the text.
   Example   **Student** Is number 1 'musicians'?
   Teacher Yes, correct. Write it in!

   It's National Navy Day in Russia, and here in Moscow, people are celebrating and having fun. It's a sunny day. There are two ¹ _musicians_ . One ² _____'s ³ _____ the ⁴ _____ and the other's ⁵ _____ the ⁶ _____. A ⁷ _____'s ⁸ _____ with a ⁹ _____. The ¹⁰ _____'s ¹¹ _____ are ¹² _____ and the other people are ¹³ _____ the celebrations.

15 8C.4▶ Listen to another radio news programme. What are the differences?

16 Read the audio script on ≫ p.155 and underline the differences.

ABCD Put it all together

17 Work with a partner. Find the differences.
   Student A Look at the picture on ≫ p.130.
   Student B Look at the picture on ≫ p.134.

I can say what's happening.
Tick ✓ the line.   with a lot of help   with some help   on my own   very easily

THE CONVERSATION

The Directors Company presents

GENE HACKMAN
in
"THE CONVERSATION"

Co-starring JOHN CAZALE · ALLEN GARFIELD · CINDY WILLIAMS · FREDERIC FORREST
Music scored by DAVID SHIRE · Co-producer FRED ROOS · Written, Produced and Directed by FRANCIS FORD COPPOLA
Color by TECHNICOLOR® · A Parambunt Pictures Release

By Francis Ford Coppola
Starring Gene Hackman

Golden Palm Award, Cannes Film Festival 1974

Rating ★ ★ ★ ★ ★
Don't miss it!

THE STORY

Gene Hackman is Harry Caul, a spy. He watches people. He listens to their conversations and makes tapes. Then he phones his customers and he takes the tapes to them. He doesn't understand the conversations – they aren't his problem. He just makes the tapes, takes the money, and takes the bus home.

Harry knows other people's secrets. That is his work. But other people don't know Harry's secrets. He lives alone. He hasn't got any friends. He never talks to his girlfriend. In the evening he listens to jazz and plays the saxophone.

One day, Harry is listening to a conversation. The people are talking about a murder plan. This is a problem for Harry. He doesn't like murders. But Harry is making a mistake. He thinks he is listening to other people, but really they are listening to him.

A great story!

1

2

3

4

How to describe actions

G present simple and present continuous   P contrastive stress

A Read for detail

1 Look at **The Conversation** opposite. Where do you think the text is from? Choose one or more of these.

a book   a magazine   the Internet   a newspaper
a poster   an email   a DVD box

2 **8D.1▶** Read and listen to the short text below. Find words for the things in pictures a–f.

Example a = tape

a b c d e f

A spy with a secret ... a tape ... a murder ...
The Conversation ... a Francis Ford Coppola movie,
with Gene Hackman and Harrison Ford ...
coming soon to a cinema near you!

3 Read **The Conversation**. Write *true* or *false*.

1 The star of the film is Gene Hackman.   *True*
2 Harry understands the conversations.
3 Harry doesn't talk to his girlfriend.
4 Harry lives with his friends.
5 Harry plays the piano.

4 Read **The Conversation** again. What is Harry doing in photos 1–4 opposite?

Example 1 = He's listening to a conversation.

B Listen for key words

5 **8D.2▶** Listen and put the actions in order.

Every evening, Harry ...
- [ ] goes to the kitchen
- [ ] has a drink
- [ ] plays the saxophone
- [ ] has a shower
- [ ] listens to jazz
- [1] arrives home
- [ ] opens the door

6 Read the audio script on **»** p.155 and check your answers.

7 **8D.3▶** Listen to the sounds. Say what is happening now.

Example Number 1 – Harry's arriving home.

C Grammar present simple and present continuous

8 Complete the grammar box.

present simple (usually)	present continuous (now)
I (usually) go to work by bus.	Today I'_____ to work by train.
He listens to people.	Now people _____ to him.
What do you do at the weekend?	What are you _____ now?

9 Complete with the present simple or continuous.

1 Usually, people *don't phone* Harry at home.
  But now, the phone *is ringing*.   not phone / ring
2 Harry usually _____ to other people. Now they _____ to him.   listen / listen
3 **A** Listen – Harry _____ a shower.   have
  B Yes. He always _____ a shower at 7.00.   have
4 Somebody _____ Harry. Harry usually _____ other people.   watch / watch
5 Harry always _____ the bus. He never _____.   take / drive
6 In this picture, he _____ on a chair and he _____ the saxophone.   sit / play

10 Work with a partner. Ask questions and find three or more differences between your habits and routines.

Examples What do you watch on TV?
What music do you listen to?
How do you go to work / school?

11 You 'change lives' with your partner for one day. Write sentences.

Example I usually drink tea for breakfast, but today I'm drinking coffee.

More practice? **Grammar Bank »** p.143.

D Pronunciation contrastive stress

12 Complete the sentences below.

I'm listening to **you**, but **you** aren't listening to **me**.
We're listening to **them**, but ...
He's listening to **her**, but ...

13 **8D.4▶** Listen and check.

14 Listen again and underline the stressed words. Listen and repeat. Copy the stress.

ABCD Put it all together

15 You win a competition. The prize is a holiday anywhere in the world.

Think about your normal life. What do you usually do?
Now think about your holiday. Where are you?
What are you doing?

I usually	work in the morning	but today	I'm sitting by the pool.
	drink ...		I'm drinking champagne.
	eat ...		I'm ...
	wear ...		

16 Tell your partner.

17 Tell another partner about your first partner.

Example Elena usually works in an office, but today she's sitting on a beach.

I can describe actions.

Tick ✓ the lines.   with a lot of help   with some help   on my own   very easily

Writing Moment poems

A Read for general meaning

1 Match the titles with photos a–d.

A Busy Moment **An Exciting Moment**
A Quiet Moment **A Boring Moment**

2 Write titles from exercise 1 for these four poems.

1 _____
   It's five o'clock in the morning
   The street's sleeping, the house is dark
   I'm in bed but I'm not sleeping
   I'm listening to the fridge and the clock
   And the wind in the trees

2 _____
   It's nine o'clock in the morning
   I'm sitting on a bus in a river of cars
   We aren't moving
   I haven't got a newspaper or an iPod
   The light's green but nothing's moving

3 _____
   It's twelve o'clock in the morning
   Everybody's moving, everybody's talking
   I'm working in the shop
   The phone's ringing, customers are waiting
   I'm not thinking – there isn't time

4 _____
   It's seven o'clock in the evening
   I'm home again and I'm looking in the mailbox
   There's a letter for me
   It's big and fat and it isn't from the bank
   What's in it?

3 Read the poems again. Write *true* or *false*.
   1 The writer gets up at five o'clock. *False*
   2 There are trees near the writer's home.
   3 The writer goes to work by car.
   4 The writer works in a shop.
   5 There's a letter from the bank in the mailbox.

B Get ideas for writing

4 Think of a quiet / busy / exciting / boring moment in a normal day for you. <u>Underline</u> the best answer or write other answers.
   1 What time is it?
     5 o'clock / 9 o'clock / midnight / other ...
   2 Where are you?
     in bed / at home / in a park / other ...
   3 What are you doing?
     sitting in bed / having lunch / reading / other ...
   4 Are there other people near?
     no / yes / my family / other ...
   5 What's happening?
     the birds are singing / the sun's going down / other ...
   6 What are you watching or listening to?
     nothing / I'm listening to ... / I'm watching ...

5 Ask your partner questions. What moment are they describing?

6 Choose another moment. Do the activity again.

C Write a simple poem

7 Write a poem in five lines with this structure.
   Title   A Quiet Moment
   Line 1 It's ... (What time is it?)
   Line 2 ... -ing and ... -ing (2 things which are happening)
   Line 3 I'm ... (Where are you?)
   Line 4 I'm ... -ing and ... -ing (2 things which you are doing)
   Line 5 I'm not ... -ing ... (1 thing which you aren't doing)

   Example   **A Quiet Moment**
            It's 8 o'clock in the evening
            The birds are singing ...

D Check your grammar

8 This writer forgot the verb *be* (*'m, 's, are*). Write in five more missing words.
   A Quiet Moment
   It‸'s 8 o'clock in the evening
   The birds singing and the sun going down
   I on a quiet beach
   I drinking fruit juice and watching the boats
   I not thinking about work

9 Check your partner's poem from exercise 7.

ABCD Put it all together

10 Write a poem about another moment. Read your poem to your partner. What moment is your partner describing?

I can write about things happening now. ▬▬▬▬

Tick ✓ the line.   with a lot of help   with some help   on my own   very easily

Unit 8 Review

R8

A Grammar

1 Imperatives What do these signs mean?
Write an imperative.
Example 1 = Don't walk on the grass.

2 Present continuous Complete the text with these verbs.
Check your spelling.

do leave play read sit sleep watch

Oh, hi Mum! Yeah, we're sitting on the train ...¹we'__ _____ the station now. Yeah, ²Earl'__ _____ next to me. ³He'__ _____ a game on his mobile. Me? ⁴I'__ _____ a magazine. Sorry, can't hear you ... there are lots of children on the train and they're jumping on the seats. ⁵What _____ you _____? Watching TV? ⁶What _____ you _____? Is Dad watching it too? Oh, ⁷he'__ _____ – typical! OK, bye Mum. Love you too. Bye!

3 Present simple or continuous? Complete the sentences.

1 Dad usually works in the morning but today *he's working in the evening.* evening
2 He usually watches the news at 6 o'clock but today he _____. football
3 Today I'm sitting near the window but I usually _____. door
4 Today my parents are having dinner at a restaurant but they usually _____. at home
5 We usually go to the cinema on Fridays but today we _____. theatre
6 You usually wear a sweater but today you _____. jacket and tie
7 Today she's having a bath but she usually _____. shower
8 He's wearing boots today but he usually _____. shoes

B Vocabulary

4 Social phrases Find three more questions and answers. Write three more questions to ask your partner.

1 I'm	going	for	a	to	come?
going	to	the	pizza,	like	Yes,
2 I'm	3 I'm	park,	would	you	I'd
to	going	would	to	come?	love
the	4 I'm	you	like	Sorry,	to.
cinema,	going	you	like	I	to.
would	for	would	to	can't.	love
you	a	coffee,	come?	Yes,	I'd
like	to	come?	Sorry,	I	can't.

5 Family Write the word.

1 my mum's sister = *my aunt*
2 my son's sister =
3 my mum's brother =
4 my sister's son =
5 my brother's daughter =
6 my sister's husband =

6 Clothes and activities Do the crossword with a partner.

Student A Look at the clues on >> p.131.
Student B Look at the clues on >> p.135.

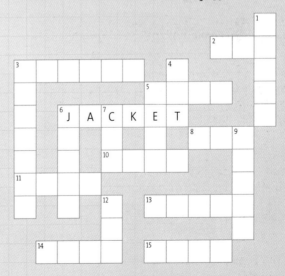

85

Transport

airport   bus   bus station
departure gate   plane
platform   taxi   train
train station
underground station

1 — train
2 — taxi
3 — METRO / M
4 — gate 6 →
5 — plane
6 — platform 1 →
7 — train station
8 — bus
9 — A ✈ (airport)
10 — bus station

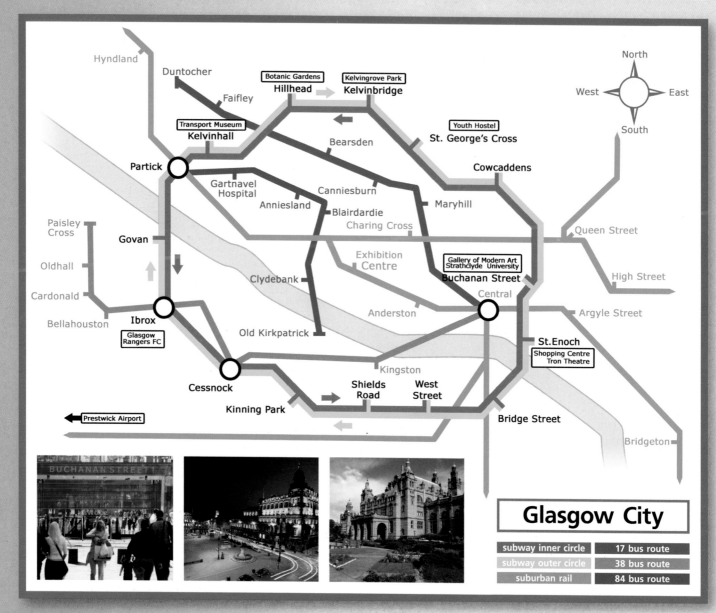

Glasgow City

subway inner circle	17 bus route
subway outer circle	38 bus route
suburban rail	84 bus route

Ana in Glasgow

Ana's in West Street, Glasgow ...

Ana Excuse me, how can I get to Buchanan Street, please?

Man Sorry?

A How do you say this, please?

M Oh – Buchanan Street!

A Buchanan Street. How can I get to Buchanan Street?

M Well, it's three stops on the underground. The station's just over there, look. Take the Inner Circle line.

A The Inner Circle line? OK, thanks.

How to ask for transport information

v transport; instruction phrases **P** polite intonation

A Vocabulary transport

1 **9A.1▶** Look at **Transport** opposite. Listen and say which picture.
Example **Audio** Airport. **You** 9!

2 Correct one letter in each <u>underlined</u> word.

You can <u>talk</u> there in an hour	1 _walk_
Or <u>make</u> the underground	2 _____
There's a bus every <u>fine</u> minutes	3 _____
And <u>she</u> ticket's just a pound	4 _____
When you <u>got</u> to the station	5 _____
Find the platform, <u>wake</u> the train	6 _____
When you get <u>no</u> the airport	7 _____
Find the gate and take the <u>plate</u>	8 _____

3 **9A.2▶** Listen and check. Listen again and repeat.

B Listen and follow directions

4 Look at the map opposite. Write *true* or *false*.
1 It's two stops from Bridge Street to Buchanan Street on the Inner Circle line.
2 Buchanan Street is twelve stops from West Street on the Outer Circle line.
3 West Street is north of the river.
4 Bridge Street is the stop after West Street on the Outer Circle line.

5 **9A.3▶** Don't look at the page opposite. Listen to Ana's conversation. Does the man answer Ana's first question?

6 Listen again and find Ana's way on the map.

7 Read **Ana in Glasgow** opposite and check.

C Read for detail

8 Work with a partner. You are at West Street station in the map opposite. Follow these instructions and complete the questions.
1 How can I get to _____ _Cross_ ?
It's four stops on the underground. Don't take the Inner Circle – take the Outer Circle. Get off at Ibrox. Take the number 38 bus and go to the end of the line.

2 How can I get to _____ _____?
Take the Inner Circle line three stops. Get off at Buchanan Street and walk to Queen Street station. Take a train one stop to the west.

3 How can I get to _____ _____?
Take the Outer Circle line six stops. Get off at Partick and change to the number 84 bus. Go to the end of the line.

9 Match 1–5 with a–e. Then check with exercise 8.
1 [c] Take the   a Partick.
2 [ ] Don't take   b the Inner Circle line.
3 [ ] Go   c ~~number 38 bus.~~
4 [ ] Get off at   d to the number 84 bus.
5 [ ] Change   e to the end of the line.

10 Work with a partner. Write directions from West Street to these places.
Bridgeton
Cardonald
Gartnavel Hospital
High Street
Transport Museum

11 With a different partner, choose two places and ask and answer.
Example Excuse me, how can I get from West Street to the Transport Museum?

12 Test a partner.
Student A Choose a destination and give directions.
Student B Say the destination.

D Pronunciation polite intonation

13 **9A.4▶** Polite or rude? Listen to the difference.

Rude intonation
Excuse me, **how** can I get to the **sta**tion, please?

Polite intonation
Ex**cuse** me, **how** can I get to the **sta**tion, please?

14 **9A.5▶** Listen and repeat the polite intonation.

ABCD Put it all together

15 Work with a partner.
Student A Look at the map on ≫ p.131. Ask student B how to get to the places on the list.
Student B Look at the map on ≫ p.135. Ask student A how to get to the places on the list.

I can ask for transport information.

Tick ✓ the line.   with a lot of help   with some help   on my own   very easily

Directions

at the corner
between
Go across the bridge.
Go out of the door.
Go past the bank.
Go straight on.

Go to the end of the street.
next to
opposite
Turn left at the corner.
Turn right at the lights.

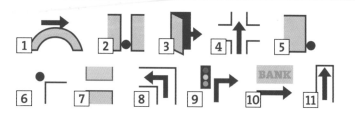

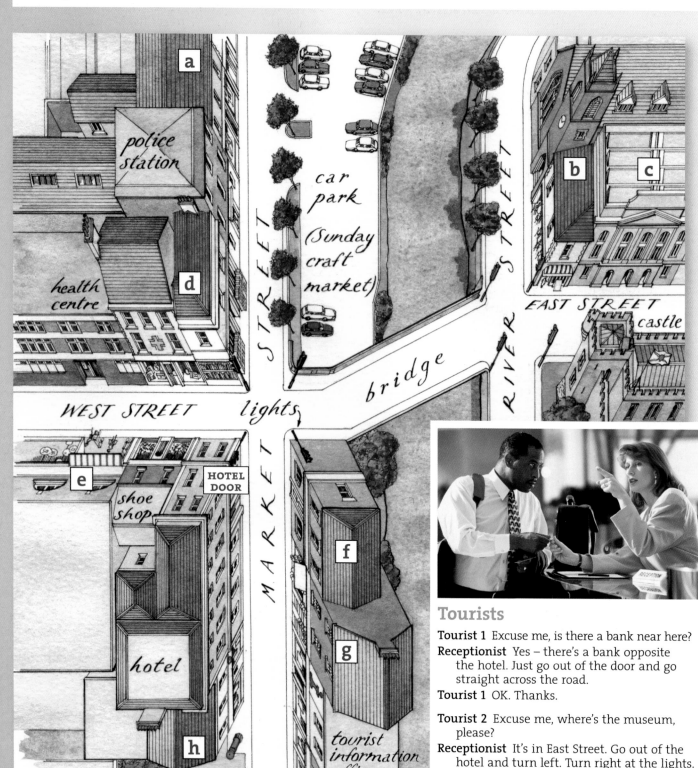

Tourists

Tourist 1 Excuse me, is there a bank near here?
Receptionist Yes – there's a bank opposite the hotel. Just go out of the door and go straight across the road.
Tourist 1 OK. Thanks.

Tourist 2 Excuse me, where's the museum, please?
Receptionist It's in East Street. Go out of the hotel and turn left. Turn right at the lights. Go across the bridge and straight on. The museum's on the left, opposite the castle.
Tourist 2 Opposite the castle? Thanks.

How to give and follow directions

v places in town; directions **P** linking words together

A Vocabulary directions

1 Look at **Directions** opposite. Work with a partner. Match the phrases with pictures 1–11.
   Example at the corner = 6

2 **9B.1▶** Listen and repeat.

3 Test a partner.
   Example **A** Picture 1? **B** Go across the bridge.

B Listen to directions

4 **9B.2▶** Don't look at the page opposite. Listen to the conversations. Write *true* or *false*.
   1 The bank is next to the hotel.
   2 The museum is opposite the castle.

5 Listen again and read **Tourists** opposite. Find the bank and the museum on the map.

6 Say the conversations with a partner.

7 **9B.3▶** The receptionist gives directions to these places. Listen and match the tourists with the places.

   art gallery   bookshop   gift shop
   ~~post office~~   restaurant   supermarket

   Tourist 3   *post office*
   Tourist 4   _____
              _____
   Tourist 5   _____
   Tourist 6   _____
   Tourist 7   _____

8 Listen again. Find the places in exercise 7 on the map.

9 Read the audio script on **»** p.156 and check.

10 Where are the places? Write *true* or *false*.
   1 The post office is next to the tourist information office.
   2 The bank is between the gift shop and the tourist information office.
   3 There's a restaurant on the corner of River Street.
   4 The supermarket is next to the shoe shop.
   5 The museum is next to the restaurant.
   6 The bookshop is between the shoe shop and the health centre.

C Pronunciation linking words together

11 **9B.4▶** Listen and repeat. (The final letter of the first word sounds like it's the first letter of the second word: *left at* sounds like *lef tat* /'lef tət/.)

   left‿at the **cor**ner /'lef tət ðə 'kɔːnə(r)/
   out‿of the **door** /'aʊ təv ðə 'dɔː(r)/
   right‿at the **lights** /'raɪ tət ðə 'laɪts/
   straight‿across /'streɪ tə'krɒs/
   walk‿across /'wɔː kə'krɒs/
   bank‿**opp**osite /'bæŋ 'kɒpəzɪt/
   post‿office /'pəʊs tɒfɪs/
   tour‿ist‿information /'tɔːrɪs tɪnfə'meɪʃn/

12 Where one word ends with a consonant sound and the next word begins with a vowel sound, write ‿.
   1 Stop at the end of the street.
   2 Turn left at the lights and walk across the street.
   3 Walk across the bridge and stop opposite the castle.

13 **9B.5▶** Listen and repeat the sentences.

D Give directions

14 Write directions from the hotel to two places on the map.

15 Work with a partner. Read out your directions. Your partner finds the place on the map.
   Example **A** Go out of the hotel and turn left. Turn left at the corner and it's on the left after the shoe shop.
   B The supermarket?
   A Yes, that's right.

ABCD Put it all together

16 Work with a partner.
   Student A Draw these on the map opposite.
      an underground station   a café
      a cash machine
   Student B Draw these on the map opposite.
      a bus stop   a newspaper kiosk   a phone box

17 Ask and give directions. You are at the hotel.
   Student A You want to find a bus stop, a newspaper kiosk, and a phone box.
   Student B You want to find an underground station, a café, and a cash machine.

   Example **A** Excuse me, is there a bus stop near here?
   B Yes, …

I can give and follow directions.

Tick ✓ the line. with a lot of help   with some help   on my own   very easily

Your **holiday** personality

On holiday

a crowded beach
cheap but dirty restaurants
a comfortable room with a sea view
exciting nightlife

friendly people
a noisy building site
a quiet pool
wet weather

 a
 b
 c
 d

Draw a ☹ if this is a problem for you.

For example:
The weather is …   a cold. ☹   b very hot.   c wet. ☹

1 In my room, there's …
  a no sea view.
  b no hot water.
  c no television.

2 In the hotel, there's …
  a no garden.
  b no lift.
  c no disco.

3 The hotel pool is …
  a noisy.
  b out of the sun.
  c small and quiet.

4 The restaurant …
  a only has fast food.
  b serves buffet food.
  c doesn't sell wine.

5 Near the hotel, there's …
  a a shopping centre.
  b a noisy building site.
  c quiet countryside.

6 The beach is …
  a crowded and noisy.
  b far from the hotel.
  c quiet and empty.

7 The sea is …
  a full of surfers.
  b very cold.
  c not safe for swimming.

8 The town is …
  a ugly and dirty.
  b full of nightclubs.
  c sleepy and quiet.

9 The local people aren't very …
  a interesting.
  b polite.
  c friendly.

Count how many ☹s you have for a, b, and c.

Mostly a = Nature
You like quiet holidays. You like going to interesting places in beautiful countryside.

Mostly b = Comfort
You go on holiday to relax. You want to be comfortable.

Mostly c = Fun
You like exciting holidays where you can meet new friends and enjoy the nightlife.

 e
 f
 g
 h

Jill's email

Hi Carla

How are things? It was so good to get home last Friday evening – home, sweet home! Our holiday was awful! We were in a horrible town called Kinalis – really ugly and dirty, and the local people were very unfriendly.

The hotel was terrible too! The rooms were small and there wasn't any hot water in the bathrooms. There was a hotel swimming pool but the water was cold and dirty. The hotel restaurant was a buffet and the food was boring, the same thing every day. It was difficult to sleep at night because it was so noisy – the hotel has three large discos … three!

The beaches were a long way from the hotel. They were dirty too, and there weren't any sunbeds. Anyway, we didn't go to the beaches because the weather wasn't very nice. It was cold and wet – we only had one sunny day all week.

Never again! I hope your holiday was good. Write soon and tell me …

Love
Jill

How to ask about and describe a holiday

G past simple of be ⊞⊟⍰ *was, were, wasn't, weren't*   V adjectives; holidays   P *is, was, are, were*

A Vocabulary adjectives

1 **9C.1▶** Look at **On holiday** opposite. Listen and match the phrases with photos a–h.
Example **Audio** A crowded beach.   **You** b!

2 Listen again and repeat.

3 **9C.2▶** Listen and write opposites from **On holiday**.
1 uncomfortable ●●●● *comfortable* ●●●
2 expensive ●●●● _____
3 unfriendly ●●●● _____
4 clean ●●● _____
5 boring ●●● _____
6 noisy ●●● _____
7 dry ● _____

4 Listen again. Write the stress patterns.

5 What do you think? Write one adjective in each gap.
Example *quiet* beaches (good) *crowded* beaches (bad)

	I like …		I don't like …
1	_____ beaches.		_____ beaches.
2	_____ rooms.		_____ rooms.
3	_____ pools.		_____ pools.
4	_____ restaurants.		_____ restaurants.
5	_____ people.		_____ people.
6	_____ weather.		_____ weather.

6 Compare your answers with other students.

B Read for detail

7 Do the **Your holiday personality** quiz opposite. Are your answers mostly a, b, or c? Compare with your partner.

8 Read **Jill's email** opposite. What information does she give about her holiday? Put the questions in order.
What was / were the …
☐ weather like?   ☐1 town like?   ☐ pool like?
☐ beaches like?   ☐ food like?   ☐ rooms like?
☐ hotel like?   ☐ people like?

9 Read **Jill's email** again. Guess her answers to the **Your holiday personality** quiz. Compare with a partner.

C Listen for key information

10 **9C.3▶** Listen to Ben talking about his holiday. Put the information in order.
☐ hotel ☐ food ☐1 weather ☐ nightlife ☐ beach

11 Listen again. What's Ben's holiday personality?
a nature   b comfort   c fun

12 Read the audio script on ≫ p.156 and check your answers.

D Grammar past simple of be ⊞⊟⍰ *was, were, wasn't, weren't*

13 Read the grammar box. Complete the information below.

+	I / He / She / It was friendly.	We / You / They were friendly.
−	I / He / She / It wasn't friendly.	We / You / They weren't friendly.
?	Was I / he / she / it friendly?	Were we / you / they friendly?

short answers	+	Yes, he was.	Yes, they were.
	−	No, he wasn't.	No, they weren't.

Remember this: *Were* is for *we* and *they* and *you*
Was is for *I*, and *he* or *she* too

The past of *am* and *is* = _____
The past of *am not* and *isn't* = _____
The past of *are* = _____
The past of *aren't* = _____

14 Complete the questions and answers about photos a–h opposite. Use *was, wasn't, were,* or *weren't.*
1 **A** What was the room like?
   B It _was_ comfortable.
2 **A** What _____ the beaches like?
   B They _____ quiet. They _____ full of people.
3 **A** What _____ the nightlife like?
   B It _____ boring.
4 **A** What _____ the restaurants like?
   B They _____ cheap but dirty.
5 **A** What _____ the weather like?
   B It _____ sunny. It _____ rainy.

More practice? **Grammar Bank** ≫ p.144.

E Pronunciation *is, was, are, were*

15 **9C.4▶** Can you hear the difference? Say A or B.

A (present)	B (past)
The beach is crowded.	The beach was crowded.
The rooms are noisy.	The rooms were noisy.
The people are friendly.	The people were friendly.
The place is nice.	The place was nice.

16 Test a partner.
Example **A** The beach was crowded.   **B** B!

ABCDE Put it all together

17 Think of (or imagine) your last beach holiday in a hotel. Write notes to answer the questions in exercise 8. Ask a partner.

I can ask about and describe a holiday.

Tick ✓ *the line.*   with a lot of help   with some help   on my own   very easily

window

stairs

rat

hill

Who's there?

BANG!

body

floor

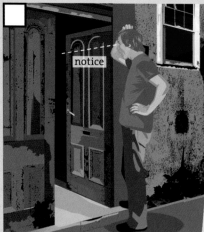

notice

bell

knock

Nightmare Hotel

I walked up the hill
To the Nightmare Hotel
I stopped at the door
But I couldn't see the bell

I knocked and I waited
In the cold and windy night
I looked in the window
But there wasn't any light

That's when I noticed
The door was open wide
Then it started raining
So I walked inside

The door closed behind me
I asked, 'Who's there?'
That's when I noticed
The rats on the stairs

I turned round to leave
But I couldn't see the door
That's when I noticed
The body on the floor

Then the body moved
The woman wasn't dead
She told me her story
This is what she said:

I also walked up
To the Nightmare Hotel...

How to tell a story

G past simple ⊞ regular -ed P -ed endings

A Read a poem

1 Tell a partner about a really good or bad hotel you know.

2 **9D.1▶** Look at the pictures opposite but don't read the story. Listen to the sounds and put the pictures in order.

3 **9D.2▶** Read and listen to **Nightmare Hotel** opposite. Check your order.

4 Answer the questions about the man in the story.
   1 The man knocked. Why? *He couldn't see the bell.*
   2 What was the weather like?
   3 He noticed the door. Why?
   4 He walked inside. Then what happened?
   5 He said something. What?
   6 He noticed some rats. Where?
   7 He noticed a body. Where?
   8 Was the woman dead?

5 What do you think? Who is the old woman? What happens next? How does the old woman's story end?

B Grammar past simple ⊞ regular -ed

6 Read the grammar box and complete the rule.

present simple	past simple
I walk to work every day.	I walked to work yesterday.
She usually closes the shop at 6.00.	She closed the shop at 8.00 last night.

To tell a story in the past, we use the past simple.

Verbs in the past simple usually end with the letters ____.

But some verbs are irregular (examples: can – could, do – did, go – went, have – had, make – made, tell – told, say – said).

Spelling: double the final consonant after a short vowel sound + one consonant (example: stop – stopped)

7 Add one, two, or three letters to make the past simple.
   ask*ed*___   knock____   notice____   turn____
   close____   look____   start____   wait____
   end____   move____   stop____   walk____

8 Tell the **Nightmare Hotel** story to your partner from memory. Did your partner forget anything?

   More practice? **Grammar Bank** >> p.144.
   Irregular verbs list >> p.148.

C Pronunciation -ed endings

9 **9D.3▶** Listen and say A or B.

A (present)	B (past)
I stop at the door.	I stopped at the door.
I knock and I wait.	I knocked and I waited.
I look in the window.	I looked in the window.
I walk inside.	I walked inside.
I turn round.	I turned round.
The body moves.	The body moved.

10 Test a partner.
   Example **A** I stop at the door.   **B** A!

11 **9D.4▶** Listen and write the sentences in the correct box.
   ~~Steve stopped.~~   Nick knocked.   Wendy ended.
   ~~Walter waited.~~   Stacy started.   Luke looked.

1-syllable verb ●	2-syllable verb ●●
Steve stopped.	Walter waited.

Complete the rule.

If the verb ends with the letters ____ or ____, the past simple ending has an extra syllable.

12 Listen to 9D.4 again and repeat.

13 Read out **Nightmare Hotel** with a partner.

D Listen for key words

14 **9D.5▶** Listen to the story. Choose the best title.
   a My Aunt's House
   b The Wrong House
   c The Old House

15 Listen again. Which verbs did you hear? Put a tick ✓.
   ✓ visited   ☐ stopped   ☐ walked   ☐ looked
   ☐ moved   ☐ started   ☐ waited   ☐ noticed

16 Read the audio script on >> p.156 and check your answers.

ABCD Put it all together

17 Work with a partner. Write notes to finish this story.
   I was on my bike one day. I was on a very quiet road. It started raining. I looked round. I noticed a small house in the trees …

18 Tell your story to another partner. Think of a title for your new partner's story.

Writing A postcard

A Get ideas to write about

1 **9E.1▶** Listen and complete the column about Avril's favourite city.

	Avril	you
city	Rio de Janeiro, Brazil	
a famous place	Sugar Loaf mountain	
the perfect weather		
a place to stay	Copacabana Palace Hotel	
three things to visit	the b_____ the f_____ the f_____ stadium	

2 Complete the column about <u>your</u> favourite city.

3 Work with a partner. Talk on the phone. B is on holiday in his / her favourite city. A asks questions about it.

A Where are you?
B In _____.
  It's great.
A Where are you staying?
B In the Hotel
  _____.
  It's near ...
A What's the weather like?
B It's _____.
A What did you do yesterday?
B I visited
  _____,
  _____,
  and _____.

4 Now change roles and have another conversation.

B Think about your reader

5 Read the postcard. Three of the sentences are not part of the postcard. ~~Cross~~ them out.

> Hi Avril,
>
> Greetings from Turkey!
>
> ¹I'm in Istanbul. It's great. ²I'm staying in a hotel near the Bosphorus. ³I started school when I was four. ⁴The weather is warm and sunny. ⁵Yesterday, I visited the Blue Mosque, the market, and the Galatasaray football stadium. ⁶My mother makes very good cakes. ⁷I'm writing this postcard in a café by the sea. ⁸Fish can swim.
>
> See you soon!
>
> Love
>
> Victor

Sultanahmet Camii (The Blue Mosque), Istanbul © Happy Cards Co., Ordu Caddesy 223, Istanbul 34475 Printed in Turkey

6 Match the other sentences to the questions in exercise 3.
  Example Where are you?   I'm in Istanbul.

7 Write three more questions to ask Victor about his favourite city.
  Example What's the food like?

8 Work with a new partner. Imagine you are in your favourite city. Ask and answer questions. Don't look at your book.

AB Put it all together

9 Write a postcard from your favourite city. Use your notes from exercise 1. Answer all the questions in exercises 3 and 7.
  Dear ...
  Greetings from ...
  I'm in ...
  I'm staying in ...
  The weather is ...
  Yesterday I visited ...
  The food here is ...
  I'm writing this postcard ...
  Love ...

10 Read other students' postcards. Which places would you like to visit?

I can write a postcard.
Tick ✓ the line.   with a lot of help   with some help   on my own   very easily

Unit 9 Review

A Grammar

1 *Was, wasn't, were, weren't* Write sentences to complete Jessica's email.

> ✉   _ □ ✕
>
> Hi Linda
>
> I went to an awful party last night …
> ¹ *The people were unfriendly.* _____. people/unfriendly
> ² _____. music/horrible
> ³ _____. food/not/very nice
> ⁴ _____. room/very hot
> ⁵ _____. nothing to drink
>
> When I decided to go, there were no taxis, so I walked home in the rain!
>
> See you soon
>
> Jessica

2 *Was / were* questions Write questions. Change some words and use *like*.

1 **A** I went to the **cinema** last night.
  B Oh really? What was the **film** like?
2 **A** I went to a Russian restaurant last night.
  B Oh really? _____?
3 **A** I went to the mountains on Sunday.
  B _____?
4 **A** I went to New York last summer.
  B _____?
5 **A** I went to a concert last night.
  B _____?

3 Past simple Complete the text with the past simple form of these verbs.

~~arrive~~ ask close knock look
notice open stop turn walk

Luke ¹ *arrived* in town at midnight. It was quiet.
He ² _____ for a place to stay. There were no hotels,
but he ³ _____ a big grey house with a board saying
'Bed and Breakfast'. He ⁴ _____ his car in front of the
house. He ⁵ _____ to the door, ⁶ _____, and waited.
A strange old woman ⁷ _____ the door. 'Have you got
a room for the night?' Luke asked. The woman said
'Sorry, we're full,' and ⁸ _____ the door. Luke ⁹ _____
round and went to sleep in his car. The next day, he
¹⁰ _____ a man at a local shop about the old woman
and the house. The man said 'Nobody lives in that house
now – the old woman died last year.'

B Vocabulary

4 Instructions Find five more sentences.

¹Take	off	at	Market	Street.
the	²Get	³Go	to	⁴Change
number	two	bus.	the	to
⁵Go	the	of	end	the
across	line.	⁶Go	Line.	Circle
the	bridge.	past	the	bank.

5 Directions Where are these places? Write sentences using these words.

at the corner   between   next to   opposite

1 bookshop   *There's a bookshop next to the hotel.*
2 supermarket _____
3 craft market _____
4 bar _____
5 theatre _____

6 Directions Write directions from the hotel to the station.
Go out of the door and ...

7 Adjectives Underline the best word.
1 Buses are often crowded/friendly/polite.
2 Big stations are usually very quiet/cheap/noisy.
3 Five-star hotels are usually dirty/comfortable/wet.
4 Five-star hotels are usually cheap/friendly/expensive.
5 Libraries are usually exciting/crowded/quiet.
6 Waiting for a bus is usually polite/boring/expensive.
7 Underground stations are often comfortable/wet/crowded.

Ana's bag

TIME
SEAT
MAY
ODEON
CINEMA

blakes wine bar
ADMIT ONE
£10·00
26th May
THE GALLERY

Paul—
Blake's,
Wed 8:30

An Inspector Calls
Sat, 28 May at 7:30 PM
20.70
FOOTLIGHTS
01659 3354467

Luigi's
110 The High, Great Milton 02078/3290

Friday 27th May

Spaghetti Carbonara — 4.10
Garlic Bread — 1.20
Mineral Water — 1.0

Total — 6.30

Thank you – serv.

FITNESS CENTRE
★★★
Mon 23rd May
Swimming pool
#8.00

NEXT
100% COTTON
34L
Jeans
£24.99
KN/092

Paul Chan
Actor
Phone: 604 482 390
Email: paulchan@wondermail.com

BRASIL CHILL
£9.99

THU 26 MAY
Thames Buses
ADULT RETURN #15.00
OXFORD TO LONDON, VICTORIA
Thank you for travelling

ODEON PRESENTS
RIVER OF
SCREEN 1 ROW —
PRICE 4.50 DATE FRI 27
YOU WERE SERVED BY: EF AT TERMI

NEXT
TUES 24TH MAY 3:02PM

995657393 SIZE 34L   24.99
JEANS
                      24.99
TOTAL
VISA   **** ***
EXP 08/09
AMOUNT
PLEASE KEEP
FOR YOUR REC

Virgin megastores
WWW.VIRGINMEGASTORES.CO.UK

DATE: TUE 24 MAY

11432 CD   9.99
BRAZIL CHILL

                 9.99
TOTAL

MASTERCARD
**** ****
EXP09.0
AUTH

Colombian Coffee House
Sugar

HAPPY BUDDHA RESTAURANT
SAT 28TH MAY
SPRING ROLLS   3.50
VEGETABLE   4.75
FRIED RICE   9.50
CHICKEN CURRY   2.78
GREEN TEA   8.30
WINE
                 28.83
TOTAL
SERVICE NOT INCLUDED

A good weekend

Jim Hi Ana. Did you have a good weekend?

Ana Oh, hi Jim. Yes, I went to the theatre on Saturday.

J Oh really? What did you see?

A 'An Inspector Calls'. It was very good. What did you do?

J Not a lot. I went to Blake's on Friday. Do you know Blake's?

A Yes, I was there last Wednesday night.

J Oh yeah? OK, well, I can't stop. My class started three minutes ago. See you!

A OK, bye Jim. Have a good class!

How to continue a conversation

G past simple ?; wh- questions   P stress in wh- questions

A Read and find information

1 Look at **Ana's bag** opposite and read **A good weekend**. Where did Ana go? Match the places with the dates.

~~to an art gallery~~   to a Chinese restaurant
to the cinema   to an Italian restaurant   to London
to the pool   to the shops   to the theatre   to a wine bar

Mon 23rd	Tue 24th	Wed 25th	Thu 26th	Fri 27th	Sat 28th
			to an art gallery		

2 Look at the pictures again. What did Ana do in these places? Work with a partner and make sentences.

Example   She went to the Fitness Centre and had a swim.

She went to	the Fitness Centre the cinema the Footlights Theatre London Virgin Records	Next Luigi's the Happy Buddha Blake's wine bar
and	visited the Tate Gallery. had vegetable fried rice. had spaghetti carbonara. saw 'An Inspector Calls'. met an actor called Paul Chan.	bought a CD. had a swim. saw 'River of Time'. bought some jeans.

3 Find the past of these irregular verbs in exercise 2.
1 meet *met*   2 go   3 buy   4 see   5 have

B Grammar past simple ?

4 Complete the examples in the grammar box.

present simple	past simple
Make questions in the present with *do* or *does*:	Make questions in the past with *did*:
Do you go out on Fridays?	Did you go out last Friday?
_____ go on Mondays?	Where did you go last Monday?
What do you drink?	_____ drink last night?
Who does she meet for lunch?	_____ yesterday?
_____ ?	When did his class start?

5 Complete the questions.
1 *Who did you meet* at Blake's? I met Paul Chan.
2 _____ at the cinema? I saw 'River of Time'.
3 _____ at Luigi's? I had spaghetti carbonara.
4 _____ at Next? I bought some jeans.
5 _____ in London? I visited the Tate Gallery.
6 _____ on Tuesday? I went to the shops.

More practice? **Grammar Bank** >> p.145.

C Pronunciation
stress in wh- questions

6 10A.1▶ Listen and say A or B.

A				B			
●	•	•	●	●	•	•	●
What	do	you	**think?**	**What**	did you		**think?**
What	does he		**drink?**	**What**	did he		**drink?**
Who	does she		**know?**	**Who**	did she		**know?**
Where	do	you	**go?**	**Where**	did you		**go?**
What	do	they	**eat?**	**What**	did they		**eat?**
Who	does he		**meet?**	**Who**	did he		**meet?**

7 10A.2▶ Listen and repeat. Keep the rhythm!

8 Test a partner.
Example   A **What** did you **think?**   B B!

D Practise conversations

9 Which responses are better, a or b?
1 Did you go out last night?
   a Yes.
   b Yes. I went to the cinema with Paul.
2 Did you have a good weekend?
   a Yes. We went away.
   b Yes. We went away. What about you?
3 I went to the cinema last Saturday.
   a Oh.
   b Oh really? What did you see?
4 Where did you go?
   a I went to a wine bar with a friend.
   b I went to Blake's with Paul.

10 Match these tips with the conversations in exercise 9.
a Don't just answer – ask too.
b Don't answer just 'yes' or 'no'.
c Use names of people or places.
d Respond with a question.

11 10A.3▶ Listen and read **A good weekend** opposite. Find an example of each tip.
Example   Yes. I went to the theatre on Saturday. = tip b

12 With a partner, write a conversation similar to **A good weekend**. Use true information for you and the four tips. Practise saying your conversation.

13 Close your book and change partners. Have a similar conversation from memory.

ABCD Put it all together

14 Look at the diary on >> p.127. What did you do last week? Ask and answer with a partner.

I can continue a conversation.

Tick ✓ the line.   with a lot of help   with some help   on my own   very easily

TV6 presents

A job interview

1

Interviewer Come in and sit down.
Robin Thank you.
I And you are Mr Banks?
R Yes. Robin Banks.

2

I Now, some questions about your career, Mr Banks. When did you leave school?
R Ehm, let's see ... I left school in ... 1995.

3

I And what did you do after that?
R I was with the police for a while.
I Oh, you joined the police?

4

R No. I took a police car and drove it into a wall.
I Oh, I see ...

5

I And what did you do after that?
R I went to Oxford.

6

I What, Oxford University?
R No, Oxford bus station.

7

I Were you a bus driver?
R No. I took mobile phones out of people's bags. Then I sold them in the market. I worked there for six months.

8

I Oh! And what did you do after that?
R A job in a bank.
I Ah, very good! You got a job in a bank. Were you there for a long time?

9

R No, only 15 minutes. Then the police arrived.
I Hmmm, I see. Well, thank you for coming to the interview, Mr Banks. Goodbye.

10

R It's for you.

Robin's career

a   b   c   d   e

How to talk about a career

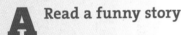
G past simple regular and irregular   V careers   P *wrote* /t/ or *rode* /d/

A Read a funny story

1 Work with a partner. Write a list of jobs.
Example   doctor …

2 Read **A job interview** opposite. Do you think Robin got the job?

3 Look at **Robin's career** opposite. Match pictures a–e with parts of **A job interview**.
Example   a = 7

4 Write *true* or *false*.
1 Robin left school in 1995.   *True*
2 Robin joined the police.
3 Robin went to Oxford University.
4 Robin took mobile phones from bags.
5 Robin worked in a bank for a long time.

5 **A job interview** is part of a TV show. Guess the places where people laugh.

6 10B.1▶ Listen to the show and check your answers.

7 Say the **A job interview** conversation with a partner.

B Grammar past simple regular and irregular

8 Read **A job interview** again. Find the past of these verbs.

1 join *joined*	4 work	7 go
2 leave	5 arrive	8 get
3 take	6 drive	9 sell

9 Write the verbs from exercise 8 in the grammar box.

regular	irregular
join – joined	drive – drove

10 Find the past of these verbs in your dictionary.
become   drink   give   know   make
pay   ride   send   think   write

> **think** 0━ /θɪŋk/ *verb* (thinks, thinking,
> (thought) /θɔːt/, has thought)
> **1** to have an opinion about something; to
> believe something: *I think it's going to rain.* ◊
> '*Do you think Sara will come tomorrow?*' '*Yes, I
> think so.*' (= I think that she will come) ◊

Oxford Essential Dictionary

More practice? **Grammar Bank** ≫ p.145.

C Pronunciation
wrote /t/ or *rode* /d/

11 **10B.2**▶ Listen and say A or B.

A /t/	B /d/
She wrote 'horses'.	She rode horses.
I can't write very well.	I can't ride very well.
I sent a lot of emails.	I send a lot of emails.
There's a 't' in 'lift'.	There's a 'd' in 'lived'.

12 Test a partner.
Example   **A** She rode horses.   **B** B!

D Vocabulary careers

13 Match the people a–c with their careers 1–3.

My career in four lines

1 I … joined the army.
   stayed there for two years.
   got a job as a mechanic.
   started a small business.

2 I … went to university.
   studied medicine.
   became a doctor.
   got a job in a hospital.

3 I … got married.
   worked at home.
   had a child.
   wrote a book.

14 Write a 'career in four lines'. It can be your own career, the career of somebody you know, or one you would like. Use your dictionary.

ABCD Put it all together

15 Add three more events to your 'career in four lines'.

16 Interview your partner. Remember the tips for a good conversation on ≫ p.97! Then ask two more students.
Example   **A** When did you leave school?
           B I left school in 1998.
           A Oh really? And what did you do after that?
           B I went to university.

I can talk about a career.
Tick ✓ the line.   with a lot of help   with some help   on my own   very easily

WHODUNNIT!

THE PEOPLE

Ernie Fortune

… was born in a poor family, but he made a lot of money in the newspaper business. He married a woman called Clara when he was 40, and they had a baby daughter, Lisa. Five years later, Clara left Ernie. She went to Australia with her new boyfriend, Nigel. Ernie and Lisa lived together in Ernie's big country house.

Lisa Fortune

… liked expensive things. She wanted expensive clothes and her father bought them for her. When she wanted an expensive car, her father bought it for her. On her 21st birthday, she wanted a flat in the city. Her father bought it for her. Every month, Lisa's father gave her money.

Jackie Potts

… was good-looking. She was also poor and worked as a maid in the flat of a young woman called Lisa Fortune. Lisa was rich, but she paid Jackie very badly. Jackie saw Lisa's expensive things and she wanted them. She wanted to be rich. When Ernie visited Lisa one day, he met Jackie. He fell in love with her and asked her to marry him. Jackie had a boyfriend called Bob, but Bob was poor. Ernie was very rich. Jackie was only 24 and Ernie was 65, but she married him.

THE CRIME

Now Jackie was rich and she remembered that Lisa paid her badly when she was her maid. She hated Lisa. She talked to Ernie, and Ernie stopped Lisa's money. 'You must get a job and work,' he said. Lisa was very angry. She planned to kill Jackie with poison, but her plan went wrong. Somebody died, but it wasn't Jackie!

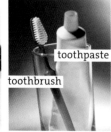

toothpaste

toothbrush

a bottle of poison

a maid

How to talk about what happened

G past simple ☐⁇ P *didn't*

A Read for detail

1 Read **Whodunnit!** opposite and write the names.
1 Ernie's first wife   *Clara*
2 Clara's boyfriend
3 Ernie's daughter
4 Ernie's second wife

2 Read it again and put these sentences in order.
- ☐ Jackie married Ernie.
- ☐ Ernie's wife Clara left him.
- 1 Ernie got rich in the newspaper business.
- ☐ Ernie stopped Lisa's money.
- ☐ Ernie and Clara had a child.
- ☐ Ernie bought a flat for Lisa.
- ☐ Ernie got married when he was 40.
- ☐ Lisa wanted to kill Jackie.
- ☐ Lisa didn't pay Jackie well.
- ☐ Jackie worked for Lisa.

3 Write answers to the questions.
1 Where did Lisa's mother go?   *She went to Australia.*
2 Where did Lisa's father live?
3 What did Lisa get on her 21st birthday?
4 Who did Jackie work for?
5 Who did Jackie hate?
6 Who did Lisa want to kill?

B Grammar past simple ☐⁇

4 Complete the grammar box.

+	Jackie died.	Jackie saw Lisa.	
–	Jackie didn't die.	Jackie _____	Lisa.
?	Did Jackie die?	_____ Jackie _____	Lisa?
answer	No, she didn't.	Yes, she did.	

5 Answer the questions.
1 Did Lisa buy a car?
  No, she didn't. Her father bought a car for her.
2 Did Lisa give money to her father?
3 Did Jackie work for Lisa?
4 Did Jackie pay Lisa badly?

6 Complete the sentences.
1 Ernie *didn't have* a son; he *had* a daughter.   have
2 He _____ his wife; she _____ him.   leave
3 His wife _____ to America; she _____ to Australia.   go
4 Lisa _____ the flat; Ernie _____ it.   buy

More practice? **Grammar Bank** >> p.145.

C Pronunciation *didn't*

7 **10C.1▶** Listen and repeat. Notice that *didn't* is stressed.
Jackie **want**ed **mon**ey
She **did**n't **want** a **job**
She **did**n't **want** to **work**
So she **did**n't **marry Bob**

D Listen for key facts

8 Work with a partner. Read all the questions. Can you guess any answers?
1 Did Lisa buy a bottle of poison?
2 Where did she put it?
3 Did Jackie use the toothpaste?
4 Did Ernie use it?
5 Did Jackie see Lisa with the poison?
6 What did Jackie do?
7 What did Jackie say on the phone?

9 **10C.2▶** Listen to the questions and make a note of the answers.

10 Listen again. Who died?

11 Ask and answer the questions with a partner.

ABCD Put it all together

12 Read **Whodunnit!** again and choose seven key words.

13 Compare with a partner. Choose ten key words from your lists.

14 Work together and make notes about the story.
Examples   Ernie, money, newspapers
         Ernie + Clara: baby

15 Practise telling the story from your notes.

I can talk about what happened.

Tick ✓ the line.   with a lot of help   with some help   on my own   very easily

Alfred Nobel

A Alfred returned to Sweden in 1863 and he worked with chemicals. He made the first 'dynamite' in 1867. He made a lot of money and started businesses in a lot of different countries.

B Then he went abroad and studied in France and in the USA. He returned to Saint Petersburg in 1852 and worked in his father's business.

C **1** Alfred Nobel was born in Stockholm, Sweden, in 1833. He was the son of Immanuel Nobel, an engineer, and his wife Andriette.

D He died in 1896, and he left a lot of money for a peace prize. He also left money for prizes in physics, chemistry, medicine, and literature.

E When he was nine, in 1842, the family moved to Saint Petersburg. His father became rich, and Alfred had a good education. When he was 17, he could speak Swedish, Russian, French, English, and German.

Nobel Prize winners

1921
Albert Einstein
1879 • Ulm • Germany

1991
Aung San Suu Kyi
New York • 1945 • Rangoon

1962
Francis Crick
England • Cambridge • 1916

1903
Marie Curie
1891 • Paris • 1906

1964
Martin Luther King
1929 • Atlanta • Boston

1979
Mother Teresa
1929 • 1997 • Agnes

1993
Nelson Mandela
1918 • Transkei • Robben Island

1971
Pablo Neruda
Santiago • 1904 • Isla Negra

1992
Rigoberta Menchú
1959 • Guatemala • Mexico

1987
Susumu Tonegawa
Tokyo • Nagoya • 1939

1993
Toni Morrison
Ohio • 1931 • Houston

1986
Wole Soyinka
1934 • Ibadan • Nigeria

How to talk about life stories

v years; education   **P** /s/ or /z/

A Pronunciation /s/ or /z/

1 **10D.1▶** Listen and say which picture.

the prize of peace

the prize of peas

the price of peas

the price of peace

2 Test a partner.
Example **A** The price of peas.   **B** c!

B Read for detail

3 What do you know about Alfred Nobel? Work with a partner and <u>underline</u> the facts.
1 He was a businessman / a scientist / an engineer.
2 He was from Switzerland / Sweden / Russia.
3 He spoke Russian / Spanish / Italian.

4 Read **Alfred Nobel** opposite and check your facts.

5 Put the **Alfred Nobel** text in order.

6 Complete this 'time line' of Alfred Nobel's life.
1833 *Alfred Nobel was born.* _____
1842 _____
1852 _____
1863 _____
1867 _____
1896 _____

C Say years

7 Write the years in numbers.
1 nineteen sixty-seven *1967*
2 nineteen fourteen
3 eighteen ninety
4 nineteen oh five
5 nineteen hundred
6 two thousand and three

8 Ask about your partner's life. Then ask other students.
Example **A** When were you born?   **B** I was born in ...

9 **10D.2▶** Listen and follow the years from start to end.

START → 1990	1955	1750	1960
1919	1909	1949	1843	1915
1999	1945	1833	1916	1980
1995	2010	1830	1918	1981
2001	2004	2003	1930	**END**

10 Work with a partner. Say another way from start to end.

D Vocabulary education

11 Write these words in the correct column.
a certificate   chemistry   a degree   a diploma
~~high school~~   history   literature   primary school
secondary school   university

go to + place, leave + place	study + subject	get + qualification
high school		

12 Add more words. Use your dictionary.

E Listen for key facts

13 **10D.3▶** Read and listen. Is this:
a part of a news programme?
b part of a story?
c a quiz game?

'OK, first one, number one ... He was born in, ehm ... in 1929. He left school, ehm ... secondary school, when he was, ehm ... 15, and went to a university in Atlanta, Georgia ... that's in the United States. He got his degree, his, ehm ... university degree, in 1948 ...'

14 When speaking, people often repeat words, for example 'school' in the text above. Find another example.

15 **10D.4▶** Listen to the quiz. Which of the **Nobel Prize winners** opposite is the woman describing? When you know the answers, don't say them – write them!

16 When did you first know the answers? Read the audio script on ›› p.157 and find the place. Compare with a partner.

ABCDE Put it all together

17 Work in groups. Talk about a Nobel Prize winner.
Student A Go to ›› p.127.   **Student C** Go to ›› p.131.
Student B Go to ›› p.128.   **Student D** Go to ›› p.135.

I can understand and talk about life stories.

Tick ✓ the lines.   with a lot of help   with some help   on my own   very easily

Writing Biodata

A Read for key facts

1 Look at the words below. Ask your teacher questions to find out about the poet Pablo Neruda. Your teacher can only say *yes* or *no*.

Example **You** Was he born in 1904?
  Teacher Yes.
  You Did he ... ?

Pablo Neruda

13 years old
1973
1971
a town called Temuco
Rangoon, Burma
French
Literature
1904
Chile
first poem

2 Complete the text with words from exercise 1.

Twenty Poems of Love
Pablo Neruda

About the Author

Pablo Neruda was born in ¹ *Chile* in ² _____.
His real name was Neftalí Reyes Basoalto. His father worked for the railways. His mother died when he was a baby and his father married again. They went to live in ³ _____. He wrote his ⁴ _____ when he was ⁵ _____. When he was 20, he changed his name to Pablo Neruda.

He studied ⁶ _____ at the University of Chile in Santiago. He became a diplomat in ⁷ _____. Then he worked in many other countries. He returned to Chile in 1952 and he lived in a town by the sea called Isla Negra. He won the Nobel Prize for ⁸ _____ in ⁹ _____ and he died in ¹⁰ _____. People remember him now as one of the greatest Spanish-language poets of the 20th century.

B Get ideas for writing

3 Think of five key dates, names, and places from your life. Write a list.

4 Play a guessing game with a partner. Look at your partner's list and ask yes / no questions about it.

Example **A** Were you born in Gdańsk?
  B No, I wasn't.

C Organize ideas for writing

5 Look at the table below and read the biodata for Pablo Neruda in exercise 2. Put these words in the 'topic' column.

~~early life~~ ~~education~~ now born work

	topic	Pablo Neruda	me
1		Chile	
2	early life		
3	education		
4		diplomat in _____	
5		greatest Spanish-language poet of the _____ century	

6 Complete the 'Pablo Neruda' column with notes from his biodata.

7 Complete the table with information about yourself.

ABC Put it all together

8 Use your notes from exercise 7 to write your biodata. Start like this:
  I was born in ...

9 Give your biodata to your partner. Ask your partner two questions about their biodata.

10 Check your partner's writing. Has he / she included all the topics?

I can write my biodata.
Tick ✓ the line. with a lot of help with some help on my own very easily

Unit 10 Review

A Grammar

1 **Irregular verbs** Find a way from start to end. <u>Don't</u> cross a square with a regular verb in it.

START	live	drive	go	get
leave	think	take	return	sell
visit	close	stop	move	write
want	pay	give	make	become
die	have	walk	study	ask
like	buy	**END**	marry	hate

2 Write the past simple of the irregular verbs in exercise 1.

3 **Past simple** ? Write the questions.

1 **A** _What did Lisa buy_ ? what Lisa buy
  B Some poison.
2 **A** _____? who Lisa hate
  B Jackie.
3 **A** _____? where Lisa put poison
  B Lisa put the poison in Jackie's toothpaste.
4 **A** _____? Jackie see this
  B Yes, she did.
5 **A** _____? what Jackie do
  B She phoned Lisa.
6 **A** _____? what Jackie say
  B She said, 'Somebody put poison in my toothpaste, but Ernie used it and died.'
7 **A** _____? Ernie use the toothpaste
  B No, he didn't, but Lisa thought, 'Oh no – I killed my father!'
8 **A** _____? what Lisa do
  B She drank the poison and died.

4 **Past simple** + – Complete the sentences to make them true for you.

Example _I went OR I didn't go_ to bed early last night. go

1 _____ to the cinema last week. go
2 _____ a cup of tea this morning. have
3 _____ English last weekend. study
4 _____ late this morning. get up
5 _____ an email yesterday. write
6 _____ a newspaper yesterday. buy
7 _____ last August. work
8 _____ the house before 8.30 this morning. leave

B Vocabulary

5 **Life stories** Find the best match.

1 [g] We got   a a baby.
2 [ ] She had   b a book.
3 [ ] I joined   c a Nobel Prize.
4 [ ] He started   d a small business.
5 [ ] She wrote   e abroad.
6 [ ] He won   f certificate.
7 [ ] They studied   g ~~married~~.
8 [ ] She went to   h medicine.
9 [ ] I got a school i Oxford University.
10 [ ] They went   j rich.
11 [ ] He became   k the Army.

6 Write six true sentences about you, your family, or famous people. Use ideas from exercise 5.

Examples   My sister studied history.
             J.R.R. Tolkien wrote books.

1 _____
2 _____
3 _____
4 _____
5 _____
6 _____

7 **Years** How do you say these years? Write the words.

1 1999   _nineteen ninety-nine_
2 2005   _____
3 1980   _____
4 1851   _____
5 1905   _____

8 **Education** Complete the biodata text with these words.

~~born~~ certificate chemistry engineer history joined literature physics Secondary subjects university

Robin Banks was [1] _born_ in Bristol in 1979. His father was an [2] _____. Robin went to Mayfields [3] _____ School. He liked science [4] _____. His favourite subjects were [5] _____ and [6] _____. He hated [7] _____ and English [8] _____. He [9] _____ the school football team. He got his [10] _____ and left school in 1995. He didn't go to [11] _____ and didn't get a degree.

ACCOMMODATION IN THE AREA

BED AND BREAKFAST

Freshnest Farm

Friendly, welcoming accommodation near the attractive fishing village of West Bay. Single and double rooms complete with bathroom, telephone, and TV. Full English breakfast between 7.30 and 9.30. Only ten minutes' drive from beautiful quiet beaches.

Tel. 01473 628722
From £25.75 to £45.50 per person

CAMPING

Erin Valley Campsite

Family-run campsite in a peaceful wooded valley next to the beautiful River Erin. Full bathroom facilities with free hot showers. Kitchen area with cookers and fridge. Washing machines available. Free fishing.

Tel. 01478 288690
From £3.75 to £6.25 per person per night. From £22.50 to £37.50 per week

HOTELS

The Five Ways Hotel
★★★★

Modern 250-room hotel. Complete with bar, nightclub, two restaurants, swimming pool, sauna, gym, Jacuzzi, golf. Wedding parties welcome. Large, comfortable rooms with satellite TV and Internet access.

For more information, see www.fivewayshotel.com.
Tel. 01473 889010
Double rooms from £175.00

The Clifftops Hotel
★★

Friendly family-run hotel near the village of West Bay. Fantastic sea views from all rooms. Comfortable double and single rooms complete with shower and tea-/coffee-making facilities. Try the delicious local recipes in our cosy restaurant.

Tel. 01471 017395
Rooms from £45.50 to £55.00

SELF-CATERING

Millside Farm

Next to the pig shed on this dirty working farm. Only a 90-minute walk from the ugly little village of Cowpatt. Relax in our uncomfortable and expensive one-room apartment, complete with two chairs and a kitchen sink (cold water only). Excellent views of the motorway.

Tel. 01473 628741
Sleeps up to five
Minimum stay 1 week
From £202.50 to £320.50 per week

Brackenhall Apartment

Next to the shop and the pub in the beautiful village of Brackenhall. Excellent country walks and horse riding. Relax in our comfortable one-bedroom apartment, complete with TV, video, CD player, oven, microwave, fridge, bedsheets and towels, and parking space.

Tel. 01477 071919
Sleeps up to three
Minimum stay 1 week
From £260.00 to £395.00 per week

Good idea!

Jim Hi Ana. Planning a holiday?
Ana Hi Jim. Yes, I want a weekend in the country, but the hotels are too expensive.
J Oh. You could stay in a self-catering place.
A Yeah, I know, but they're usually for one week minimum. And I hate cooking!
J I see. Well, why don't you stay at a campsite?
A The weather isn't warm enough – it's too cold.
J Right. You could stay in a bed and breakfast. Here's one, look … 'Freshnest Farm'.
A The breakfast's too early. I don't get up before ten at the weekend!
J Ana, can I make a suggestion? Why don't you just stay at home?!
A Ha ha ha! Good idea!

How to make suggestions

G *too big, not big enough* V holiday accommodation; suggestions P stress in long words

A Vocabulary holiday accommodation

1 Match the words with meanings 1–5.
- [ ] self-**cater**ing a**part**ment [ ] bed and **break**fast
- [ ] accommo**da**tion [1] **camp**site [ ] **ho**tel

1 ~~You sleep outside in a tent.~~
2 You stay in a flat and you clean and cook.
3 You stay in a room and you don't clean or cook. You can stay all day.
4 You stay for the night and have breakfast, but usually you can't stay all day.
5 A place where you can stay.

a tent

2 Which type of accommodation do you prefer when you go on holiday? Why? Tell your partner.

B Read and find

3 Look at **Accommodation in the area** opposite. One of the adverts is a joke (not real, just for fun). Find it.

4 Find the best accommodation for these people.
1 I want to play golf. *The Five Ways Hotel*
2 I want to go swimming in the sea.
3 I want a cheap room for one person.
4 I'd like a cheap apartment for three people.
5 I'd like a fishing holiday.
6 I'd like to stay in a quiet hotel, but not too expensive.

5 **11A.1▶** Don't look at the page opposite. Listen to Ana and Jim. Write Ana's problems with the accommodation.

accommodation	problem
hotel	*too expensive*
self-catering	
campsite	
bed and breakfast	

6 Read **Good idea!** opposite and check.

C Grammar *too* + adjective; *not* + adjective + *enough*

7 Complete the grammar box.

too	*not ... enough* /ɪˈnʌf/
The bed's too small.	The bed isn't big enough.
The tent's _____ short.	The tent _____ long _____.

8 Complete the sentences. Use *too* or *enough*.
1 Why don't you go swimming in Alaska? warm
  The water isn't *warm enough* _____.
2 Why don't you stay in five-star hotels? expensive
  They're _____.
3 Why don't you leave at three in the morning? early
  It's _____.
4 Why don't you sleep in your car? big
  It isn't _____.
5 Why don't you buy a home in Hollywood? rich
  I'm not _____.

More practice? **Grammar Bank** >> p.146.

D Make suggestions *You could ..., Why don't you ...?*

9 Read **Good idea!** again. Underline Jim's four suggestions.
Example Jim Oh. You could stay in a self-catering place.

10 **11A.2▶** Listen and repeat the four suggestions.

11 Say the **Good idea!** conversation with a partner.

12 Work with a partner. A is planning a holiday.
Student A Make sentences from the box on >> p.131.
Student B Make suggestions from the box on >> p.135.

E Pronunciation stress in long words

13 Underline these adjectives in **Accommodation in the area**. Are they positive ☺ or negative ☹?
- ☺ attractive
- ○ delicious
- ○ fantastic
- ○ peaceful
- ○ beautiful
- ○ excellent
- ○ friendly
- ○ ugly
- ○ comfortable
- ○ expensive
- ○ modern

14 Look at /fænˈtæstɪk/ below. What is the meaning of the ' ?

> **fantastic** /fænˈtæstɪk/ *adjective* (*informal*)
> very good; wonderful ➷ SAME MEANING
> **great** or **brilliant**: *We had a fantastic holiday.*

Oxford Essential Dictionary

15 **11A.3▶** Listen and write the adjectives in the table.

●●			
●●●	*attractive*		
●●●			

16 **11A.4▶** Listen and check. Listen again and repeat.

ABCDE Put it all together

17 With a partner, have a conversation like in **Good idea!**.
Student A Suggest accommodation from **Accommodation in the area**.
Student B Say what the problems are.

I can make suggestions. ▬▬▬▬
Tick ✓ the lines. with a lot of help with some help on my own very easily

The Estate Agent

108 11B

How to say what's wrong

A Vocabulary rooms and furniture

1 Which furniture do you have in these rooms at home?

bathroom bedroom dining room
hall kitchen living room

Example bedroom – a cupboard, a chair, a bed …

2 **11B.1▶** Look at the pictures in **The Estate Agent** opposite for one minute, but don't read the text. Close your book. Listen and say *true* or *false*.

Example **Audio** There's a shelf in the bathroom.
  You False!

3 The dictionary shows pronunciation with phonetic letters. Can you guess these furniture / room words? Write them.

1 /bed/ *bed*   5 /hɔːl/   9 /ˈsəʊfə/
2 /tʃeə(r)/   6 /ʃelf/   10 /ˈteɪbl/
3 /ˈkʊkə(r)/   7 /ˈʃaʊə(r)/   11 /ˈtɔɪlət/
4 /ˈkʌbəd/   8 /sɪŋk/   12 /ˈwɒʃbeɪsn/

4 **11B.2▶** Listen, check, and repeat.

B Pronunciation long and short vowel sounds

5 Write more examples from exercise 3 in the box.

short vowel sounds	long vowel sounds	
1 vowel symbol	2 vowel symbols	1 vowel symbol + :
bed /bed/	sofa /ˈsəʊfə/	hall /hɔːl/

6 Find these words in your dictionary. Is the vowel sound short or long?

bath enough fridge mouse room space stairs too

C Listen to a conversation

7 **11B.3▶** Don't look at the page opposite. Listen to the conversation. Why doesn't the woman like the flat?

a It's too big.   b It's too expensive.   c It's too small.

8 Listen again. Write *true* or *false*.

1 The lift doesn't work. *True*
2 The living room is very light.
3 The bedroom's big enough for a double bed.
4 There isn't a fridge.
5 There's a bath in the bathroom.

9 Read **The Estate Agent** opposite. Match these problems with things in the flat.

1 It's too small. *the living room, the window, the bedroom*
2 There aren't enough plates.
3 There isn't enough light.
4 There isn't a bath.
5 There isn't a fridge.
6 There isn't enough space.
7 It doesn't work.

10 Say the conversation with a partner.

D Grammar *too much / many* + noun, *not enough* + noun

11 Complete the grammar box with these words.

noise plates space spiders

countable	uncountable
¹There are too many _____.	³There's too much _____.
²There aren't enough _____.	⁴There isn't enough _____.

12 Look at **The Estate Agent** and underline the correct word.

1 There isn't enough water / light / chairs in the living room.
2 There aren't enough tables / chairs / music in the living room.
3 There's too much baths / water / noise in the bathroom.
4 There are too many beds / space / spiders in the bedroom.

13 Work with a partner. What's wrong in these situations? Write sentences with *too* and *enough*.

1 There are 500 books and one shelf.
   There are too many books. There aren't enough shelves.
2 There are four chairs and six people.
3 There are 20 cups of tea but only one cup of coffee.
4 There are three sofas but space for only one.
5 There are only four people at the party but there are ten pizzas and eight cakes.

More practice? **Grammar Bank** >> p.146.

ABCD Put it all together

14 Work with a partner. You are flatmates and you want to find a new flat.

Student A Look at the flat plan on >> p.131.
Student B Look at the flat plan on >> p.135.
Choose the best flat.

I can say what's wrong.
I can describe a home.

Tick ✓ the lines. with a lot of help with some help on my own very easily

Ricky's office

Frank's office

Envy

A bigger flat	A smaller flat
A warmer bed	A colder bed
A fatter cat	A thinner cat
And fresher bread	Older bread
Sweeter cakes	Harder chairs
And greener grass	And smaller plates
Bigger steaks	Higher stairs
And business class	And longer waits
Expensive wine	Cheaper wine
A better view	A worse TV
The first in line	The last in line
Is always you	Is always me

How to compare things

G comparatives   v adjectives   P -er endings

A Vocabulary adjectives

1 Work with a partner. Match the opposites.

big clean comfortable expensive fat good
~~long~~ new old-fashioned rich soft warm

1 short *long*	5 modern	9 uncomfortable
2 dirty	6 cheap	10 hard
3 old	7 small	11 cool
4 bad	8 thin	12 poor

B Grammar comparatives

2 Look at the pictures opposite. Then read the grammar box and complete the sentences below.

-er than (short adjectives)	more ... than (long adjectives)
Ricky is richer than Frank.	Ricky's office is more modern than Frank's.

spelling	irregular forms
short – shorter (add –er)	good – better
dirty – dirtier (change y to i and add -er)	bad – worse
big – bigger (double the consonant)	

1 Frank poor Ricky
2 Ricky's office comfortable Frank's

3 Write the comparative forms of the adjectives in exercise 1 in the table.

+ -er	more + adjective
short – shorter	modern – more modern

double the consonant	irregular	change y to i + -er
big – bigger	good – better bad – worse	dirty – dirtier

4 Work with a partner. Make sentences about the pictures opposite.

Example Ricky's view is better than Frank's.

Ricky's	view	is	more modern	than Frank's.
Frank's	cupboard	are	more comfortable	than Ricky's.
	plants		dirtier	
	chair		better	
	phone		smaller	
	shelves		bigger	
	table		longer	

5 Look at the pictures again for one minute. Close your book. With a partner, say sentences to compare the offices.

Example A Ricky's sofa is, ehm ...
         B Longer?
         A Yes, Ricky's sofa is longer than Frank's.

More practice? **Grammar Bank** >> p.146.

C Read a poem

6 **11C.1▶** Read and listen to the poem **Envy** opposite. What does *envy* mean?
   a You've got something good and you're happy.
   b Another person has got something good and you're happy.
   c Another person has got something good and you want it.

7 What things does the writer compare? Write the words.
   1 home and garden *flat, grass, view*
   2 food and drink
   3 furniture

8 Work with a partner. Write more lines about:

   car clothes friends holidays house job shoes

   Examples A faster car
            More expensive shoes

9 Think of five things you've got that you'd like to change. Tell a partner.
   Example I've got an old computer. I'd like a better computer.

D Pronunciation -er endings

10 Look at the pronunciation of *better* in the dictionary.

> **better**[1] 0▬ /ˈbetə(r)/ *adjective* (good, better, best)
> **1** of a higher standard or quality; not as bad as something else: *This book is **better than** that one.*

Oxford Essential Dictionary

Remember! The vowel sound of the -er ending is /ə/, and the /r/ sound is optional.

11 Listen to **Envy** again. Does the speaker say the r in -er?

12 Practise saying the poem.

ABCD Put it all together

13 Look at the picture on >> p.127 for one minute. Close your book and draw the picture from memory.

14 Work with a partner. Compare your pictures.
   Example My tree is taller than your tree.

I can compare things.

Tick ✓ the line.   with a lot of help   with some help   on my own   very easily

FurnitureMegaStores
WINTER SALE
EVERYTHING FROM OLD-FASHIONED COMFORT TO MODERN STYLE
CHEAPEST PRICES GUARANTEED!

VISIT OUR SOFA SHOWROOM
FREE DELIVERY!

a
Picasso
Take home this stylish sofa for only £699!

b
Standard
Available in a range of 15 colours, price down to only £389. Hurry while stocks last!

c
Comfort Zone
Relax in style. Only £565!

d
Elegance
We have the biggest range of antique sofas in the Midlands, from only £650.

VISIT OUR CHAIR SECTION
CHECK OUT OUR PRICES

e
Director
Comfort and versatility. Available in black, white, and green. Take home 4 for only £119!

g
Classic
Take a look at our collection of elegant dining chairs, from only £40 each.

f
Avant Garde
Strong and simple design, only £49.

h
Van Gogh
This farmhouse-kitchen dining chair only £24.99, available in pine or mahogany.

DISCOUNT DECORATION!

Professional decorator's paints, over 150 colours, discount prices!

TOP TABLES
UNBEATABLE PRICES!

i
Milano
This Italian-style ebony table for only £399!

j
Country Kitchen
Only £499!

k
Ruskin
These beautiful handmade tables for only £599.

l
Favourite
Available in three colours, only £99.50.

MAKE A HOME OFFICE SPACE!

m
Victoria
Pure elegance, only £369.

n
Work Station
Practical workspace with storage, for only £129.

o
Century
Clean modern design, available in white or wood finish, only £239.

p
Tradition
Pine-finish desks with drawer space, only £149.

How to make an appointment

v signs; times of the day   p intonation to ask and confirm

A Read and find

1 Look at **People** opposite. Match the jobs with photos a–h.
Example   a = bank manager

2 Look at **Signs** opposite. Match signs 1–8 with the jobs in **People**.
Example   sign 1 = men's hairdresser

3 Look at signs 1–8 again. Read these sentences and write the jobs.
1 You can call him 24 hours a day, 7 days a week.
   mechanic
2 He went out for ten minutes.
3 He works till late.
4 She has one hour for lunch.
5 She works with two other people.
6 He finishes work at 6.00 on weekdays.
7 She can prepare new contact lenses for you while you are in the shop.
8 You can make an appointment to see her between 9.00 and 4.00 on weekdays.

4 Compare the opening and closing hours in the signs to the hours in your country.
Example   In Spain, the banks open earlier and close later.

B Vocabulary times of the day

5 Look at **Times of the day** opposite. Now find the way from start to end – go past the times in the correct order.

START	→ first thing tomorrow morning	mid-morning tomorrow
mid-afternoon tomorrow	early tomorrow afternoon	late tomorrow morning
late tomorrow afternoon	the day after tomorrow	next week
early tomorrow evening	tomorrow night	**END**

6 **12A.1▶** Listen and check. Listen again and repeat.

7 **12A.2▶** Don't look at the page opposite. Listen. When's Jim's appointment with the dentist?
a tomorrow morning
b tomorrow afternoon
c mid-morning, the day after tomorrow

8 Read **At the dentist's** opposite and check.
More practice? **Grammar Bank** >> p.147.

C Pronunciation intonation to ask and confirm

9 **12A.3▶** Listen and repeat.

A asking	B confirming
This after**noon**?	This after**noon**.
To**mo**rrow **morn**ing?	To**mo**rrow **morn**ing.
The **day** after to**mo**rrow?	The **day** after to**mo**rrow.

10 **12A.4▶** Listen. Does the speaker ask (A) or confirm (B)?
Example   **Audio** This afternoon.   **You** B!

11 Test a partner.
Example   **A** Twelve o'clock?   **B** A!

12 Work with a partner. Say the **At the dentist's** conversation.

D Listen for key facts

13 **12A.5▶** Listen to two people making appointments. Who do they want to see?
1 a a mechanic   b a dentist   c an optician
2 a a hairdresser   b a doctor   c a mechanic

14 Listen again. What time are the appointments?

15 Read the audio script on >> p.158 and check.

ABCD Put it all together

16 Work with a partner. Take turns to be A and B.
Student A You want an appointment with Ms Steel.
Student B You are Ms Steel's receptionist.

Start the conversation like in **At the dentist's**. Use different times.

17 Close your books. Say the conversation again.

I can make an appointment.

Tick ✓ the line.   with a lot of help   with some help   on my own   very easily

File　Edit　View　Favourites　Tools　Help

C Back　Next　Stop　Refresh　Home　Search　Favourites

Address　http://www.news-online/todaystopic

The body

arm　back　foot　hand　head
heart /hɑːt/　ill / sick　leg　neck
stomach /'stʌmək/　well

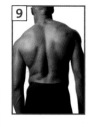

Phoning in sick

How often do you phone in sick when you're well? The results of a new study show:

- The average person takes eight days a year off sick. People who work in the public sector, for example education, take more time off than other people. The highest figure is in the police force. The average worker in the police force takes 12 days sick leave a year.

- The most common excuses are flu, back pain, headache, and stomach ache. 40% of days off result from flu.

- Of all people who take time off sick, about one in five are not really ill.

- Every year, 22 million people get sick notes from their doctors. Of these people, 9 million are perfectly well.

- 50% of sick days are on Monday or Friday. The number of people off sick is also higher when there are important football matches or other events.

- There are also problems with school kids taking time off sick. There are plans to make parents pay £100 a day if their kids take time off sick, for example to go on holiday.

Are you going to take a day off sick this month? Tell us what you think about sick days.

Your comments:

'They want us to work longer hours and they don't pay us enough. So sometimes we take days off when we're not really sick. What's wrong with that?'
Derek, Middlesborough

'I never take days off. These days, people feel tired after a late night and they phone in sick. I think it's disgusting. If you don't want to work, leave!'
Marge, Leeds

'I hate people coming into the office with flu. Two weeks later, we've all got it. When I get flu, I stay in bed and phone in sick. But I don't agree with people taking days off when they're not ill. I think that's like stealing from your company.'
Robert, Northampton

'In our office, we get a bonus if we don't take sick days over Christmas and New Year. So I take my sick leave in February!'
Beverly, Guildford

'I get really bad headaches. But I hate phoning in sick. The boss thinks I'm lying because the others in the office are taking days off to go shopping or whatever. That's the problem.'
Sheila, Motherwell

'I'm always ill in the holidays or at weekends. I think it's because I work too hard, I get really tired and stressed, and then I get sick in my free time. So I take a few days off and say I'm sick. That's fair enough, isn't it?'
Russ, Swansea

flu

stomach ache

back pain

headache /'hedeɪk/

How to **say how you feel**

v the body; health **P** short and long vowels

A Vocabulary the body

1 Look at **The body** opposite. Work with a partner. Match the words with numbers 1–11.

Example 1 = head

2 **12B.1▶** Listen and check. Listen again and repeat.

B Read for general meaning

3 Look at **Phoning in sick** opposite. Read the article quickly. What do you think the title means?

a Phoning your friend to ask if he / she is feeling well.
b Telephoning your boss to say you're ill.
c Telephoning the doctor.

4 Read the article again. Write *true* or *false*.

1 People who work in education take most time off sick.
2 20% of people who take time off aren't really ill.
3 Doctors give notes to people who aren't ill.
4 Derek thinks he doesn't get enough pay.
5 Beverly doesn't usually take time off sick over Christmas.
6 Russ works very hard at weekends.

5 Find words or phrases in the article with these meanings.

1 time off work when you are ill   *sick leave*
2 a letter from the doctor to say you are ill
3 take a day off work when you are ill
4 a pain in the head
5 a stomach problem
6 extra money
7 9,000,000
8 taking something and not paying for it
9 not telling the truth

6 Read **Phoning in sick** again. The article is about Britain. Do people do the same in your country? Tell a partner.

C Pronunciation short and long vowels

7 **12B.2▶** Listen and say A or B.

A short vowel sounds	B long vowel sounds
Put your hand on your hat. /æ/	Put your hand on your heart. /ɑː/
I've got a pen in my hand. /e/	I've got a pain in my hand. /eɪ/
I can't fill my stomach. /ɪ/	I can't feel my stomach. /iː/
I see the doctor's not there. /ɒ/	I see the doctor's note, there. /əʊ/
There's no fun in the office. /ʌ/	There's no phone in the office. /əʊ/

8 Test a partner.

Example **A** Put your hand on your hat. **B** A!

D Vocabulary phrases to say how you feel

9 **12B.3▶** Listen and repeat.

I **don't** feel **well**
I **think** it's **flu**
I **feel** really **ill**
What shall I **do**?

Don't go to **work**
Stay **home** in**stead**
Phone in **sick**
And **stay** in **bed**

10 Complete the conversation with phrases from exercise 9.

A ¹ *I don't feel well* .
B Why? What's wrong?
A I've got a headache and back pains. ² _____.
B Flu? You look fine to me.
A I'm not. ³ _____.
B OK. ⁴ _____. ⁵ _____.
A Can you phone for me?
B Oh, all right ... How do you feel now?
A Much better, thanks. Let's go out!

11 **12B.4▶** Listen and check.

12 Say the conversation with a partner. Take turns to be A and B.

E Listen for key words

13 **12B.5▶** Listen to the conversation. Who goes to the shop, the man or the woman?

14 Which words and phrases did you hear? Put a tick ✓.

✓ milk   ☐ not dressed   ☐ stay in bed
☐ bread   ☐ headache   ☐ stay home
☐ coffee ☐ back pains   ☐ phone work

15 Read the audio script on **≫ p.158** and check your answers.

ABCDE Put it all together

16 Work with a partner. You are flatmates. You need something but you don't want to go to the shop. Write a similar conversation.

17 Practise saying your conversation. Then close your book and act your conversation for another pair.

I can say how I feel.

Office Life

Episode two

1

Holly   You don't look very well. Are you OK?
Justin Yeah, I'm fine. I'm just acting ill for Mr Minnit. I'm taking Friday off sick so I'm preparing him for the phone call!
Holly   Oh, I see! Ha ha, very good.

2

Holly   So what are you doing on Friday?
Justin 'Officially', I'm seeing the doctor.
Holly   And what are you doing really?

3

Justin I'm going to Paris for the weekend with Debbie.
Holly   Oooh, very nice! How are you getting there?
Justin On the train.

4

Holly   And where are you staying?
Justin We booked a cheap hotel on the Internet. What's wrong with your mouth?

5

Holly   Nothing. I'm taking Friday morning off too.
Justin What for?

6

Holly   'Officially', I'm going to the dentist's.
Justin And really?
Holly   I've got an appointment at the hairdresser's … Quick, Mr Minnit's coming!

7

Holly   Oh, hello Mr Minnit!
Justin Hello Bister Biddit! Achooo!
Boss   You two look terrible! Never mind. Friday's a holiday, so you've got a long weekend to rest!

8

Justin/Holly   What!!

How to **talk about future arrangements**

G present continuous future   **P** sentence stress in questions

A Read a conversation

1 Read **Office Life** opposite and answer the questions.
   1 What's wrong with Justin?
      a He's got flu.   b Nothing.
   2 What's wrong with Holly?
      a Nothing.   b She's got toothache.

2 Answer the questions with a partner.
   1 When's Justin taking a day off sick? *On Friday.*
   2 What's Justin doing on Friday?
   3 Who's he going with?
   4 How is he travelling to Paris?
   5 Where are they staying?
   6 What's Holly doing on Friday morning?
   7 Who is 'Bister Biddit'?
   8 What is Mr Minnit's good news?

3 **Office Life** is a TV show. Guess the places where people laugh.

4 **12C.1▶** Listen and check.

5 Say the **Office Life** conversation with a partner.

B Grammar present continuous future

6 Read the grammar box. <u>Underline</u> seven more examples of the present continuous for future arrangements in **Office Life**.

The present continuous has two uses ...	
present action	future arrangements
I'm just acting ill for Mr Minnit.	I'm taking Friday off sick.
Mr Minnit's coming!	What are you doing on Friday?

7 Complete the sentences with the correct form of these verbs.

   go have sit talk

   1 We*'re going* tomorrow morning on the 10 o'clock train.
   2 Justin and Holly _____ about their plans for Friday.
   3 I _____ lunch with Debbie tomorrow.
   4 Holly _____ to the hairdresser's on Friday morning.
   5 Justin _____ on his chair in the office.
   6 Justin _____ to Paris at the weekend.

8 Work with a partner. Which sentences in exercise 7 are future arrangements?

More practice? **Grammar Bank** >> p.147.

C Pronunciation sentence stress in questions

9 **12C.2▶** Listen and repeat.
   Where are you **go**ing this **eve**ning?
   What are you **doing**   to**night**?
   Who   are you **meet**ing?
   When are you **eat**ing?
   Who   are you **see**ing   to**night**?

10 Write three or more questions.

What	are you	doing	after the lesson?
Where		having	this evening?
When		going	for dinner?
			tomorrow?
			next weekend?

11 Ask and answer with a partner.
   Example   **A** What are you doing after the lesson?
               B I'm going home. And you?

More practice? **Grammar Bank** >> p.147.

D Listen for key facts

12 **12C.3▶** Listen to Holly and Justin. Answer the questions.
   a Who's having dinner with Dave?
   b Who's meeting Debbie?

13 Put the conversation in order.
   ☐ Holly   OK, what are you doing on Wednesday evening?
   ☐ Holly   I'm having dinner with Dave tonight. How about tomorrow?
   ☐ Holly   Yes, good idea.
   ☐ Holly   OK, fine. See you on Wednesday, then.
   [1] Justin   Let's go out for a drink one evening.
   ☐ Justin   Nothing. Let's meet on Wednesday.
   ☐ Justin   What are you doing tonight?
   ☐ Justin   Tomorrow's good. Oh no, wait a moment – that's no good. I'm meeting Debbie tomorrow.

14 Listen again and check. Say the conversation with a partner.

ABCD Put it all together

15 You are a very busy person. Complete your diary for next week. Write *free* in only three squares.

	Mon	Tues	Wed	Thurs	Fri
morning					
afternoon					
evening					

16 Work with one or two partners. Find one morning, afternoon, or evening to meet next week.

I can talk about future arrangements.

Tick ✓ the line.   with a lot of help   with some help   on my own   very easily

Three
steps to healthy living
by Dr Patricia Carlsson

We often start the year with the best of intentions. But too often, we forget them after the first month. So, what can we do to make our good intentions come true?

1 *Be realistic.*

Don't say … 'I'm going to lose 20 kilos next month.'
Say … 'I'm going to lose 1 kilo.'

2 *Give details.*

Don't say … 'I'm going to do something about my health.'
Say … 'I'm going to run for 20 minutes every day.'

3 *Think positive.*

Don't say … 'I'm going to eat boring salads and have no social life.'
Say … 'I'm going to eat fresh fruit every day.'

Go on, **you can do it!**

Good Intentions

I'm going to **quit**, I'm not **jok**ing
I'm **go**ing to quit **smok**ing
I **quit**, that's **it**!
Yes, I'm **go**ing to get **fit**

No **stay**ing out **late**
And I'm **go**ing to lose **weight** /weɪt/
Less **sug**ar in my **tea**
Fat-**free**, that's **me**!

Good, good, good
Good intentions!

I'm **go**ing to join a **gym**
I'm going to **run**, I'm going to **swim**
Less **stress**, less **mess**
I'm going to **learn** to play **chess**

I'm going to **drink** green **tea**
Watch **less** TV
Fat-**free**, stress-**free**
Smoke-**free**, that's **me**!

Good, good, good
Good intentions!

GLOSSARY		
1	q_____	= stop doing something
2	f_____	= well, strong, healthy
3	w_____	= 🛍 KG
4	l_____	= opposite of *more*
5	*chess*_____	= a game with ♟♞♝
6	s____-____	= without stress

How to talk about intentions

G *going to* for future intentions   V lifestyle   P fast speech

A Vocabulary lifestyle

1 Work with a partner and add more things to this list. Use your dictionary.

It's good for you ...	It's bad for you ...
fruit	stress
exercise	smoking

2 **12D.1▶** Listen and read **Good Intentions** opposite. Complete the glossary.

3 Listen again and repeat.

4 Don't look at the page opposite. Complete these phrases.
  1 I'm going to quit _____ .
  2 I'm going to _____ fit.
  3 I'm going to _____ weight.
  4 I'm going to _____ a gym.
  5 I'm going to _____ to play chess.

B Read for key information

5 Read **Three steps to healthy living** opposite. Write *true* or *false*.
  1 People often have good intentions in April.
  2 We sometimes forget our good intentions.
  3 Good intentions are better if we are realistic, positive, and think about the details.

6 Work with a partner. Look at these sentences and give some advice. Use *Be realistic*, *Give details*, and *Think positive*.
  1 I'm going to live to be 150.   *Be realistic!*
  2 I'm not going to pass my exams.
  3 I'm going to eat healthy food.
  4 I'm going to do more exercise.
  5 I'm not going to enjoy meals.
  6 I'm going to win 30 Olympic gold medals.

C Grammar *going to* for future intentions

7 Complete the grammar box.

+	I'm going to get fit.	They're going to swim.	She _____ fruit.
–	I'm not going to get fit.	They _____ .	She isn't going to eat fruit.
?	Are you going to get fit?	Are they going to swim?	_____ she _____ fruit?

8 Read the box and underline the present continuous or *going to* in sentences 1–7.

arrangements	intentions
Have you got a ticket?	Is it a plan in your head?
Have you got an appointment?	Did you decide alone?
Did you arrange it with other people?	If 'yes' → choose *going to*
If 'yes' → choose **present continuous**	

  1 I'm having / going to have lunch with Ana tomorrow.
  2 I'm quitting / going to quit smoking.
  3 I'm relaxing / going to relax more next year.
  4 I'm going / going to go out with James on Friday.
  5 I'm doing / going to do more exercise next year.
  6 I'm meeting / going to meet my sister at two o'clock.
  7 I'm playing / going to play tennis with Tony tonight.

9 Choose one intention for you in the next year – a, b, c, or d. Underline it.

1 learn	a Arabic	b German	
	c Italian	d *other*	
2 visit	a Rio de Janeiro	b London	
	c Moscow	d *other*	
3 stop	a eating potatoes	b watching TV	
	c using my mobile phone	d *other*	
4 learn to play	a chess	b the violin	
	c the saxophone	d *other*	
5 be	a happier	b more friendly	
	c stress-free	d *other*	

10 Compare your intentions with a partner.
  Example   **A** I'm going to learn German.
         B Really? Me too. And I'm going to ...

  More practice? **Grammar Bank** ≫ p.147.

D Pronunciation understand fast speech

11 **12D.2▶** When we say *going to* and *want to* fast, they sound like 'gonna' and 'wanna'. Listen to the difference.

A normal	B fast
I'm going to have a good time.	I'm gonna have a good time.
What do you want to do?	What do you wanna do?

12 **12D.3▶** Listen and say *normal* or *fast*.

ABCD Put it all together

13 Think of three or four intentions for you in the next year. Use the ideas in exercise 9 or **Good Intentions** and make notes.
  Example   get fit – join a gym, lose weight, no sugar

14 Work with two or three other students. Talk about your intentions and decide whose intentions will come true.

Writing Thank-you letters

A Read thank-you letters

1 Look at photos a–j. Find good presents for these people.
  1 ☐ *h* 'I'm going to drink green tea.'
  2 ☐ 'I'm going to make my arms stronger.'
  3 ☐ 'I'm going to lose weight.'
  4 ☐ 'I'm going to learn to play chess.'
  5 ☐ 'I'm going to become a vegetarian.'

2 Match the thank-you letters with three of the photos.
  1 ☐ *j* Gemma gave these to Vince.
  2 ☐ Caroline gave this to Gemma.
  3 ☐ Vince gave this to Caroline.

3 Gemma, Vince, and Caroline want to improve their health. What are they going to do?
  Example Gemma's going to cook healthier food. She's going to eat more vegetables.

4 Work with a partner. Look at the language in the three letters. How do they start? How do they finish?
  Example They all begin with the word _____.

B Check your writing

5 Caroline gave Vince present *c*. Ask the teacher questions to complete his thank-you letter.
  Example **You** Is number 9 'present'? **Teacher** Yes, it is.

¹D_____ Caroline,

²I'_____ ³w_____ ⁴t_____ ⁵t_____ ⁶y_____ ⁷f_____ ⁸y_____
⁹p_____. ¹⁰I_____ ¹¹w_____ a ¹²l_____ ¹³s_____. ¹⁴I'_____
¹⁵g_____ ¹⁶t_____ ¹⁷l_____ ¹⁸t_____ ¹⁹p_____ ²⁰c_____
²¹s_____ ²²t_____ ²³i_____ ²⁴p_____ ²⁵f_____ ²⁶m_____.

I ²⁷h_____ ²⁸y_____ ²⁹a_____ ³⁰w_____.

³¹L_____ ³²o_____ ³³l_____,

Vince

6 Read your partner's letter in exercise 5. Check the spelling.

7 Work with a partner. Choose another thank-you letter from exercise 2. <u>Underline</u> this information in the letter and write 1, 2, or 3 next to the sentence(s) in the letter.
  1 the writer says thank you
  2 the writer says why he/she likes the present
  3 the writer says what he/she's going to use it for and why

AB Put it all together

8 Work with a partner. Give a small present to another pair (or draw it on a piece of paper). Here are some ideas:

9 Write a polite thank-you letter for your present. Give your letter to the students who gave you the present.

10 Check the spelling. Is all the information in exercise 7 included?

Dear Gemma,

I'm writing to thank you for your present. It was a fantastic surprise. They're really comfortable, and I love the colour. I'm going to use them this afternoon. In fact, I want to go swimming every week, so they're going to be very useful. Pool water is bad for the eyes. So thank you very much.

I hope you're well.

Lots of love,

Vince

Dear Caroline,

I'm writing to thank you for your present. It was a lovely surprise and it's got lots of interesting ideas. I'm going to use it a lot because I want to cook healthier food this year. I'm going to stop eating red meat, and I'm going to eat more vegetables. I always wanted to eat more carrots but I didn't know how to cook them, so this book is perfect for me!

I hope you are well. Write soon!

Best wishes,

Gemma

Dear Vince,

I'm writing to thank you for your present. It's on the coffee table now, and it looks great. I love the colour, and it's really easy to clean. In fact, I'm going to use it as a paperweight because I'm going to quit smoking.

I hope you're well.

Love,

Caroline

Ideas for presents ...

I can understand and write thank-you letters.

Tick ✓ the line.   with a lot of help   with some help   on my own   very easily

Unit 12 Review

A Grammar

1 Arrangements Write sentences with the present continuous future.

1 Iris and Sue have got train tickets to travel to London on Saturday. travel

 They're travelling to London on Saturday.

2 Jim's got an appointment with the dentist for 10.45 on Wednesday. go

3 Justin and Debbie booked to stay in a hotel in Paris for the weekend. stay

4 Ana arranged to play tennis with Jim tomorrow. play

5 I booked a table for dinner this evening at an Italian restaurant. have

2 Intentions Complete the text. Use *going to* and these verbs.

do drink eat join ~~lose~~ quit run watch

Good intentions

This year, everybody in my family wants to live a healthier life. My ¹ sister *'s going to lose* weight. My ² brother_____ more fruit and vegetables. My parents ³ _____ a gym. Mum ⁴ _____ smoking and ⁵ Dad_____ less beer. I ⁶ _____ more exercise. I ⁷ _____ for 20 minutes every day. And we ⁸ _____ less TV. Let's see if we can keep our good intentions!

3 Write three sentences about your good intentions.

4 Make questions and complete the conversation.

What	are you going to	travel?	get money?
Where		stay?	eat?
When		come home?	leave?
How			

A I'm going to travel round the world next year.
B ¹ _____ ?
A In January, probably.
B ² _____ ?
A Oh, by bus, train, boat ... anything, really.
B ³ _____ ?
A I don't know. Cheap hotels, campsites ...
B ⁴ _____ ?
A I'm going to find work in bars, on boats, whatever.
B ⁵ _____ ?
A Anything, really. Whatever the local people eat.
B ⁶ _____ ?
A In August or September.
B Wow! Well, have a good time!

B Vocabulary

5 Health Do the crossword.

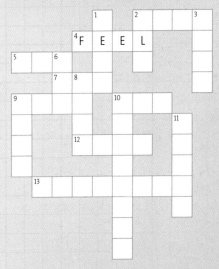

Across

2 the end of your leg
4 I don't ____ very well today.
5 Justin's taking Friday ____ sick.
7 not fine, the opposite of 'well'
9 If you're off school, get a doctor's ____.
10 Stay in ____ and rest.
12 I'm going to phone in ____.
13 a pain in your head

Down

1 fine, the opposite of 'ill'
2 40% of days off work are because of this.
3 Some people ____ days off work when they aren't sick.
6 healthy, well, strong
8
9 You wear a tie around your ____.
10 a pain in the back
11 a stomach ache = an ____ stomach

6 Appointments Complete the conversation.

A This is Dr Brittan's surgery. Can I ¹ *help* you?
B Yes, I'd like to ² _____ an appointment with Dr Brittan, please.
A OK. How ³ _____ tomorrow?
B Sorry, that's no ⁴ _____. I've got another appointment.
A OK, the day ⁵ _____ tomorrow?
B Yes, that's fine.
A How about early ⁶ _____, say 2.30?
B Can it be a ⁷ _____ later, say 3.30?
A Yes, that's ⁸ _____. Can you give me your name, please?

Pairwork

1C Exercise 15
Smith and Jones

Jim Smith		**Tom Jones**	
Ireland		Wales	
23 Market Street Newtown		10 West Street Newmarket	
599 9955		595 5959	
Anne Jones		**Jacky Smith**	
Scotland		Wales	
10 West Street Newmarket		23 Market Street Newtown	
595 5959		599 9955	
Jane Smith		**Sam Jones**	
England		Ireland	
10 West Street Newmarket		10 West Street Newmarket	
955 5599		995 5599	
Liz Jones		**Mark Smith**	
Scotland		England	
23 Market Street Newtown		23 Market Street Newtown	
995 5599		955 5599	

1D Exercise 14

2C Exercise 16
Houses

4B Exercise 4
Months

January's the first month
It's easy to remember
The tenth and the eleventh
Are _____ and _____

_____'s the fourth month
And _____ is the third
_____'s the second month
A short month, a long word

_____ is the sixth month
It's easy to say
The eighth month is _____
The fifth month is _____

_____ is the seventh month
The ninth is _____
And finally, the twelfth month
The last month, _____

4B Exercise 11
Puzzle answers

1 In the dictionary!
2 September.
3 The letter Y.
4 These months have more days (31).

6D Exercise 11

How	many	books do you read	in a	day?
	much	fruit do you eat		week?
		coffee do you drink		month?
		butter do you use		
		eggs do you eat		
		water do you drink		
		salt do you use		
		hamburgers do you eat		
		wine do you drink		
		fish do you eat		
		your own ideas		

Answers
A lot. Not much. Not many. I don't (eat / drink / read / use) any. None.

10A Exercise 14
Diary

Write last week's dates in the diary. Write things you did on each day. You can invent some!

Ask your partner. Remember the four conversation tips in exercise 10 on >> p.97!

Example **A** What did you do last Monday?
  B Not a lot. I watched TV. How about you?
  A I went to …

Mon	Tue	Wed	Thu	Fri	Sat

11C Exercise 13
Picture

11D Exercise 11
Puzzle

Do this puzzle.

There are five hotels – the Wilton, the Pilton, the Vilton, the Bilton, and the York. The Bilton is cheaper than the Wilton. The Wilton is more expensive than the York and cheaper than the Pilton. The Vilton is more expensive than the Wilton and cheaper than the Pilton. The York is more expensive than the Bilton. Which hotel is the cheapest? And the most expensive?

7B Exercise 16
Student A Suggestions

Have conversations. Agree on one suggestion for each day.

Example **A** What shall we do?
  B I don't know. What's the weather like?
  C It's hot and sunny.
  B How about playing football?
  C No, let's go for a swim.
  A Or how about going for a walk?

day	weather	🙂	🙁
1		football walk *your idea*	swim
2		sailing cinema *your idea*	shops
3		DVD skiing *your idea*	park
4		table tennis roller-skating *your idea*	run

10D Exercise 17
Student A Life story notes

Tell this life story to your partners. Your partners say which Nobel Prize winner you are talking about.

Example This person was born in … He was …

Albert Einstein	
born	1879, Ulm, Germany son of a bed salesman
education	secondary school, Munich, Institute of Technology, Zurich
work	scientist, thinker
Nobel Prize	1921 Prize for Physics
died	1955

Pairwork

10D Exercise 17
Student B Life story notes

Tell this life story to your partners. Your partners say which Nobel Prize winner you are talking about.

Example This person was born in ... She was ...

Toni Morrison	
born	1931, Ohio, USA; 2nd of four children; working-class family
education	first degree, Howard University second degree, Cornell University
work	writer of novels; first novel 1970
Nobel Prize	1993 Prize for Literature

1B Exercise 16
Student A Names and numbers

	1	2	3
name	Gemma		
phone	71 733 7374		
email	gem@pal.es		

	4	5	6
name	Bruce		Serge
phone	774 6626		837 1192
email	brujo@jazz.au		serlo@dep.fr

2A Exercise 17
Student A Classroom

1
2 clock
3 tree
4
5 bike
6
7
8 tap
9
10 umbrella

3A Exercise 16
Student A Map

Ask your partner questions and find:

the cash machines   the music shop   the pub
the restaurant   the taxis   the telephones

Write the words on your map.

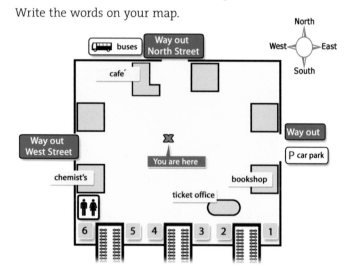

4B Exercise 15
Student A Birthday List

Ask your partner and complete the birthday information.

Example A When's Kofi Annan's birthday?
B It's on April the eighth.

Rigoberta Menchú		Kofi Annan	
Jackie Chan	April 7	Maria Sharapova	April 19
Penelope Cruz		Nelson Mandela	
Nicole Kidman	June 20	Madonna	August 16
Salma Hayek		Ronaldo	
Agatha Christie	September 15	Cervantes	September 29
Gandhi		Woody Allen	December 1
Paul Simon	October 13	Brad Pitt	
Tiger Woods	December 30	Picasso	October 25
Antonio Banderas		John Lennon	

Now answer the questions below.

True or false?

1 Mandela's and Madonna's birthdays are in the same month.

2 Gandhi's and Paul Simon's birthdays are in the same month.

3 The people with birthdays in April are not Americans.

4 The people with birthdays in December are all actors.

4C Exercise 16
Student A Eric's morning

Work with a partner. Find eight differences.

Example **A** Eric gets up at eight o'clock.
B Oh, in my picture Erica gets up at eight thirty. That's one difference …

5B Exercise 12
Student A

My best friend   **My neighbour**

5D Exercise 11
Student A Jude and Mike

	Jude	Mike
car	no	yes
wine	no	yes
perfume	yes	no
computer	yes	no
cook	yes	no
mobile phone	no	yes
chocolate	no	no
ski	no	no

Example **A** I need a gift for my friend Jude. Have you got any ideas?
B Has she got a car?
A No, she hasn't …

6A Exercise 15
Student A

You have €5. You want to buy some food and drink.
Choose from:

an apple a coffee crisps a packet of biscuits
a packet of sandwiches soup tea water a yogurt

Ask student B the prices. Be careful. Remember the **Six tips for shoppers** on ≫ p.56.

Example **A** How much are the sandwiches, please?
B €4.50.
A That's expensive. How much is the yogurt?

Now change roles. Look at your price list on ≫ p.135.

6C Exercise 15
Student A Find the differences

6D Exercise 18
Food in the Kitchen 1

You've got …	You've also got …
tea coffee pizza sugar milk water	

Pairwork

6R Exercise 5
Student A Crossword

Read your clues to your partner. Complete the crossword.

Across

2 An orange 'gap', please. (5)
3 I'd like 'gap' apple, please. (2)
5 a yellow fruit (6)
7 French onion 'gap' (4)
8 See you 'gap' Friday for lunch. (2)
9 a cup of 'gap' or coffee (3)
12 'gap', thank you. I don't like coffee. (2)
13 Greek, Russian, or fruit 'gap' (5)
14 small green vegetables (4)
16 You use these to make an omelette. (4)
17 Sue's got a lot of dog 'gap'. (8)
18 not cheap (9)
21 Two 'gap' of coffee, please. (4)
23 The 'gap' is 5.99. (5)
25 'Gap', there aren't. (2)
26 'gap' and chips (4)
27 a 'gap' of pizza (5)

7B Exercise 16
Student B Suggestions

Have conversations. Agree on one suggestion for each day.

Example **A** What shall we do?
　　　　　 B I don't know. What's the weather like?
　　　　　 C It's hot and sunny.
　　　　　 B How about playing football?
　　　　　 C No, let's go for a swim.
　　　　　 A Or how about going for a walk?

day	weather	☺	☹
1		football walk *your idea*	swim
2		cinema shops *your idea*	sailing
3		park skiing *your idea*	DVD
4		run table tennis *your idea*	roller-skating

7D Exercise 16
Your likes and dislikes

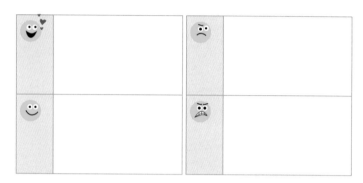

8B Exercise 18
Student A Clothes tips

Ask for and give clothes tips.

What clothes shall I take ...	**What shall I wear ...**
to Hawaii?	for a walk in the mountains?
to Greenland?	to a dinner party?
to New York?	to go skiing?
your ideas	*your ideas*

Example **A** I'm going for a walk in the mountains.
　　　　　　 What shall I wear?
　　　　　 B Wear boots and a warm coat. Don't wear a
　　　　　　 short skirt.

8C Exercise 17
Student A Carnival

Describe your picture and find eight differences.

Example **A** In my picture there's a musician.
　　　　　　 He's playing the guitar.
　　　　　 B Oh, in my picture, he's playing the
　　　　　　 saxophone. That's one difference ...

8R
Exercise 6
Student A Crossword

Read your clues to your partner. Complete the crossword.

Across
2 What shall I take 'gap' a walk in the mountains? (3)
3 Take 'gap' to Hawaii. First letter 's'. (6)
5 What shall I wear to 'gap'? A suit and tie?
   First letter 'w'. (4)
6 Take a coat or a 'gap' to England. First letter 'j'. (6)
8 Take a 'gap' when you go for a drive.
   First letter 'm'. (3)
10 Wear shoes for a walk in the 'gap'. First letter 'p'. (4)
11 Wear a 'gap' dress to a wedding. First letter 'l'. (4)
13 Don't wear a 'gap' and tie to the beach.
   First letter 's'. (5)
14 Don't take a 'gap' to Hawaii. First letter 'c'. (4)
15 Don't 'gap' a coat in Brazil in the summer. (4)

9A
Exercise 15
Student A Map

the transport museum   the football stadium
West Park   the airport   the sports centre

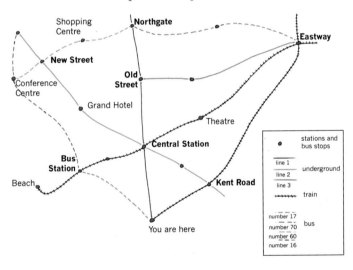

10D
Exercise 17
Student C Life story notes

Tell this life story to your partners. Your partners say which
Nobel Prize winner you are talking about.

Example   This person was born in ... She was ...

Rigoberta Menchú	
born	1959, Chimel, Guatamala daughter of a farmer
education	Catholic secondary school
work	human rights worker
Nobel Prize	1992 Peace Prize

11A
Exercise 12
Student A Problems

The train	's	too expensive.
The buses	isn't	too slow.
The hotels	are	quick enough.
My tent	aren't	good enough.
The weather		big enough.
your ideas		too small.
		too wet.
		warm enough.
		your ideas

11B
Exercise 14
Student A Flat plan

Tell your partner about the flat in the picture.

Example   It's got a big hall. The living room's very small ...

Have a conversation about the good points and the problems
with the flats. Choose the best flat.

Example **A** I think there's too much noise from the
          railway in Flat B.
          B Yes, but Flat A's on the 6th floor and there
          isn't a lift.
          A Mmm, but there isn't enough ...

Pairwork

1B Exercise 16
Student B Names and numbers

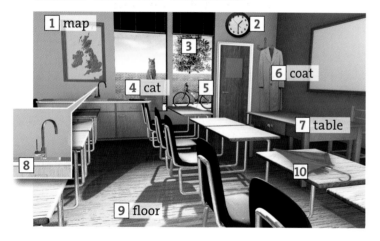

	1	2	3
name		Craig	Irvina
phone		827 4637	77 33 74
email		crg@it.uk	ervas@pin.ru

	4	5	6
name		Colleen	
phone		826 8827	
email		collan@fir.ir	

2A Exercise 17
Student B Classroom

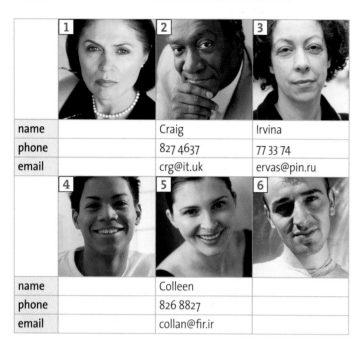

1 map
2 [clock]
3 [cat]
4 cat
5 [bicycle]
6 coat
7 table
8 [sink]
9 floor
10 [chair]

3A Exercise 16
Student B Map

Ask your partner questions and find:

the bookshop   the buses   the café
the chemist's   the ticket office   the toilets

Write the words on your map.

North
West — East
South

Way out
North Street

music shop

pub

restaurant

Way out

Way out
West Street

P car park

You are here

taxi

6 5 4 3 2 1

4B Exercise 15
Student B Birthday List

Ask your partner and complete the birthday information.

Example **A** When's Kofi Annan's birthday?
            B It's on April the eighth.

Rigoberta Menchú	January 9	Kofi Annan	April 8
Jackie Chan		Maria Sharapova	
Penelope Cruz	April 28	Nelson Mandela	July 18
Nicole Kidman		Madonna	
Salma Hayek	September 2	Ronaldo	September 22
Agatha Christie		Cervantes	
Gandhi	October 2	Woody Allen	
Paul Simon		Brad Pitt	December 18
Tiger Woods		Picasso	
Antonio Banderas	August 10	John Lennon	October 9

Now answer the questions below.

True or false?

1 Mandela's and Madonna's birthdays are in the same month.
2 Gandhi's and Paul Simon's birthdays are in the same month.
3 The people with birthdays in April are not Americans.
4 The people with birthdays in December are all actors.

4C Exercise 16
Student B Erica's morning

Work with a partner. Find eight differences.

Example **A** Eric gets up at eight o'clock.
B Oh, in my picture Erica gets up at eight thirty. That's one difference …

5B Exercise 12
Student B

My best friend   **My neighbour**

5D Exercise 11
Student B Rose and Pete

	Rose	Pete
car	yes	no
wine	yes	yes
perfume	yes	no
computer	no	yes
cook	no	yes
mobile phone	no	yes
chocolate	no	yes
ski	no	yes

Example **B** I need a gift for my friend Rose. Have you got any ideas?
A Has she got a car?
B Yes, she has …

6A Exercise 15
Student B

Student A wants to buy some food and drink in your café. This is your price list:

Café
price list

soup €3.50
special offer: two for the price of one today

sandwiches €4.50
a yogurt €0.79
a coffee €2.50
water €1.25
crisps €1.33
biscuits €1.75
an apple €2.50
tea €0.75
with milk €1.99

Now change roles. You have €5. You want to buy some food and drink. Ask Student A the prices. Be careful. Remember the **Six tips for shoppers** on ≫ p.56!

Example **B** How much are the crisps, please?
A €2.30.
B That's expensive! How much is …

6C Exercise 15
Student B Find the differences

Pairwork

6D Exercise 18
Food in the Kitchen 2

You've got ...	You've also got ...
bread and ham water coffee milk sugar	

6R Exercise 5
Student B Crossword

Read your clues to your partner. Complete the crossword.

Down
1   French 'gap' soup (5)
2   bread and 'gap' (3)
4   'Gap', there isn't any milk in Turkish coffee. (2)
6   a 'gap' of coffee (3)
7   ham and cheese 'gap' (10)
10   green and red fruit, plural (6)
11   a 'gap' sandwich (3)
14   a 'gap' of cheese (5)
15   fish and 'gap' (5)
17   My dog likes dog 'gap'. (8)
19   Many Italians like this. (5)
20   a 'gap' burger (6)
22   Potatoes or 'gap'? (4)
24   I'd like 'gap' orange, please. (2)

7B Exercise 16
Student C Suggestions

Have conversations. Agree on one suggestion for each day.

Example   **A** What shall we do?
　　　　　B I don't know. What's the weather like?
　　　　　C It's hot and sunny.
　　　　　B How about playing football?
　　　　　C No, let's go for a swim.
　　　　　A Or how about going for a walk?

day	weather	☺	☹
1		swim walk *your idea*	football
2		cinema sailing *your idea*	shops
3		DVD skiing *your idea*	park
4		table tennis roller-skating *your idea*	run

8B Exercise 18
Student B Clothes tips

Ask for and give clothes tips.

What clothes shall I take ...
to Egypt?
to Britain?
to Buenos Aires?
your ideas

What shall I wear ...
to play tennis?
to my English class?
for a walk in the park?
your ideas

　　　Example   **A** I'm going for a walk in the mountains.
　　　　　　　　　　　What shall I wear?
　　　　　　　　B Wear boots and a warm coat. Don't wear a
　　　　　　　　　　　short skirt.

8C Exercise 17
Student B Carnival

Describe your picture and find eight differences.

　　　Example   **A** In my picture there's a musician. He's
　　　　　　　　　　　playing the guitar.
　　　　　　　　B Oh, in my picture, he's playing the
　　　　　　　　　　　saxophone. That's one difference ...

8R Exercise 6
Student B Crossword

Read your clues to your partner. Complete the crossword.

Down

1 What shall I wear for a 'gap' in the car? First letter 'd'. (5)
3 Don't wear 'gap' when you go for a drive. First letter 's'. (7)
4 Don't take a warm hat to Egypt in the summer. It's very 'gap'. (3)
5 I'm going to play tennis. What should I 'gap'? (4)
6 Wear 'gap' to a party. First letter 'j'. (5)
7 Wear a hat or a 'gap' in the park. First letter 'c'. (3)
9 Don't wear shorts to a dinner 'gap'. First letter 'p'. (5)
12 Take a cap or a 'gap' when you go fishing. First letter 'h'. (3)

9A Exercise 15
Student B Map

the shopping centre   the theatre   the beach
the Grand Hotel   the conference centre

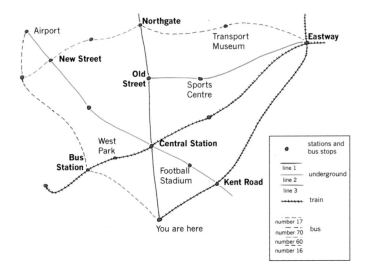

10D Exercise 17
Student D Life story notes

Tell this life story to your partners. Your partners say which Nobel Prize winner you are talking about.

Example   This person was born in ... He was ...

Wole Soyinka	
born	1934, Nigeria
education	secondary school in Ibadan University College, Ibadan Leeds University
work	writer of books and plays
Nobel Prize	1986 Prize for Literature

11A Exercise 12
Student B Suggestions

Why don't you	go by train?
You could	buy a new one?
	stay in a self-catering place?
	stay at home?
	your ideas

11B Exercise 14
Student B Flat plan

Tell your partner about the flat in the picture.
   Example   It hasn't got a hall. The living room's very big ...

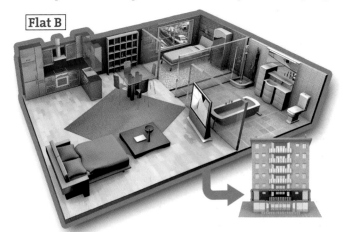

Flat B

Have a conversation about the good points and the problems with the flats. Choose the best flat.
   Example   A I think there's too much noise from the railway in Flat B.
   B Yes, but Flat A's on the 6th floor and there isn't a lift.
   A Mmm, but there isn't enough ...

6A Exercise 15
Student A

Student B wants to buy some food and drink in your café. This is your price list:

Café
price list

an apple €2.50
a yogurt €2.50
special offer: three for the price of two today

a coffee €3.99

water €1.50
soup €1.89
biscuits €1.50
crisps €2.30
sandwiches €1.50
half-price today

tea €1.50

Grammar Bank

1B possessives *my, your, his, her*, etc.

Use possessive adjectives (*my, your, his, her*) to describe nouns. They tell us who / what something belongs to.

possessives			
my	My name's Joanna.	his	How do you spell his name?
your	What's your name?	her	Her name's Maria.

• Use possessive adjectives before a noun.

>> Now go to **exercise 1.1** to practise.

1C subject pronouns *I, you, he, she*, etc.

Use subject pronouns (*I, you, he, she, it, we, they*) to talk about someone or something. They tell us who / what a sentence is about, or who / what does something.

subject pronouns			
I	I'm from Belgium.	it	It's from London.
you	You're from France.	we	We're from Paris.
he	He's from Spain.	they	They're from Mexico.
she	She's from China.		

• Use subject pronouns before a verb in a positive ⊞ statement.
• Always use a capital letter for *I*.
• Use *I, you, he, she, we, they* for people.
• Use *it, they* for things.

>> Now go to **exercise 1.2** to practise.

1C subject pronouns and possessives

subject pronouns	I	you	he	she	it	we	they
possessives	my	your	his	her	its	our	their

>> Now go to **exercise 1.3** to practise.

1C present simple of *be* ⊞

short form	full form	
I'm	I am	I'm from America.
You're	You are	You're from England.
He's	He is	He's from Spain.
She's	She is	She's from Poland.
It's	It is	It's from Belgium.
We're	We are	We're from Germany.
They're	They are	They're from Canada.

• Use short forms in conversation or in informal writing.

>> Now go to **exercise 1.4** to practise.

1D present simple of *be* ⊞ ⊟ ？

+	– (n't = not)	?
I'm a teacher.	I'm not a teacher.	Am I a teacher?
You're in my class.	You aren't in my class.	Are you in my class?
He / She / It's late.	He / She / It isn't late.	Is he / she / it late?
We're students.	We aren't students.	Are we students?
They're from Spain.	They aren't from Spain.	Are they from Spain?

short answers			
Yes, I am.	No, I'm not.	Yes, we are.	No, we aren't.
Yes, you are.	No, you aren't.	Yes, they are.	No, they aren't.
Yes, he / she / it is.	No, he / she / it isn't.		

>> Now go to **exercises 1.5 and 1.6** to practise.

1.1 Order the words to make sentences.
Example name 's his what ? *What's his name?*
1 telephone her 's number what ?
2 website address his 's what ?
3 's name what your ?
4 email my address samir@teleline.uk is
5 Alan name his 's
6 mobile her 91 456 2110 number 's

1.2 Complete the sentences. Use a subject pronoun.
Example My name's Sam. *I* 'm Sam.
1 Holly and Justin are from England. _____'re from England.
2 You're from Germany. I'm from Germany. _____'re from Germany.
3 Tatiana's from Russia. _____'s from Russia.
4 Where's Pablo from? Where's _____ from?
5 Where are Julia and Gemma from? Where are _____ from?
6 John's from France. _____'s from France.

1.3 Right or wrong? Tick (✓) or correct the sentences.
Example I name's Ana. *My name's Ana.*
1 Our names are Sue and Iris.
2 She's first name's Derya. She's from Turkey.
3 My address is 27 Market Street.
4 What's you email address?
5 What are they first names?
6 We're all from Europe.

1.4 Underline the correct word.
Example Paola 's / are from Italy.
1 My partner am / 's Tina.
2 His email address is / are crg@it.uk.
3 They 's / 're my friends.
4 Our address are / is 44 New Street.
5 Their phone number 's / are 773374.
6 I 'm / 's from Spain.
7 Our names are / is Jenny and Craig.
8 My phone number am / 's 9955599.

1.5 Write short answers.
Example Are you and Paul married? No, *we aren't* .
1 Is Mr Minnit married? Yes, _____.
2 Are Jim and Satomi in the bar? No, _____.
3 Sam, are you from America? Yes, _____.
4 Is Maria in Italy? No, _____.
5 Am I late for your class? Yes, _____.
6 Sandy, are you from Spain? No, _____.

1.6 Match 1–7 with a–g.
1 ☐d Are they in a coffee bar?
2 ☐ Is their teacher from New York?
3 ☐ Are you in their class?
4 ☐ What's your first name?
5 ☐ Is he married?
6 ☐ Is this seat free?
7 ☐ Is your surname Banks?

a Peter, and my surname's Jones.
b No, she's from Washington.
c Yes, we are.
d No, they're in a taxi.
e No, it isn't.
f No, it's Jones.
g No, he isn't. He's single.

2A imperatives ⊞

Use imperatives to tell someone what to do and to give instructions.

infinitive	to close	to listen	to open
imperative	Close the door.	Listen to the teacher.	Open your books.

• The imperative form is the same as the infinitive without *to*.
>> Now go to **exercise 2.1** to practise.

2B possessive *'s*

Use the possessive *'s* to say who something belongs to.

after a singular noun	apostrophe + s	Gilly's book the girl's mother
after a plural noun that doesn't end with s	apostrophe + s	the children's books
after a plural noun that ends with s	apostrophe	the students' books

>> Now go to **exercise 2.2** to practise.

2B demonstratives *this, that, these, those*

this	that	these	those
+ singular noun (near you)	+ singular noun (not near you)	+ plural noun (near you)	+ plural noun (not near you)
This is my sister.	That's my brother.	These are my children.	Those are my children.

• The short form of *that is* = *that's*.
• There is no short form of *this is*, *these are*, or *those are*.
>> Now go to **exercise 2.3** to practise.

2C adjectives

Use adjectives to describe people and things.

adjective	be + adjective	adjective + noun
rich	She's rich.	She's a rich woman.
young	He's young.	He's a young man.
old	It's old.	It's an old taxi.
married	They're married.	They're a married couple.
retired	We're retired.	We're retired doctors.
single	I'm single.	I'm a single woman.

• There are no plural adjectives. *They're old.* not *They're olds.*
>> Now go to **exercises 2.4 and 2.5** to practise.

2C articles *a, an*

a	before a **consonant sound**	She's a dentist. He's a Spanish actor.
an	before a **vowel sound**	She's an actress. He's an English singer.

• Use *a / an* before a singular noun.
>> Now go to **exercise 2.6** to practise.

2D prepositions of time

at	+ a time	at six o'clock.
on	+ a day	on Monday on Tuesday evening
no preposition	+ some time expressions	this afternoon tonight tomorrow morning

• Use *this morning, this afternoon, this evening*, and *tonight* to talk about parts of today.
• For more information about prepositions of time, see **lesson 4B**.
>> Now go to **exercise 2.7** to practise.

2.1 Match 1–9 with a–i.

1	☑ d Read	a	at the board.
2	☐ Open your	b	the words slowly.
3	☐ Look	c	with a partner.
4	☐ Write your name	d	the text.
5	☐ Work	e	book at page 24.
6	☐ Answer the	f	questions on page 5.
7	☐ Swap	g	and address on the form.
8	☐ Say	h	the tape and repeat the words.
9	☐ Listen to	i	information with a partner.

2.2 Right or wrong? Tick (✓) or correct the sentences.
Example   Sandy's Bobs wife.   *Sandy's Bob's wife.*

1   He's Steve father.
2   They're Johns' books.
3   She's my friend's teacher.
4   We're Simons students.
5   Sandra's Bob's childrens teacher.
6   They're Julia's sisters.

2.3 Underline the correct words.
Example   This / <u>These</u> are my students.

1   These / Those are my books on that desk.
2   This / That girl with those people is my sister.
3   What is this book / these books about?
4   That / Those students are from Russia.
5   These / That man in the bar is Jim's father.
6   Who are that man / those men?

2.4 Order the words to make sentences.
Example   married my isn't sister
         My sister isn't married.

1   retired he office worker a 's
2   rich are parents your ?
3   isn't rich woman a she
4   old my is car
5   old Jaime is man an ?
6   young Elena a doctor 's

2.5 Complete the sentences with a suitable adjective.
Example   Mr and Mrs Jones are *married*.

1   He isn't married or divorced. He's _____.
2   His daughter is five years old. She's _____.
3   He's _____. His wife is a doctor.
4   My father is _____. He's 85.
5   Paul is Carla's ex-husband. They're _____.

2.6 Complete the text with *a* or *an*.

Hi. My name's Jenny. I'm [1] *a* farmer. This is a photo of my family and my friends. This is my sister. She's [2] _____ engineer. That's my brother. He's [3] _____ footballer. Our father's [4] _____ actor and our mother's [5] _____ singer. That girl's my friend. She's [6] _____ doctor and her husband's [7] _____ English teacher.

2.7 Right or wrong? Tick (✓) or correct the sentences.
Example   Our English class is on four o'clock.
         Our English class is at four o'clock.

1   The next Spanish lesson is at Friday.
2   My tennis lesson is on Thursday morning.
3   The quiz is at tonight.
4   The next class is tomorrow evening.
5   The news is on half past seven.

3B articles *a, an, the*

the	only one	Is Venice the capital of Italy?
a	more than one, and the next word begins with a consonant sound	I'm from a big town in Spain. He's a singer.
an	more than one, and the next word begins with a vowel sound	Kenya is an African country. This is an umbrella.

>> Now go to **exercises 3.1 and 3.2** to practise.

3C plurals

To form plurals		
most singular nouns	+ *s*	name > names shop > shops
nouns that end with *ch, s, sh, x*	+ *es*	church > churches actress > actresses brush > brushes fax > faxes
nouns that end with consonant + *y*	*y* + *ies*	family > families nationality > nationalities
irregular nouns		child > children person > people

>> Now go to **exercises 3.3 and 3.4** to practise.

3C prepositions of place *in, on*

Use prepositions of place to describe where something / someone is, e.g. *They're on the bus. He's in the restaurant.*

3D present simple ⊞-⊡? *do, don't*

Use the present simple to talk about things that happen sometimes or all the time, and things that are generally true, e.g. *My class starts at 6 o'clock. Mark speaks Italian.*

+	– (n't = not)	?
I understand German.	I don't understand German.	Do I understand German?
You live in a flat.	You don't live in a flat.	Do you live in a flat?
We speak French.	We don't speak French.	Do we speak French?
They like coffee.	They don't like coffee.	Do they like coffee?
They're from Spain.	They aren't from Spain.	Are they from Spain?

short answers	
Yes, I / you / we / they do.	No, I / you / we / they don't.

>> Now go to **exercises 3.5 and 3.6** to practise.

3D adverbs of degree *quite, very*

Use adverbs of manner (e.g. *well*) to say how someone does something.
Use an adverb of degree (e.g. *very, quite*) to modify the adverb of manner.

+++	very well	You speak English very well.
++	well	They speak English well.
+	quite well	She speaks English quite well.
–	not very well	I don't speak English very well.

- Use an adverb of degree before an adverb.
- Use an adverb of manner at the end of a sentence.

>> Now go to **exercise 3.7** to practise.

3E conjunctions *and, but*

Use the conjunctions *and* and *but* to join two sentences.

and	I speak Spanish. I speak Italian.	I speak Spanish and Italian.
but	I speak English. I don't speak French.	I speak English but I don't speak French.

- When you use *and* to join two sentences, it isn't necessary to repeat the verb or noun.

>> Now go to **exercise 3.8** to practise.

3.1 Underline the correct word.
Example   Is she <u>a</u> / an teacher at your school?
1 The / A capital of Australia is Canberra.
2 Is the / a currency of Japan the / a yen?
3 Is Milan the / a big city?
4 What's the / a language of Brazil?
5 Jim is a / an English teacher.
6 Carmen Maura is a / an Spanish actress.
7 Jamaica is the / an island and the / a capital is Kingston.

3.2 Right or wrong? Tick (✓) or correct the sentences.
Example   It's an French restaurant.   *It's a French restaurant.*
1 He's an Italian designer.
2 Mary isn't a vet. She's an doctor.
3 The bank is near the station.
4 Marbella is the town in Spain.
5 Is the euro a currency of Australia?
6 My husband is an office worker.
7 Ecuador is a country in South America.

3.3 Write the plural.
1 watch _____   4 designer _____
2 language _____   5 capital city _____
3 email address _____   6 that _____

3.4 Write the singular.
1 currencies _____   4 classes _____
2 trees _____   5 people _____
3 toilets _____   6 cash machines _____

3.5 Order the words to make sentences.
Example   understand Arabic do they ?
            Do they understand Arabic?
1 two speak I languages
2 do coffee like you ?
3 understand they English don't
4 we Cairo like
5 live they don't a in city
6 speak do you Polish ?

3.6 Answer the questions. Use the blue words.
Example   Do you like Spain?   <u>Yes, we do.</u>   yes we
1 Do you live in an old house? _____   yes I
2 Do they like football? _____   no they
3 Do you understand Italian? _____   yes we
4 Do you speak another language? _____   no I
5 Do they live in Tokyo? _____   yes they
6 Do you like big cities? _____   no we

3.7 Order the words to make sentences.
Example   well do speak very Spanish you
            Do you speak Spanish very well?
1 very understand I German well
2 well don't they Italian speak
3 do English well they understand ?
4 understand well French quite we
5 you speak Portuguese do well very ?

3.8 Rewrite the sentences using *and* or *but*.
Example   I like Spain. I like China.   *I like Spain and China.*
1 They speak English very well. They speak French very well.
2 The telephones are upstairs. The toilets are upstairs.
3 I understand Spanish. I don't speak it very well.
4 We like tennis. We don't like football.
5 Jorge is a doctor. His wife is a doctor.
6 I don't speak Russian. I speak a little Polish.

4A prepositions of place *at*

Use prepositions of place to describe where something / someone is, e.g. *I'm at school. They're at the beach.*

4B prepositions of time *at, in, on*

at	+ a time	at six o'clock
	+ a point in time	at the end of July
	+ certain phrases	at the weekend
on	+ a day	on Monday on Wednesday afternoon
	+ a date	on July 17th
in	+ a month	in September
	+ a part of the day	in the afternoon

>> Now go to **exercises 4.1 and 4.2** to practise.

4C present simple with *he / she / it*

+	– (doesn't = does not)	?
He lives in Germany.	He doesn't live in Germany.	Does he live in Germany?
She understands Italian.	She doesn't understand Italian.	Does she understand Italian?
It opens at 9 p.m.	It doesn't open at 9 p.m.	Does it open at 9 p.m.?

short answers	
Yes, he does.	No, he doesn't.
Yes, she does.	No, she doesn't.
Yes, it does.	No, it doesn't.

>> Now go to **exercises 4.3 and 4.4** to practise.

4C spelling: present simple with *he / she / it*

most verbs	+ s	live > He lives in Spain. work > Sheila works in Milan.
verbs that end with *ch, o, s, sh, x*	+ es	press > He presses 'snooze'. brush > She brushes her hair. go > Harry goes to work.
verbs that end with consonant + *y*	*y* + *ies*	study > She studies French.
irregular verbs		have > He has a shower. be > Jane is a doctor.

>> Now go to **exercise 4.5** to practise.

4D adverbs of frequency

Use adverbs of frequency to say how often something happens.

100%				0%
always	usually	often	sometimes	never

Put an adverb of frequency after the verb *be*.	He's usually in his office at 9 a.m.
Put an adverb of frequency before other verbs.	I sometimes read the newspaper in the morning.
Put an adverb of frequency between an auxiliary verb and a verb.	I don't always have breakfast. Does he often work on Saturday?
Don't use *never* with a negative auxiliary.	He doesn't never watch TV. ✗ He never watches TV. ✓

>> Now go to **exercise 4.6** to practise.

4.1 <u>Underline</u> the correct form.
Example   Christmas is on December / <u>December 25th</u>.
1 We play football in the end of June / the morning.
2 The party is on midnight / Friday.
3 The play starts at eight o'clock / Friday evening.
4 Their office is closed at the afternoon / the weekend.
5 The term ends in July / the end of July.
6 Our German class is on Monday / the morning.

4.2 Complete the sentences with *at, in,* or *on*.
Example   My birthday's _at_ the end of July.
1 My English class starts _____ nine o'clock.
2 Paul's birthday's _____ 8th May.
3 The museum isn't open _____ the afternoon.
4 My holiday is _____ August.
5 The exam is _____ Wednesday morning.
6 The film finishes _____ midnight.

4.3 Order the words to make sentences.
Example   she does TV morning in watch the ?
Does she watch TV in the morning?
1 doesn't football he play
2 gets at o'clock she up seven
3 Alan listen radio the does to ?
4 brother in hospital works my a
5 read does the evening the he newspaper in ?
6 live Holly doesn't Spain in

4.4 Complete the sentences with the verbs in the correct form.
Example   Henri _goes_ to school at 8.30 a.m. go
1 She _____ a shower in the morning. not have
2 Pablo _____ football on Sunday morning. play
3 He _____ English and Italian at university. study
4 The class _____ at four o'clock. not finish
5 The bookshop _____ at 6 p.m. close
6 She _____ TV in the evening. not watch
7 Sam _____ coffee and yogurt for breakfast. have

4.5 Write the opposite.
Example   She doesn't finish work at 5 o'clock.
She finishes work at 5 o'clock.
1 Ana doesn't watch TV in the morning.
2 Iris doesn't have a shower in the evening.
3 Jim teaches English.
4 Sally doesn't write emails at home.
5 Chen studies French in Paris.

4.6 Rewrite the sentences using the red words.
Example   My brother is late for school. sometimes
My brother is sometimes late for school.
1 Mary has coffee in the morning. always
2 Do you watch TV in the evening? usually
3 We go to the theatre. never
4 Does she listen to the radio? often
5 That shop opens on Sunday. never
6 He leaves the house at 7.30 a.m. always
7 Jon and Ian play football on Sunday. sometimes
8 The London train is late. usually

5A prepositions of place *next to, opposite*

Use prepositions of place to say where someone/something is.

next to	My friend is next to me.	
opposite	Pete is opposite Jude.	

5A object pronouns

Use a subject pronoun to say who/what does an action.
Use an object pronoun to say who/what 'receives' the action.

subject pronouns	object pronouns	
I	me	She phones me at the weekend.
you	you	I know you.
he	him	She likes him.
she	her	He speaks to her in French.
it	it	She watches it in the evening.
we	us	David teaches us English.
they	them	We usually see them on Sunday.

- Use an object pronoun in the place of a noun.
- Put an object pronoun after the verb.

>> Now go to **exercises 5.1 and 5.2** to practise.

5B order of adjectives

Adjectives are the same with singular or plural nouns.	a red book > two red books an old man > four old men
Adjectives go before the noun.	a small car an English teacher
Colour adjectives go after other adjectives.	a big green house a new black bag

>> Now go to **exercise 5.3** to practise.

5C *I / you / we / they have got*

Use *have got* to talk about possessions.

+ ('ve = have)	– (haven't = have not)	?
I've got a computer.	I haven't got a computer.	Have I got a computer?
You've got a phone.	You haven't got a phone.	Have you got a phone?
We've got a TV.	We haven't got a TV.	Have we got a TV?
They've got a dog.	They haven't got a dog.	Have they got a dog?

short answers	
Yes, I / you / we / they have.	No, I / you / we / they haven't.

>> Now go to **exercise 5.4** to practise.

5D *he / she / it has got*

+ ('s = has)	– (hasn't = has not)	?
He's got a blue bag.	He hasn't got a blue bag.	Has he got a blue bag?
She's got a clock.	She hasn't got a clock.	Has she got a clock?
It's got a battery.	It hasn't got a battery.	Has it got a battery?

short answers	
Yes, he / she / it has.	No, he / she / it hasn't.

>> Now go to **exercises 5.5 and 5.6** to practise.

5.1 Complete the conversations with an object pronoun.
Example **A** Mr Brown is a very good teacher.
B I don't know _him_. Is he new?

1 **A** Do you often listen to the radio?
B Yes, I listen to _____ in the morning.
2 **A** Do you use computers in your school?
B Yes, we use _____ to learn English.
3 **A** Hi. My name's Jane.
B Pleased to meet _____.
4 **A** Do you and John know Mary?
B Yes, she works with _____.
5 **A** Why don't you talk to Pablo?
B He doesn't like _____ and I don't like _____.

5.2 Rewrite the sentences using an object pronoun.
Example She works with Justin and Holly.
She works with them.

1 Do you understand John?
2 He doesn't like coffee.
3 She knows me and my brother.
4 Listen to Mrs Jones.
5 He teaches Ana and Satomi.

5.3 Right or wrong? Tick (✓) or correct the sentences.
Example He drives a red old car.
He drives an old red car.

1 She's got long brown hair.
2 He's got big blues eyes.
3 They live in a house white.
4 I've got two black cats.
5 She's a tall thin woman with grey long hair.
6 We've got a small black dog and four browns cats.
7 My mother has got black short hair.
8 We've got a big yellow clock.

5.4 Match 1–6 with a–f.
1 [a] Have you got a computer at home?
2 [ ] Oh no! I haven't got any money.
3 [ ] What sort of car have they got?
4 [ ] Have we got any tea?
5 [ ] What's 'book' in Spanish?
6 [ ] Have we got any homework?

a No, I haven't, but I've got one in my office.
b A Fiat Punto.
c That's okay. I've got a credit card.
d Yes, we have. Exercise 4 in the workbook.
e I don't know. I haven't got a dictionary.
f No, we haven't, but we've got some coffee.

5.5 Order the words to make sentences.
Example has he blond got hair ?
Has he got blond hair?

1 your has car GPS got ?
2 my has car friend got a blue
3 Gemma green has eyes got ?
4 he any children got has ?
5 Andy new 's phone got mobile a
6 alarm got 's an it

5.6 Answer the questions.
Example Has Henry got blond hair? No, _he hasn't._
1 Have they got a car? Yes, _____.
2 Have you got a daughter? No, _____.
3 Has Sheila got a boyfriend? Yes, _____.
4 Has the hotel got a good restaurant? No, _____.
5 Have the classrooms got computers? No, _____.
6 Has Marco got a watch? Yes, _____.

6A countable and uncountable

countable nouns (C)	
A countable noun is one that you can count.	One cat, two cats, etc.
They can be singular or plural.	a book > books

uncountable nouns (U)	
An uncountable noun is one that you can't count.	water ✓ two waters ✗
They can't be singular or plural.	soup ✓ a soup ✗ soups ✗

- Use *is* before a singular countable noun or an uncountable noun, e.g. *This coffee is cold. My book is new.*
- Use *are* before a plural countable noun, e.g. *There are two computers in the classroom.*
- Don't use *a / an* before an uncountable noun.
- Countable and uncountable nouns are not the same in all languages. For example, *news* and *information* are uncountable in English but countable in Spanish.

>> Now go to **exercises 6.1 and 6.2** to practise.

6B some, any

	+	–	?
plural countable nouns	I've got some oranges.	I haven't got any apples.	Have you got any eggs?
uncountable nouns	I've got some wine.	I haven't got any coffee.	Have you got any bread?

- Use *some* in positive statements with plural countable nouns and uncountable nouns.
- Use *any* in negative statements with plural countable nouns and uncountable nouns.
- Use *any* in questions with plural countable nouns and uncountable nouns.

>> Now go to **exercise 6.3** to practise.

6C there is, there are

+	–	?
There's some wine.	There isn't any sugar.	Is there any fruit?
There are some cups.	There aren't any oranges.	Are there any chips?

short answers	
Yes, there is.	No, there isn't.
Yes, there are.	No, there aren't.

>> Now go to **exercise 6.4** to practise.

6D much, many, a lot of

	+	–	?
plural countable nouns	There are a lot of sausages.	There aren't many eggs.	How many oranges are there?
uncountable nouns	There's a lot of red wine.	There isn't much white wine.	How much water is there?

- Use *is* with uncountable nouns.
- Use *are* with plural countable nouns.

>> Now go to **exercise 6.5** to practise.

6E or, with

Use *or* when there are two or more things to choose from.	Do you want tea or coffee? Do you want oranges, apples, or bananas?
Use *with* when there are two or more things together.	I'd like tea with milk. Do you want a biscuit with your coffee?

>> Now go to **exercise 6.6** to practise.

6.1 Look at the words. Write *C* for countable or *U* for uncountable.

Example ☐*C* dictionary

1 ☐ person
2 ☐ coffee
3 ☐ soup
4 ☐ water
5 ☐ sandwich
6 ☐ euro

6.2 Right or wrong? Tick (✓) or correct the sentences.

Example How much is the biscuits?   *How much are the biscuits?*

1 Can I have a cup of coffee?
2 A sandwich is four euros.
3 Do you usually drink wines?
4 How much are the oranges?
5 I don't like soups.
6 How much is these computers?

6.3 Complete the sentences with *some*, *any*, *a*, or *an*.

Example We've got _some_ apples.

1 Have you got _____ eggs?
2 We haven't got _____ bread.
3 Can I have _____ sausages, please?
4 Do you want _____ orange?
5 I'd like _____ glass of wine.
6 He doesn't want _____ sugar in his coffee.
7 Can I have _____ piece of pizza, please?
8 I've got _____ steak for our dinner.
9 They want _____ chocolate ice cream.

6.4 Match 1–9 with a–i.

1 ☐*c* Have we got any eggs?
2 ☐ Is there any sugar?
3 ☐ What's for breakfast?
4 ☐ Are there any tomatoes in this soup?
5 ☐ There's a new computer shop in the town centre.
6 ☐ There aren't any apples.
7 ☐ What have we got to drink?
8 ☐ There are some books on your desk.
9 ☐ Is there any water?

a There's wine or orange juice.
b Yes, there are. They're in the bag on the table.
c ~~Yes, there are some in the fridge.~~
d Oh, those are the new dictionaries.
e Well, there's some toast and some jam.
f Yes, there's some in the cupboard.
g Yes, there's a bottle in the kitchen.
h Have they got any cheap printers?
i No, there aren't.

6.5 Order the words to make sentences.

Example much water you how do drink ?
How much water do you drink?

1 week a hours they in work many do how ?
2 salt a use lot I of usually
3 meat do much eat they ?
4 much homework don't we do
5 are a there students of in lot class your ?
6 a sugar in there tea of lot 's this
7 do you films many watch ?

6.6 Complete the sentences with *or* or *with*.

Example Do you want some ice cream _with_ your apple pie?

1 Use a black _____ blue pen.
2 There's red _____ white wine.
3 Do you want some chips _____ your hamburger?
4 Can I have coffee _____ milk and two sugars?
5 I love toast _____ jam.
6 Does he want meat _____ fish for dinner?

7B Let's ... , How about ...

Use *Let's* or *How about* to make a suggestion.

Let's (let's = let us)	+ verb	Let's go to the cinema.
How about	+ noun	How about a cup of tea?
	+ -*ing* form	How about going to the pub?

>> Now go to **exercise 7.1** to practise.

7B -*ing* forms

To make -*ing* forms		
most verbs	+ *ing*	speak > speaking
verbs ending *e*	e + *ing*	write > writing
verbs ending *ie*	ie + *ying*	tie > tying
one-syllable verbs ending with one vowel + one consonant	double the consonant + -*ing*	run > running

>> Now go to **exercise 7.2** to practise.

7C can, can't

Use *can* or *can't* to talk about ability.

+	– (can't = cannot)	?
I can cook.	I can't cook.	Can I cook?
You can play the guitar.	You can't play the guitar.	Can you play the guitar?
He / She / It can run fast.	He / She / It can't run fast.	Can he / she / it run fast?
We can skate.	We can't skate.	Can we skate?
They can speak Greek.	They can't speak Greek.	Can they speak Greek?

short answers	
Yes, I / you / we / they can.	No, I / you / we / they can't.
Yes, he / she / it can.	No, he / she / it can't.

- Use a verb after *can*.
- Don't use *to* after *can*.

>> Now go to **exercise 7.3** to practise.

7C adverbs of manner

Use adverbs of manner to say how someone does something.

To make adverbs		
most adjectives	+ *ly*	slow > slowly
adjectives that end consonant + *y*	*y* + *ily*	easy > easily
irregular		good > well fast > fast

- Use an adverb of manner at the end of a sentence e.g. *Do your homework quickly.*

>> Now go to **exercises 7.4 and 7.5** to practise.

7D like doing, like sth

I / You / We / They like He / She / It likes	+ -*ing*	cooking reading
	+ noun	sport chocolate ice cream

love   like / enjoy   don't like   hate

>> Now go to **exercise 7.6** to practise.

7E also

Use *also* to connect ideas in positive sentences.

I like fish. I also like meat.
I go swimming and I also play tennis.

- Use *also* before the second verb. *I like football. I also like tennis.*
- Use *also* after the verb *be*. *He's rich. He's also handsome.*
- Use *also* after an auxiliary. *Does she also speak French?*

>> Now go to **exercise 7.7** to practise.

7.1 ~~Cross out~~ the wrong word.

Example How about ~~to~~ going to the park?

1 Let's to go to the theatre tomorrow.
2 How about going to shopping?
3 How about we going to London?
4 Let's us have a party.
5 How about to seeing a film tonight?
6 Let's go for skiing.
7 How about have a cup of coffee?
8 Let's going play cards.

7.2 Write the -*ing* form.

Example shop _shopping_

1	take _____		5	drive _____
2	swim _____		6	listen _____
3	dance _____		7	stop _____
4	play _____		8	get _____

7.3 Complete the conversations. Use *can* or *can't*.

Example **A** Have you got a car? **B** No, I _can't_ drive.

1 **A** Does he know any foreign languages?
  B Yes, he _____ speak Italian.
2 **A** I've got a new guitar.
  B _____ you play it?
3 **A** Do you do a lot of cooking?
  B No, I _____ cook.
4 **A** What's the matter?
  B This exercise is difficult. We _____ do it.
5 **A** _____ they swim?
  B Yes, they _____.

7.4 Rewrite the sentences. Use the red words.

Example Her English isn't very good.   badly
She speaks English badly.

1 He's a fast runner.   fast
2 You're a quick worker.   quickly
3 I'm not a fast walker.   slowly
4 They're good singers.   well
5 He's a quiet speaker.   quietly

7.5 Adjective or adverb? Underline the correct word.

Example I can sing, but not very well/good.

1 She's a good/well teacher.
2 You write very quick/quickly.
3 Listen careful/carefully.
4 They can swim, but badly/bad.
5 Can you speak slow/slowly, please?
6 Is she a quiet/quietly student?

7.6 Underline the correct sentence.

Example a Do you like skiing? b Do you like ski?

1 a I hate cook.   b I hate cooking.
2 a I enjoy sport.   b I enjoy sporting.
3 a We love swimming.   b We love swim.
4 a Does he enjoy reading? b Does he enjoy to read?
5 a I don't like writting emails. b I don't like writing emails.

7.7 Write sentences with *also*.

Example I play football basketball
I play football and I also play basketball.

1 Robin study Maths Physics
2 She speak Arabic Chinese
3 We like Chinese food Indian food
4 He can drive car bus
5 My daughter have got mobile phone laptop
6 They like play cards watch DVDs

8A *for* and *to*

to	+ a place	I'm going to school. They usually walk to work.
for	+ an activity	She's going for a swim.
	+ a thing	She's going for a sandwich.

>> Now go to **exercise 8.1** to practise.

8A *I'd like ... , Would you like ... ?*

Use *would like* to make an offer or an invitation, or to say that you want something / want to do something.

offers	*would like* + noun	Would you like a glass of wine?
invitations	*would like* + infinitive	Would you like to come to the cinema with us?
to say you want something	*would like* + noun	I'd like a glass of wine. ('d = would)
to say you want to do something	*would like* + infinitive	I'd like to go to Italy.

>> Now go to **exercise 8.2** to practise.

8B imperatives

Use imperatives to tell someone what to do or what not to do.

+	−
Listen carefully. Drink lots of water.	Don't talk. Don't write on the desk.

>> Now go to **exercise 8.3** to practise.

8C present continuous ⊞⊟⁇

Use the present continuous to describe what's happening now.

+	−	?
I'm wearing jeans.	I'm not wearing jeans.	Am I wearing jeans?
You're walking to work.	You aren't walking to work.	Are you walking to work?
He / She / It's working.	He / She / It isn't working.	Is he / she / it working?
We're watching a film.	We aren't watching a film.	Are we watching a film?
They're dancing.	They aren't dancing.	Are they dancing?

short answers	
Yes, I am.	No, I'm not.
Yes, you / we / they are.	No, you / we / they aren't.
Yes, he / she / it is.	No, he / she / it isn't.

• For information on how to make -*ing* forms, see 7B.

>> Now go to **exercise 8.4** to practise.

8D Present simple and present continuous

Use the present simple to talk about things that happen sometimes or all the time, and things that are generally true.
Use the present continuous to talk about what's happening now.

present simple	present continuous
They work from nine to five.	They're working in London this week.
I do my homework in the evening.	Be quiet. I'm doing my homework.
He usually has a shower in the morning.	He's having a shower at the moment.

>> Now go to **exercise 8.5** to practise.

8.1 Complete with *for* or *to*.

Example Do you want to go *for* a swim?

1 We're going _____ a pizza after work.
2 Are you going _____ the supermarket now?
3 My brother always goes _____ a run in the evening.
4 Let's go _____ a drink.
5 I'm going _____ the shop _____ some sugar.
6 They're going _____ the park _____ a game of football.

8.2 Match 1–6 with a–f.

1 ☑ *f* We're going to the pub tonight. Would you like to come?
2 ☐ I'd like a glass of wine.
3 ☐ Would you like to come to London on Saturday?
4 ☐ Would you like a cup of tea?
5 ☐ Would you like to come to Spain next month?
6 ☐ Would you like one of my ham sandwiches?

a I'm sorry, I can't. I usually work at the weekend.
b Yes, please. With milk and sugar.
c I'd love to, but I haven't got a passport.
d Red or white?
e No, thanks. I don't eat meat.
f ~~Sorry, I can't. I've got an exam tomorrow.~~

8.3 Complete the conversations with these verbs.

buy don't eat don't go go make run take wash ~~wear~~

Example A I'm cold. B *Wear* a hat.

1 A It's raining. B _____ an umbrella.
2 A I haven't got any money. B _____ to the bank.
3 A I've got a lot of homework. B _____ out tonight.
4 A This soup is horrible. B _____ it.
5 A These jeans are dirty. B _____ them.
6 A There's no milk. B _____ some.
7 A I'm late. B _____.
8 A There's no cheese for my sandwiches.
   B _____ a ham sandwich.

8.4 Complete the conversations. Use the verbs in the present continuous.

Example A Where are they?
          B They're on the train. *They're going* to Oxford. go

1 A Can I speak to John?
   B No, sorry, _____ a shower. have
2 A Do you and Jamie want to come to the pub?
   B No thanks, _____ this film. watch
3 A What's the matter with your mobile phone?
   B _____. not work
4 A It's nine o'clock. Why are you in bed, Sally?
   B _____ ill. feel
5 A Why _____ ? smile
   B I'm happy.
6 A That smells nice. What _____ ? you cook
   B A Spanish omelette.
7 A Who _____ to? she talk
   B Her boyfriend.

8.5 Underline the correct form.

Example Mr Minnit speaks / *'s speaking* to his secretary now.

1 Listen. The teacher talks / 's talking.
2 They have / 're having breakfast now.
3 We always go / are going to school by car.
4 I have / 'm having a shower every morning.
5 We go / 're going to the theatre now. Do you want to come?
6 He's Spanish. He comes / 's coming from Madrid.
7 I'm on the train. I go / 'm going to Berlin.
8 Shhh! Be quiet. The children sleep / are sleeping.

9C past simple of *be* [+][-][?] *was, were, wasn't, weren't*

Was / were is the past simple of the verb *to be*.
Use *was / were* to talk about the past.

+	– (wasn't = was not, weren't = were not)	?
I was late.	I wasn't late.	Was I late?
You were happy.	You weren't happy.	Were you happy?
He / She / It was nice.	He / She / It wasn't nice.	Was he / she / it nice?
We were cold.	We weren't cold.	Were we cold?
They were friendly.	They weren't friendly.	Were they friendly?

short answers	
Yes, I was.	No, I wasn't.
Yes, you / we / they were.	No, you / we / they weren't.
Yes, he / she / it was.	No, he / she / it wasn't.

>> Now go to **exercises 9.1 and 9.2** to practise.

9D past simple [+] regular *-ed*

Use the past simple to talk about actions that are finished.

Regular past simple forms finish with *-ed*
I watched TV last night.
You cooked dinner yesterday.
He walked home.
She started work at 9 a.m.
It closed at four o'clock.
We looked at the photos.
They stopped work at 5.30.

• The past simple is the same for all subject pronouns.

9D spelling: *-ed* endings

most verbs	+ *ed*	work > worked
verbs ending *e*	+ *d*	dance > danced
verbs ending consonant + *y*	*y* + *ied*	study > studied
one-syllable verbs ending in one vowel + one consonant (except verbs ending *w, x, y, z*)	double the consonant + *ed*	stop > stopped

>> Now go to **exercises 9.3 and 9.4** to practise.

9.1 Right or wrong? Tick (✓) or correct the sentences.
Example The weather weren't very nice.
The weather wasn't very nice.

1 The film was very good.
2 The people wasn't very friendly.
3 Her English were very good.
4 Your children were late for school this morning.
5 He wasn't at work last week.
6 I were tired yesterday.
7 The restaurants wasn't very cheap.
8 They weren't at the park.
9 Where was you at ten o'clock?
10 Was Simon and Clare at Sue's party?

9.2 Complete the questions with *was* or *were*. Then match 1–10 with a–j.

1 [*i*] What _was_ the weather like?
2 ☐ Where _____ Pablo yesterday?
3 ☐ _____ the lessons interesting?
4 ☐ _____ Gemma at work last week?
5 ☐ Why _____ they late?
6 ☐ When _____ their wedding?
7 ☐ _____ the hotel nice?
8 ☐ _____ the exams difficult?
9 ☐ How much _____ those shoes?
10 ☐ Where _____ the party?

a No, she was ill.
b He was at school.
c Seventy euros.
d At a hotel in the town centre.
e Yes, the rooms were very comfortable.
f No, the questions were easy.
g In January.
h No, they were boring.
i ~~It was very cold.~~
j There was a problem with the bus.

9.3 Right or wrong? Tick (✓) or correct the past forms.

	infinitive	past simple	
Examples	close	closed	✓
	walk	walkd	_walked_
1	arrive	arrivd	_____
2	work	worked	_____
3	stay	staied	_____
4	live	lived	_____
5	snow	snowwed	_____
6	reply	replyed	_____
7	shop	shoped	_____
8	finish	finished	_____

9.4 Complete the sentences. Put the verbs in the past simple.
Example We _started_ work at 8 o'clock this morning. start

1 I _____ *The Legend of Zorro* last night. watch
2 They _____ the meal at that new restaurant. enjoy
3 They _____ the chocolate cake. finish
4 We _____ in a lovely hotel. stay
5 I _____ Holly yesterday. phone
6 Sheila _____ her mother last week. visit
7 He _____ to France in 2005. move
8 Arif _____ our bags to the airport. carry
9 It _____ yesterday. rain
10 They _____ for hours at Ana's party. dance

10A past simple ?

past simple questions	Did I arrive late? Did you walk to school? Did he visit the Blue Mosque? Did she phone you yesterday? Did it finish late? Did we close the door? Did they ask the teacher?
	When did you see John? What did he wear to the party? Why did she leave work at 12.00? Who did she meet? Where did they go on holiday? How much did it cost?

>> Now go to **exercises 10.1 and 10.2** to practise.

10B past simple regular and irregular

regular verbs	+ *ed* (see **9D** for spelling rules)	arrive > arrived join > joined walk > walked
irregular verbs		drive > drove go > went leave > left

- Use the irregular past form in positive sentences only, not in negative sentences or questions.
- For a list of irregular verbs, see >>148.

>> Now go to **exercises 10.3 and 10.4** to practise.

10C past simple -?

+	– (didn't = did not)	?
I worked in an office.	I didn't work in an office.	Did I work in an office?
You phoned him last night.	You didn't phone him last night.	Did you phone him last night?
He / She / It arrived yesterday.	He / She / It didn't arrive yesterday.	Did he / she / it arrive yesterday?
We danced at the party.	We didn't dance at the party.	Did we dance at the party?
They played the saxophone.	They didn't play the saxophone.	Did they play the saxophone?

short answers	
Yes, I / you / we / they did.	No, I / you / we / they didn't.
Yes, he / she / it did.	No, he / she / it didn't.

>> Now go to **exercises 10.5 and 10.6** to practise.

10.1 Order the words to make questions.
Example enjoy did holiday you your
Did you enjoy your holiday?

1 homework he do his did last night
2 did what she at buy supermarket the
3 they yesterday go did out
4 yesterday time did finish he what work
5 Eiffel Tower they see the did
6 go why to you did Prague
7 wife did meet where his he

10.2 Match 1–8 with a–h.

1 [c] Where did you go?
2 ☐ When did you go?
3 ☐ How did you get there?
4 ☐ How much did the flights cost?
5 ☐ Who did you go with?
6 ☐ Where did you stay?
7 ☐ What did you do?
8 ☐ Did you take your camera?

a Yes, I did.
b By plane.
c ~~To Malta.~~
d In March.
e My best friend, Jenny.
f £150.
g We went to the beach and we visited Valletta.
h In a little hotel in Sliema.

10.3 Write the past form of the verbs in the correct column.
~~die~~ have make play study teach walk write

regular	irregular
died	

10.4 Complete the sentences with the past form of the verbs in exercise 10.3.
Example JK Rowling _taught_ English in Portugal.

1 Penelope Cruz _____ her first film in 1993.
2 Mother Theresa was born in 1910 and _____ in 1997.
3 Paulo Coelho _____ a book called *The Alchemist*.
4 Madonna _____ her first child in 1996.
5 American astronaut Neil Armstrong _____ on the moon.
6 Bill Clinton _____ at Georgetown University.
7 Pelé _____ football for Brazil.

10.5 Make the sentences negative.
Example I went to a party on Saturday.
I didn't go to a party on Saturday.

1 We saw a film last night.
2 She bought a new jacket.
3 They got married last year.
4 Satomi found some money in the classroom.
5 He went to university in Paris.
6 The teacher gave us a lot of homework.
7 Robin Banks left school when he was 15.

10.6 Complete the conversations. Use the red words.

1 A _Did you go_ to the theatre last night? you go
  B No, _____ a film at home. we watch
2 A Where _____ in Barcelona? they stay
  B I don't know.
3 A Where _____ his new girlfriend? he meet
  B I think _____ to the same university. they go
4 A What _____ for the wedding? she wear
  B Oh, _____ a new dress. she buy
5 A _____ the hotel? you like
  B No, _____. we not

11A too, not enough

Use *too* when something is more than you want or need.	*too* + adjective	This hat is too big for me. (I need a smaller hat.)
Use *not enough* when something is less than you want or need.	*not* + adjective + *enough*	This dress isn't big enough for her. (She needs a bigger dress.)

» Now go to **exercises 11.1 and 11.2** to practise.

11B too much, too many, not enough

Use *too many* with countable nouns when there is more of something than you want or need.	*too many* + noun	He bought too many apples at the supermarket.
Use *too much* with uncountable nouns when there is more of something than you want or need.	*too much* + noun	There's too much sugar in this coffee.
Use *not enough* with countable and uncountable nouns when there is less of something than you want or need.	*not enough* + noun	We haven't got enough eggs for breakfast. There isn't enough hot water for a bath.

» Now go to **exercise 11.3** to practise.

11C comparatives

Use a comparative + *than* to compare two things, e.g. *His house is bigger than your house.*

To make comparatives		
one-syllable adjectives*	+ *er*	quick › quicker small › smaller
adjectives that end *y*	*y* + *ier*	easy › easier happy › happier
adjectives with more than one syllable	*more* + adjective	beautiful › more beautiful expensive › more expensive
irregular adjectives		good › better bad › worse

* Spelling note

one-syllable adjectives that end *e*	+ *r*	nice › nicer
one-syllable adjectives that end vowel + consonant	double the consonant + *er*	big › bigger

» Now go to **exercises 11.4 and 11.5** to practise.

11D superlatives

Use *the* and a superlative adjective to compare more than two things, e.g. *This is the most comfortable chair in the room. He's the fastest runner in the school.*

To make superlative adjectives		
adjectives with one syllable*	+ *est*	quick › quickest small › smallest
adjectives that end *y*	*y* + *iest*	easy › easiest happy › happiest
adjectives with more than one syllable	*most* + adjective	beautiful › most beautiful expensive › most expensive
irregular adjectives		good › best bad › worst

* Spelling note

one-syllable adjectives that end *e*	+ *st*	nice › nicest
one-syllable adjectives that end vowel + consonant	double the consonant + *est*	big › biggest

» Now go to **exercise 11.6** to practise.

146

11.1 Order the words to make sentences.
Example big isn't for room the people enough three
The room isn't big enough for three people.

1 shoes me small too for these are
2 got hasn't money he enough
3 my good enough English isn't
4 trousers are short your too
5 is expensive restaurant too this

11.2 Match 1–6 with a–f.

1 [c] Why didn't you do the homework?
2 ☐ Do they walk to school?
3 ☐ Do you want to come to the park with us?
4 ☐ Why did you turn the radio up?
5 ☐ Did he go to work this morning?
6 ☐ Did you win the football match?

a It wasn't loud enough for me to hear.
b No, we weren't good enough.
c It was too difficult.
d No, he wasn't well enough.
e No, it's too far.
f No, thanks. It's too cold.

11.3 Write sentences using *too much, too many,* or *not enough*.
Example There are five chairs. There are seven people.
There *aren't enough chairs*   .

1 The book is five pounds. He's got four pounds.
  He _____ to buy the book.
2 There are six people. The taxi can take five people.
  There _____ for the taxi.
3 We've got 100 books. We only have one shelf.
  There _____ for the shelf.
4 We wanted two litres of milk. You bought four litres.
  You _____.
5 There are two rooms. There are five guests.
  There _____.
6 We've got one kilo of ham. We want two kilos for the party. We _____ ham.

11.4 Write the comparatives.
Example cheap   *cheaper*

1 old   _____
2 hot   _____
3 uncomfortable _____
4 poor   _____
5 long   _____
6 heavy   _____
7 fat   _____
8 boring   _____

11.5 Match 1–7 with a–g.

1 [e] Summer is hotter than …   a … pasta.
2 ☐ Moscow is bigger than …   b … your Spanish.
3 ☐ Japan is more expensive than … c … that book.
4 ☐ My car is faster than …   d … your bicycle.
5 ☐ Fish and chips are nicer than … e … winter.
6 ☐ His English is worse than …   f … St Petersburg.
7 ☐ This book is better than …   g … Spain.

11.6 Complete the sentences. Use the superlative form.
Example We stayed in *the nicest* hotel in Paris.   nice

1 *La Dolce Vita* is _____ place to eat.   bad
2 Mount Everest is _____ mountain in the world.   high
3 Is the Sahara Desert _____ place on Earth?   hot
4 She's _____ girl in our school.   attractive
5 We bought _____ bed in the shop.   comfortable
6 It's _____ bag in the shop.   expensive
7 The _____ apple in the world weighed 1.67 kilos.   big
8 Halle Berry was _____ actress in the film.   good

12A time expressions

past	present	future
last night	today	tonight
yesterday	this week	tomorrow
the day before yesterday		the day after tomorrow
last week		next week
the week before last		the week after next

12A times of day

8AM	9AM	10AM	11AM	12PM	1PM	2PM	3PM	4PM	5PM	6PM	7PM
first thing in the morning		mid-morning				early afternoon		late afternoon			
			late morning				mid-afternoon			evening	

>> Now go to **exercise 12.1** to practise.

12C present continuous future

Use the present continuous to talk about future arrangements.

+	–	?
I'm working tomorrow.	I'm not working tomorrow.	Am I working tomorrow?
You're taking a day off next week.	You aren't taking a day off next week.	Are you taking a day off next week?
He / She / It's leaving tonight.	He / She / It isn't leaving tonight.	Is he / she / it leaving tonight?
We're meeting him for lunch.	We aren't meeting him for lunch.	Are we meeting him for lunch?
They're going home after the lesson.	They aren't going home after the lesson.	Are they going home after the lesson?

short answers	
Yes, I am.	No, I'm not.
Yes, you / we / they are.	No, you / we / they aren't.
Yes, he / she / it is.	No, he / she / it isn't.

>> Now go to **exercises 12.2 and 12.3** to practise.

12C wh- questions

Use *wh-* questions to ask for information.

Use **who** to ask about people.	Who's coming to the party tonight?
Use **what** to ask about things / activities.	What are you doing tomorrow? What are we having for dinner tonight?
Use **where** to ask about places.	Where are you meeting Peter?
Use **when** to ask about times.	When are they going on holiday?
Use **why** to ask about reasons.	Why is she leaving work early?
Use **how much / how many** to ask about quantity.	How many people are coming to the meeting? How much money are you taking on holiday?

>> Now go to **exercise 12.4** to practise.

12D going to for future intentions

Use *going to* to talk about future intentions.
An intention is something you decide to do.

+	–	?
I'm going to lose weight.	I'm not going to lose weight.	Am I going to lose weight?
You / We / They're going to join a gym.	You / We / They aren't going to join a gym.	Are you / we / they going to join a gym?
He / She / It's going to learn Japanese.	He / She / It isn't going to learn Japanese.	Is he / she / it going to learn Japanese?

short answers	
Yes, I am.	No, I'm not.
Yes, you / we / they are.	No, you / we / they aren't.
Yes, he / she / it is.	No, he / she / it isn't.

>> Now go to **exercise 12.5** to practise.

12.1 Order the activities 1–8.
a ☐ Justin got up early this morning.
b ☐ Justin's got a meeting first thing tomorrow.
c ☐ It's 11 o'clock now. Justin's having his mid-morning break.
d ☐ Justin and Holly went to the cinema last night.
e ☐ Holly's party is the day after tomorrow.
f ☐1 Justin phoned Holly <u>late yesterday afternoon</u>.
g ☐ Justin's got another meeting early tomorrow afternoon.
h ☐ Justin and Holly are going on holiday next week.

12.2 Complete the text. Use these verbs in the correct form.

drive ~~finish~~ have meet visit watch

It's Friday and Lynda*'s finishing* work early today.
[1] She_____ her husband, Paul, at four o'clock.
[2] They_____ to Edinburgh tonight. [3] They_____
Lynda's family. It's Lynda's sister's birthday and
[4] she _____ a party tomorrow evening. Paul doesn't
want to go. There's a big football match this weekend and
[5] Paul's friends _____ it in the pub.

12.3 Write sentences using the present continuous.
Example I work this Saturday *I'm working this Saturday.*
1 she meet him bus station tomorrow
2 I not have lunch Harry Friday
3 you go cinema tonight ?
4 he do anything at weekend ?
5 we buy new car Saturday
6 they arrive today tomorrow ?
7 we not go on holiday this year
8 I take my daughter dentist after lunch

12.4 Write *wh-* questions.
Example <u>Where are you going?</u> We're going to <u>the park</u>.
1 _____? Pablo and Jim are coming to <u>the pub</u>.
2 _____? I'm wearing <u>my blue dress</u> tomorrow.
3 _____? Gran's meeting Arif <u>at the airport</u>.
4 _____? Justin's catching the train to Paris <u>tonight</u>.
5 _____? <u>Thirty people</u> are coming to her party.
6 _____? I'm getting him <u>a hat</u> for his birthday.

12.5 Order the words to make sentences.
Example 're improve to English going our We
        We're going to improve our English.
1 going study I next 'm to weekend
2 Panos do is going to homework on his Sunday
3 're going we tomorrow buy car new to a
4 use to are they the this evening going Internet
5 speak going English we every day to 're
6 Satomi at the 's watch going a film weekend to
7 to learn next going Jim 's year French
8 going we to aren't this arrive afternoon late

Irregular verbs

verb	past simple
be	was
	were
break	broke
buy	bought /bɔːt/
can	could /kʊd/
come	came
cut	cut
do	did
draw	drew
drink	drank
drive	drove
eat	ate
find	found
forget	forgot
get	got
give	gave
go	went
have	had
hear	heard /hɜːd/
know	knew /njuː/
learn	learnt
	learned
leave	left
lose	lost

verb	past simple
make	made
meet	met
put	put /pʊt/
read	read /red/
ring	rang
run	ran
say	said /sed/
see	saw /sɔː/
sell	sold
send	sent
sing	sang
sit	sat
sleep	slept
speak	spoke
spend	spent
stand	stood /stʊd/
swim	swam
take	took /tʊk/
tell	told
think	thought /θɔːt/
understand	understood
wake up	woke up
wear	wore
write	wrote

« Look at the verb column.
Cover the past simple column
and test yourself.

Pronunciation

Vowel sounds

/æ/ apple /æpl/	/e/ egg /eg/	/ɪ/ fish /fɪʃ/	/ɒ/ office /'ɒfɪs/	/ʌ/ uncle /'ʌŋkl/	/ʊ/ book /bʊk/
/ɑː/ car /kɑː(r)/	/ɜː/ girl /gɜː(r)l/	/iː/ eat /iːt/	/ɔː/ four /fɔː(r)/	/uː/ two /tuː/	
/eə/ hair /heə(r)/	/ɪə/ ear /ɪə(r)/	/ʊə/ newer /njʊə(r)/	/əʊ/ phone /fəʊn/	/aʊ/ mouth /maʊθ/	
/aɪ/ ice /aɪs/	/eɪ/ eight /eɪt/	/ɔɪ/ boy /bɔɪ/	/ə/ cinema /'sɪnəmə/		

Consonant sounds

/p/ pen /pen/	/b/ bed /bed/	/t/ table /teɪbl/	/d/ door /dɔː(r)/	/tʃ/ chair /tʃeə(r)/	/dʒ/ jeans /dʒiːnz/
/f/ food /fuːd/	/v/ visit /'vɪzɪt/	/θ/ thing /θɪŋ/	/ð/ father /'fɑːðə(r)/	/k/ cup /kʌp/	/g/ garden /'gɑːdən/
/s/ sister /'sɪstə(r)/	/z/ zoo /zuː/	/ʃ/ shoe /ʃuː/	/ʒ/ television /'telɪvɪʒn/	/h/ house /haʊs/	/l/ lunch /lʌntʃ/
/m/ man /mæn/	/n/ nine /naɪn/	/ŋ/ sing /sɪŋ/	/r/ red /red/	/w/ water /'wɔːtə(r)/	/j/ young /jʌŋ/

The alphabet

A	B	C	D	E	F	G	H	I	J	K	L	M	N
/eɪ/	/biː/	/siː/	/diː/	/iː/	/ef/	/dʒiː/	/eɪtʃ/	/aɪ/	/dʒeɪ/	/keɪ/	/el/	/em/	/en/

O	P	Q	R	S	T	U	V	W	X	Y	Z
/əʊ/	/piː/	/kjuː/	/ɑː(r)/	/es/	/tiː/	/juː/	/viː/	/'dʌbljuː/	/eks/	/waɪ/	/zed/, American /ziː/

Stressed and unstressed words

Stress 'vocabulary' words ...	
nouns	*book, girl, time ...*
main verbs	*walk, speak, play ...*
adjectives	*big, green, old ...*
adverbs	*easily, fast, slow ...*
question words	*Who, What, How, ...*
negatives	*not, aren't, can't ...*

Don't stress 'grammar' words ...	
articles	*a, an, the ...*
prepositions	*in, on, of ...*
conjunctions	*and, but ...*
auxiliary verbs	*is, was, do ...*
pronouns	*you, we, them ...*
possessives	*me, your, their ...*
demonstratives	*this, that ...*

Example stress patterns

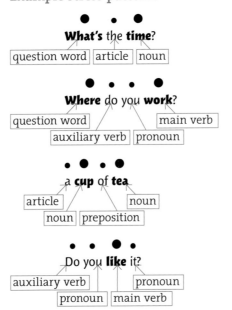

Audio scripts

1

1A.1
How are you?
I'm fine thanks.
Sorry?
Good morning.
Good afternoon.
Nice to meet you.
What's your name?
My name's Bill.
See you later!

1A.2
Day one
Jim Hi, my name's Jim. What's your name?
Satomi Hello, Jim. I'm Satomi.
J Sorry?
S Sa-to-mi. Satomi.
J Oh, OK. Nice to meet you, Satomi.
S Nice to meet you!

Day two
S Good morning, Jim. How are you?
J I'm fine, thanks, Satomi. And you?
S I'm fine. See you later.
J See you later. Bye!

Day three
J Good morning, Satomi.
S Good afternoon, Jim!
J What? Oh yes, it's afternoon. Oops!

1A.3
Hi, hell**o**. **What's** your **name**?
Hi, hell**o**. **My** name's **Wayne**.
Nice to **meet** you. **My** name's **Sue**.
Hello **Sue**. **Nice** to **meet you**!

Morning, good **morn**ing! Hell**o** again **Sue**.
Morning, good **morn**ing! **Hi**, how are **you**?
Fine thanks! **Fine** thanks! **Fine**, and **you**?
Fine thanks! **Fine** thanks! **I'm** fine **too**.

1B.1
1, 2, 3   7, 8, 9   2, 5, 8
4, 5, 6   1, 4, 7   3, 6, 9

1B.2
@   jkl   wxyz
abc   mno   dot
def   pqrs   oh
ghi   tuv   slash

1B.3
a, b …   j, k …   t, u …
d, e …   m, n …   w, x …
g, h …   p, q …

1B.4
10, 11, 12, 13, 14, 15, 16, 17, 18, 19, 20

1B.5
H, J, N, X, A, V, D, R, two

1B.6
A What's your phone number, Jacky?
B My home phone number's 082 925 8049 … and my mobile number is 607 483 double-7 52.
A What's your email address?
B My email address is smit-J – that's S-M-I-T-J – at coolmail.com.
A What's your website address?
B It's www dot jaysmith dot uk. Let me spell that for you. It's J-A-Y-S-M-I-T-H.
A Thank you.

1B.7
minerva@teleten.com
www.compulite.au
837 663 367
981 6826
www.finbar.lit
walsh@sylvan.ac.uk
bennj, that's B-E-double N-J @ 17265.com
134 276 376

1C.1
A What's your first name?
B Jacky.
A What's your surname?
B Smith.
A Where are you from?
B I'm from Wales.
A What's your address?
B It's 23 Market Street, Newtown.

A What's your first name?
B Jan.
A What's your surname?
B Kowalski.
A Where are you from?
B I'm from Poland.
A What's your address?
B It's 23 ulica Rynek, Nowe Miasto.

A What's your first name?
B Ivan.
A What's your surname?
B Kuznetsov.
A Where are you from?
B I'm from Russia.
A What's your address?
B It's 23 ulitsa Rynok, Novgorod.

A What's your first name?
B Juanita.
A What's your surname?
B Herrero.
A Where are you from?
B I'm from Mexico.
A What's your address?
B It's 23 Calle del Mercado, Villa Nueva.

A What's your first name?
B Jeannette.
A What's your surname?
B La Forge.
A Where are you from?
B I'm from Belgium.
A What's your address?
B It's 23 Rue Foire, Neuville.

1C.2
twenty-two
thirty-three
forty-four
fifty-five
sixty-six
seventy-seven
eighty-eight
ninety-nine
a hundred and ten

1C.3
first name
your **first** name
What's your **first** name?

sur**name**
your **sur**name
What's your **sur**name?

from
are you **from**
Where are you **from**?

ad**dress**
your ad**dress**
What's your ad**dress**?

1D.1
Jeff Excuse me, are you a medical student?
Anita Yes, I am.
J Yeah, me too. What's your name?
A Anita. And you?
J I'm Jeff. Where are you from?
A I'm from London, but my mum and dad aren't British. They're from China. Are you from London?
J No, I'm not. I'm from Nottingham. My mum's English but my dad isn't. He's from Trinidad.
A Oh really?
J Yeah. Oh, this is my stop. OK, bye. Nice to meet you … Sorry, what's your name again?
A Anita.
J Nice to meet you, Anita.
A Bye Jeff. See you!

1D.2
Natalia Excuse me! Are you Eddy Martinez?
Eddy Yes, that's right.
N How do you do, Mr Martinez? I love your books.
E Oh really? Thank you. Erm … What's your name?
N Natalia Dubois.
E Nice to meet you, Miss Dubois – or is it Mrs Dubois? Or Ms Dubois?
N Please just call me Natalia!
E OK. Where are you from Natalia? You aren't French …
N No. I'm from Australia, but my father's Belgian.
E Really? Are you here on holiday?
N No, I'm not. I'm here for work. I'm a teacher.
E Oh, here's my taxi. Sorry, I'm late for a meeting …
N No problem. Goodbye, Mr Martinez.
E Bye. Nice to meet you!

1D.3
1 Excuse me, are you a medical student?
2 Sorry, what's your name again?
3 How do you do, Mr Martinez?
4 Oh really? Thank you.
5 Nice to meet you Miss Dubois.
6 Or is it Mrs Dubois?
7 Or Ms Dubois?
8 Please just call me Natalia!

1E.1
Man Full name?
Satomi Satomi Sakamoto.
M How do you spell that, please?
S S-A-T-O-M-I S-A-K-A-M-O-T-O.
M Age?
S Can you repeat that, please?
M Age. How old are you?
S Oh. I'm 22.
M Marital status?
S Sorry, I don't understand.
M Are you married or single?
S Oh. I'm single.
M Country of origin?
S Japan.
M What's your home address?
S Nakanochi 13, Tokyo.
M How do you spell that please?
S N-A-K-A-N-O-C-H-I.
M Thanks. And your phone number?
S It's 81 3201 8709.
M 89 3201 8709 …
S No, 81 3201 8709.
M Oh, OK. Email?
S Email? Um, it's S-A-T-O-1 at D-I-N-J dot J-A.
M OK … and your passport number?
S Sorry, can you repeat that, please?
M Your ID. Passport number.
S Ah, yes. It's 818 220 892.
M OK, thanks.

2

2A.1
bag   door   student
board   pen   teacher
CD   pencil   window
chair   phone
desk   picture

2A.2
1 **Ana** Jim?
  Jim Yes, Ana?
  A What's that in English?
  J That's a window.
  A Ah, OK. Window.

2 **Pablo** Sorry?
  Jim Window.
  P How do you spell that?
  J Window. W-I-N-D-O-W.
  P Oh, OK. Thanks.

3 **Satomi** Can you write that, please?
  Jim Yes, sure. W-I-N-D-O-W.

4 **Jim** Now, open your dictionary, please.
  Pablo Sorry? Open what?
  J Your dictionary.
  P Can you repeat that, please?
  J Dictionary.

150

5 Ana Sorry? Can you say that slowly, please?
Jim Yes. Dic-tion-ary. OK?
A Yes. Dictionary.

2A.3

in **Eng**lish
that in **Eng**lish
What's that in **Eng**lish?

please
re**peat** that, please
Can you re**peat** that, please?

spell that
do you **spell** that
How do you **spell** that?

slowly, please
say that **slow**ly, please
Can you **say** that **slow**ly, please?

write that, please
Can you **write** that, please?

2A.4

Monday, **Tues**day
Wednesday, **Thurs**day
Friday, **Sat**urday
Sunday, **Mon**day …

2A.5

Jim OK, that's all for today. See you tomorrow.
Pablo No, tomorrow is Saturday!
J Oh yes. OK, see you on Monday!
P What's *fin de semana* in English?
J Weekend.
P Have a good weekend!
J Oh thanks. You too!

2B.1

father, **moth**er, **sis**ter, **broth**er, **wife** and **hus**band, **daugh**ter, **son**

2B.2

A OK, so this is the English singer, John Lennon…
B Yeah, John Lennon, yeah, and number 14 – that's his wife Yoko Ono.

2B.3

A OK, so this is the English singer, John Lennon…
B Yeah, John Lennon, yeah, and number 14 – that's his wife Yoko Ono.
A Yeah. She's a singer too, and ehm … OK, that's Caetano Veloso …
B Caetano Veloso?
A Yeah, he's a Brazilian singer, and this is his sister Maria Bethania …
B Number 2?
A Uh huh, yeah, Maria Bethania. She's a singer too.
B OK, so this is Enrique Iglesias, the Spanish singer …
A Right, and that's his father, number 11 – Julio Iglesias.
B Uh huh.
A OK, so next one. This is Frida Kahlo.
B Frida Kahlo?
A Yeah, you know the film *Frida*? Mexican artist.
B Oh.
A And that's her husband Diego Rivera, number 10. He's an artist too.

B Ehm. I don't know them. But this man, he's Humphrey Bogart, the American actor.
A Yeah, and number 8, that's his wife, the actress Lauren Bacall.
B Uh huh, yeah. And this is Goldie Hawn, and number 9 – that's her daughter Kate Hudson.
A They're American actresses, mother and daughter, right?
B Uh huh. OK, and the last one, I guess this is Klaus Kinski.
A Yes, he's a German actor, and number 12, that's his daughter Natasha Kinski.
B Natasha Kinski, yeah. OK, so that's it then.

2C.1

a a child, a boy
b an old man, a grandfather, a grandmother, grandparents
c a baby
d a teenager, a boy, a girl, a boyfriend, a girlfriend
e a married couple, a woman, a man
f a man
g a housewife
h an engineer
i a factory worker
j a vet
k a doctor
l an office worker
m a shop assistant
n a farmer
o a designer

2C.2

an old woman, an old woman, an old woman, an old woman

2C.3

You aren't old.
He isn't an adult.
My son isn't an engineer.

2C.4

old … told … aren't old … You aren't old
adult … nadult … an adult … tan adult … isn't an adult … He isn't an adult
engineer … an engineer … tan engineer … isn't an engineer … nisn't an engineer … My son isn't an engineer

2D.1

Paul Anila?
Anila Yes, Paul?
P What time's the news?
A It's at six o'clock, Paul.
P And what time is it now?
A It's nearly ten to five, Paul.
P Ten to nine?
A No, ten to <u>five</u>. Four fifty.
P Four fifteen?
A No, four <u>fifty</u>.
P Oh. Your watch says four fifty.
A Yes. Four fifty.
P That's strange.
A Why?
P <u>My</u> watch says ten to five!

2D.2

A thir**teen**, four**teen**, fif**teen**, six**teen**, seven**teen**, eigh**teen**, nine**teen**
B **thir**ty, **for**ty, **fif**ty, **six**ty, **sev**enty, **eigh**ty, **nine**ty

2D.3

thirty, **for**ty, **fif**teen, six**teen**, **sev**enty, eigh**teen**, **nine**ty

2D.4

1 **A** Thirteen.
   P Thirty?
   A No, thir<u>teen</u>!
2 **A** Forty.
   P Fourteen?
   A No, <u>forty</u>!
3 **A** Fifty.
   P Fifteen?
   A No, <u>fifty</u>!

2D.5

five past one
five to two
half past one
ten past one
ten to two
twenty past one
twenty to two
two o'clock
one o'clock
quarter past one
quarter to two
twenty-five past one
twenty-five to two

2D.6

Start
twenty past seven
five to nine
twelve o'clock
one thirty
five past eight
quarter to one
eleven o'clock
quarter past nine
twenty-five to seven
half past five
ten o'clock
twenty past seven
twenty to three
end

3

3A.1

bookshop
bus
café
car park
cash machine
chemist's
music shop
platform
pub
restaurant
station
taxi
telephones
ticket office
toilets
train

3A.2

1 **A** Excuse me, where are the toilets, please?
   B They're over there, near Platform 12.
   A Platform 12? OK, thanks.
2 **A** Excuse me, where's the pub, please?
   B It's upstairs.
   A Thanks.
3 **A** Excuse me, where are the taxis, please?

B Taxis? They're near the Fairfield Street exit.
A The Fairfield Street exit? OK, thank you.
4 **A** Excuse me, where's the chemist's, please?
   B It's near the Piccadilly exit.
   A OK, thank you.
5 **A** Excuse me, where's the long-stay car park exit, please?
   B It's near platform 1, over there.
   A Over there? Thank you.

3A.3

A Excuse me, where's the ticket office, please?
B Sorry, love?
A The ticket office.
B Oh, yeah. It's over there – you see?
A Yes. Thanks … a ticket to Liverpool, please.

A Excuse me, where is the café?
B Which café?
A Oh, ehm … I don't know.
B Well, Starbucks is over there, look, near Platform 12.
A Starbucks. OK, thanks … a coffee, please.

A Excuse me, is this Platform 13?
B No, this is Platform 3. Platform 13 is that way.
A OK, thanks. The Liverpool train's from Platform 13, isn't it?
B Yes, that's right. But you need to run – you've only got three minutes!
A Oh no! Thanks.

3B.1

Aus**tral**ia and **Germ**any
India, Ja**pan**
Egypt and **It**aly
Spain, **Greece**, and **France**

Russia and South **Af**rica
Canada, Bra**zil**
The US**A** and **Chin**a
Turkey and Pe**ru**

3B.2

American, Australian, Brazilian, Canadian, Chinese, Egyptian, French, German, Greek, Indian, Italian, Japanese, Peruvian, Russian, South African, Spanish, Turkish

3B.3

Where are you **from**?
What's the **cap**ital of your **coun**try?
What's your natio**nal**ity?
What's the **lang**uage of your **coun**try?
What's the **curr**ency of your **coun**try?

3B.4

OK, first question. Question one. Picture 9 is in Australia. The currency of Australia is the Australian dollar, and the language is English. But what's the capital of Australia? The capital of Australia. Is it a Sydney, b Canberra, or c Auckland? Sydney, Canberra, or Auckland?

Now, second question. Question two. Picture 13 is in Brazil. The capital of Brazil is Brasilia, and the nationality is Brazilian. But what's the language of Brazil? Is it a Portuguese, b Spanish, or c French?

Third question. Question three. Picture 16 is in Turkey. The language and nationality of Turkey is Turkish. But what's the capital of Turkey. Is it a Ankara, b Istanbul, or c Damascus? Ankara, Istanbul, or Damascus?

And now question four. Picture 3 is in Russia. The capital of Russia is Moscow, and the language is Russian. But what is the currency of Russia? The currency of Russia. Is it a the euro, b the lira, or c the rouble. The euro, the lira, or the rouble?

And now to question five. Picture 1 is in Egypt. The capital of Egypt is Cairo. The nationality is Egyptian. But what is the language? Is it a Egyptian, b Arabic, or c English? Egyptian, Arabic, or English?

And the answers are:
question one – Canberra
question two – Portuguese
question three – Ankara
question four – the rouble
question five – Arabic

3C.1
People on **bikes**
People on **bus**es
Workers in their **off**ices
Workers in their **fact**ories

Drivers in their **lorr**ies
Cars in the **car** park
Waiters in the **rest**aurant
Glasses on the **tables**

Children at **school**
Children in their **class**es
People in the **mark**et
People in their **houses**

3C.2
girls, girl, girl
bike, bike, bikes
shops, shops, shop
phone, phones, phones

3C.3
bus – buses
car – cars
school – schools
class – classes
place – places
bike – bikes
church – churches
page – pages
boy – boys

3C.4
A Hi, it's Tony here.
B Oh, hello Tony. Where are you?
A I'm in Market Street, near the bookshop. See you in about ten minutes.
B OK, see you. Bye.

3C.5
A Hi, it's Alice here.
B Oh, hello Alice. Where are you?
A I'm in the market. See you in about five minutes.
B OK, see you. Bye.

A Hi, it's Wendy here.
B Oh, hello Wendy. Where are you?
A I'm in my office. See you in about ten minutes.
B OK, see you. Bye.

3D.1
Sue and Iris are students. They live together in a student flat ...
Iris Bon Soir!
Sue Sorry?
I Oh, you don't speak French. I speak French very well.
S Really?
I Oh, yes. In Paris, they think I'm French.
S Wow! Do you speak any other languages?
I Yes, I do. I'm very good at foreign languages.
S What other languages do you speak?
I I speak German quite well. And I speak a little Russian. And Italian. *Mamma mia*, I love Italian – it's my favourite language. Do you speak Italian?
S No, I don't. I'm not very good at languages. I speak English and I understand a little Gaelic. My boyfriend's Irish.
I I don't speak Gaelic, but I speak Spanish very well. My boyfriend's from Buenos Días.
S Sorry?
I Buenos Días. It's the capital of Argentina. Oh, the phone ... Hello?

3D.2
Irish, Irish, Iris
Sue, shoe, Sue

3D.3
Are you Irish, Iris?
Is this your shoe, Sue?

3D.4
A Where are you from?
B I'm from Switzerland.
A Oh. Do you speak German?
B Yes, I do. I speak German very well. And French – I speak French very well too.
A And Italian? Do you speak Italian?
B Well, I speak a little Italian, yes. But really, German and French are my first languages.
A And do you speak any other languages? Do you speak Spanish, for example?
B Spanish – no. I don't speak Spanish. But I speak a little English!
A Yes, of course!

4

4A.1
Jim Hi Ana. How are you?
Ana So-so.
J What's wrong?
A Well, the good news is my boyfriend's here in England.
J Oh really? That's great! And the bad news?
A He's with his new girlfriend!
J Oh, I see. I'm sorry!
A Thanks. Anyway, how are you?
J Not bad. The good news is I'm in a play.
A Oh really? Well done! And the bad news?
J Tonight's the first night and I don't know my lines.
A Oh no! Good luck!

4A.2
Oh no! Good luck!
Oh really? That's great!
What's wrong?
Oh really? Well done!
Oh, I see. I'm sorry.

4B.1
January's the first month
It's easy to remember
The tenth and the eleventh
Are October and November
April's the fourth month
And March is the third
February's the second month
A short month, a long word
June is the sixth month
It's easy to say
The eighth month is August
The fifth month is May
July is the seventh month
The ninth is September
And finally, the twelfth month
The last month, December

4B.2
March, May, June
April, August
July
January, February
September, October, November, December

4B.3
tree, tree, three
eighth, eight, eighth
three, three, free
thing, sing, sing
eights, eighth, eights
six, six, sixth

4C.1
Man What do you do in the morning, Lily?
Lily Well, first, I wake up, obviously, yeah, so, ehm, I wake up and, ehm ... I get up and, ehm ... I have breakfast, like cereal or whatever ... ehm, and then after breakfast, I ehm, check my email ...
M You check your email?
L Yeah. Why not? And .... ehm, I have a shower ... Then I brush my teeth and I get dressed and then finally I, I, ehm, ... I leave the house.
M Right. Same as me really. But I don't check my email.

4C.2
Interviewer OK Jim, first question. The alarm clock rings. What do you do?
Jim That's easy. I press 'snooze' five times.
I Uh huh. OK, second question. You get up. What do you do first?
J Oh, ehm ... I sit on the bed and think.
I You sit on the bed and think, uh huh. Next question. You go to the bathroom. Somebody is there before you. What do you do?
J Ehm ... letter a or c... yes, c. I walk into the door!
I OK. And ... what do you have for breakfast?
J Breakfast? No time for breakfast. I'm always late for work!
I No breakfast, uh huh. OK, next question. What do you do first – brush your teeth, get dressed, or have breakfast?
J Well, ha ha, I ehm, I do all three together.
I All three together. OK. Next. You leave the house. What do you do next?
J Ehm ... I run to the bus and then phone work to say I'm late.
I OK, next question. You read a newspaper. Where do you read it?
J Newspaper? Oh, I read that at home in the evening.
I Right, last question. You wake up, it's a holiday. What do you do?
J It's a holiday, yeah? I don't get up, I mean, I get up at lunchtime.
I Ha ha – you get up at lunchtime ... OK ... ehm, let's see ... C, C, C ... ha ha, you're a morning monster, Jim!

4C.3
My brother gets up early.
My brothers get up early.
My sisters like morning.
My sister likes mornings.
My friends study in the morning.
My friend studies in the morning.

4D.1
Boss We usually work nine to five here, Justin. You're always late.
Justin Not always, Mr Minnit.
B Yes, you always arrive late!
J But I never leave late!
B Hmm. And how often do you have coffee breaks?
J Not very often, Mr Minnit.
B But you're always at the coffee machine with Holly.
J That's not true. I'm often at the coffee machine without Holly.
B And another thing. The lunch break is one hour. But you sometimes leave at twelve o'clock and come back to the office at two! Explain that please!
J Well, I sometimes go for lunch with Holly, and we add our lunch hours together. One and one make two!
B Justin, it's 9.35. Start work now!
J 9.35? Oh no – I'm late for my coffee break!

4D.2

Justin doesn't live with Holly.
Justin doesn't leave with Holly.
He leaves alone.
He lives alone.
Justin sits near Holly.
Justin's seat's near Holly.

4D.3

Well, I'm a writer, and, ehm ... I don't work in an office or anything, I work at home, and I usually get up at eight o'clock or sometimes at seven, and I start work. I always have a cup of tea and then I start work, ehm ... I sometimes have a break at ten, or half past, you know, a break for breakfast. I usually have lunch at one o'clock and, ehm, I watch the news on TV. I often go to bed for half an hour after lunch and then I start work again. I finish work at five or six o'clock. I never work in the evening.

4E.1

Wednesdays
work on Wednesdays
walks to work on Wednesdays
always walks to work on Wednesdays
Wendy always walks to work on Wednesdays.

February the first
Phil on February the first
phones Phil on February the first
always phones Phil on February the first
Fiona always phones Phil on February the first.

September the seventh
school on September the seventh
starts school on September the seventh
son starts school on September the seventh
Simon's son starts school on September the seventh.

5

5A.1

I know you ...
He knows her ...
We know them ...
You know them ...
He knows you ...
She knows us ...
They know me ...

5A.2

A – Kate   O – Rose
E – Pete   U – Jude
I – Mike

5A.3

This is Kate's cat and that's Pete's pet.
Mike and Mick are short for Michael.
Rose Ross knows Jude Judd.

5A.4

1 **Joe** Do you know my girlfriend Kate? Come and meet her ...
2 **Joe** Kate, this is Steve.
3 **Jude** Who's he? Do you know him?
4 **Rose** Yeah, that's Pete. He's from Amsterdam. Come and meet him.
5 **Pete** Sorry, what's your name again?
6 **Jude** Jude. It's short for Judith.
7 **Rose** Who are they? Do you know them?
8 **Jane** Yeah, that's Mike, but I don't know the other one. Let's go and meet them.
9 **Jane** Hi Mike. Do you remember me?

5B.1

a red car   black hair
blue eyes   a yellow car
blond hair   long hair
a white cat   a small bag
a green bag   a fat dog
a grey dog   big eyes
a tall man   an old car

5B.2

the man, the man, the men, the man
the tall men, the tall man, the tall men
the tall blond man, the tall blond men

5B.3

My flatmate Matt's got a fat black cat.
My best friend Jen's got ten red pens.

5B.4

a small white cat
long black hair
short blond hair
a small blue bag
a thin grey dog
a big black cat
long brown hair
a thin white dog
a short blond man
long blond hair
a big blue bag
a big green bag
short blonde men
short brown hair
a small green bag
a fat grey dog
a new yellow car
a new red car
an old yellow car
an old red car
big blue eyes
small brown eyes
short black hair
big brown eyes
a small black cat
a fat white dog
a big white cat
tall blond men
small blue eyes
a tall blond man

5B.5

Hmm, my best friend ... well, her name's Sandra and she's tall, ehm ... and she's got ... she's got short black hair, ehm ... She's got blue eyes. Ehm, let's see, what else? Oh, well, she's got a car – a small white car. And she's got a small grey cat called Felix.

Oh, and I've got a neighbour called Mr Ross – ehm, he's short, he's very short. Ehm ... black hair – he's got short black hair and brown eyes. And he's got a dog, yeah, a big brown dog, and I hate it. Horrible dog. What else? Oh, well, yeah, Mr Ross has got this really big car, a big red car – it's like a small bus, really!

5C.1

1 rulers   7 files
2 notebooks   8 printer ink
3 pens   9 a printer
4 pencils   10 paper
5 rubbers   11 CDs
6 a computer   12 batteries

5C.2

Customer Excuse me, can you help me?
Assistant Yes, of course.
C Have you got any printer ink?
A Yes, what printer have you got?
C It's an Epson. I don't know the model.
A Is it this one?
C Yes, that's it.
A OK. Black and colour?
C Just black, thanks. I've got lots of colour ink.
A OK. Here you are.
C Thanks. Oh, and I haven't got any paper ...
A OK, the paper's over there.

5C.3

Excuse me, can you help me?
Have you got any printer ink?
What printer have you got?
I've got lots of colour ink.
I haven't got any paper.

5C.4

1
Customer Excuse me, can you help me?
Assistant Yes, of course.
C Have you got a book of baby names?
A Yes, just a moment. We've got this book. It's very popular.
C Oh, OK, that's great. And have you got any books about baby care?
A Yes. We've got all these over here ...

2
Assistant Can I help you?
Customer Yes, have you got any English wine?
A English wine? Yes, we've got these two bottles.
C Oh, I see. It's red. Have you got any white?
A No, I'm afraid we haven't got English white at the moment. But we've got some good German white wine over here ...

3
Assistant Can I help you?
Customer Yes. Have you got any green tomatoes?
A Well, we've got these, but they aren't really green.
C No, I want green tomatoes.
A I'm sorry. We haven't got any.
C OK. And can I have a bag of oranges, please?
A Yes, of course.

4
Customer Excuse me, have you got any French newspapers?
Assistant Yes, I've got one copy of Le Monde here ...
C Have you got La Tribune?
A No, I'm sorry, I haven't got any other French papers. Just this one.
C OK. And some chewing gum, please.

5D.1

A I need a gift for my friend Jane. Have you got any ideas?
B Does she like wine?
A No, she doesn't.
B Has she got a DVD player?
A No, she hasn't.
B OK, give her a DVD player.
A They're very expensive.
B Oh, OK. Does she like animals?
A Yes, she does.
B OK, give her an animal calendar.
A Good idea. Thanks.

5D.2

A Ehm, I, I need a gift for my friend Jane. Have you got any ideas?
B Well, does she like wine?
A Like wine? No, she doesn't. She doesn't like wine, no ...
B OK, well, has she got, oh, has she got a DVD player?
A No, she hasn't.
B OK, give her a DVD player.
A Er ... they're very expensive.
B Oh, OK. Oh, does she like animals?
A Yes, I think she does.
B OK, then give her, er ... give her an animal calendar.
A Ehm ... good idea. Great! Thanks.

5D.3

A Ehm, I, I need, ehm ... a gift for my friend Rose. Have you got any ideas?
B Well, does she ski?
A Ski? No, she doesn't. She doesn't ski, no ...
B OK, well, has she got, ehm, has she got a car?
A No, she hasn't. She doesn't drive.
B OK. Has she got a mobile phone?
A Mobile phone? Yes, she's got a mobile phone.
B OK. Give her a mini keyboard.
A Um ... they're very expensive ...
B Does she like computer games?
A Yes, I think she does ...

5D.4

She's **got** a guitar but she **has**n't got a **car**.
He's **got** a **car** but he **has**n't got a guitar.

5E.1

A Self-portrait
by Mike Campbell

I've got black hair, I've got brown eyes
I don't like hats and I don't like ties
I've got an old bike but I haven't got a car
I live in a flat and I work in a Spar
I drink white wine but never Champagne
My favourite food's chicken chow mein
I listen to jazz but I don't like blues
I always watch the nine o'clock news
I haven't got a dog but I've got a small cat
My favourite place is my little flat

6

6A.1
Start
five euros fifty
seven euros thirty
three euros fourteen
nine euros sixteen
six euros forty
two euros fifty
thirteen euros seventy
two euros fifteen
thirty euros seventeen
fifteen euros fifty
fifty euros fifteen
end

6A.2
How **much** are the **bis**cuits?
How **much** is the **tea**?
The **tea's** one pound **fif**ty
The **bis**cuits are **free**

6A.3
Waitress Can I help you?
Jim How much are the sandwiches, please?
W Three pounds fifty.
J OK, a sandwich, please.
W Here you are. Would you like anything to drink?
J How much is the tea?
W Ninety p.
J OK, I'd like a cup of tea, please.
W That's four pounds forty, please.
J Here you are.
W And here's your change. Thank you.

6B.1
The Greasy Spoon
Sausages with chips and eggs
Tomato salad
Chicken legs
Tea or coffee
Bread and jam
Toasted sandwich
Cheese or ham
Breakfast in the afternoon
Here at 'The Greasy Spoon'
A piece of pizza (extra cheese!)
Fish and chips with beans or peas
Potatoes, onions, carrots, and steak
Apple pie or chocolate cake
Morning, night, and afternoon
Here at 'The Greasy Spoon'!

6B.2
W Can I help you?
J Yes. I'd like some sausages with beans and bread, please.
W Sorry, we haven't got any bread today.
J OK, then can I have sausages with beans, please?
W Sorry, we haven't got any beans.
J Have you got any sausages?
W No, sorry.
J OK. I'd like a pizza …

6C.1
1 There are some apples.
2 There are some chips.
3 There are some sandwiches.
4 There's some sugar.
5 There's some fruit.
6 There's some jam.
7 There isn't any milk.
8 There isn't any soup.
9 There isn't any cake.
10 There aren't any sausages.

6C.2
1 Is there any yogurt in a Greek salad? No, there isn't.
2 Is there any cheese in a Greek salad? Yes, there is.
3 Are there any potatoes in a Russian salad? Yes, there are.
4 Are there any peas in a fruit salad? No, there aren't.

6C.3
1 Are there any apples in a Russian salad?
2 There are green apples and red apples. But are there blue apples?
3 There's usually meat in paella. But are there any vegetables in paella?

6C.4
1 There are potatoes in a Russian salad. But are there any potatoes in a Greek salad? No, there aren't.
2 There's cheese in a Greek salad. But is there any cheese in a fruit salad? No, there isn't.
3 Is there any ham in a hamburger? No, there isn't.
4 There's usually meat in paella. But are there any vegetables in paella? Yes, there are.
5 There are yellow bananas and green bananas. But are there red bananas? Yes, there are.
6 Is there any apple juice in wine? No, there isn't.
7 Are there any apples in a Russian salad? No, there aren't.
8 There's white bread and brown bread. But is there black bread? Yes, there is.
9 Are there any tomatoes in a fruit salad? No, there aren't.
10 There are green apples and red apples. But are there blue apples? No, there aren't.
11 Is there any jam in a ham sandwich? No, there isn't.
12 Carrots are normally red or orange. But are there green carrots? No, there aren't.
13 Is there any cheese in Mexican chilli con carne? No, there isn't.
14 Oranges are usually orange in colour. But are there green oranges? Yes, there are.
15 Is there any sugar in an Indian curry? No, there isn't.
16 There's sugar in fruit. But is there any sugar in a carrot? Yes, there is.
17 Is there any milk in Turkish tea? No, there isn't.
18 Are there any apples in a fruit cake? No, there aren't.

6C.5
Waiter, **wai**ter!
There's **but**ter in my **wa**ter
And **su**gar on my **piz**za
And **pas**ta on my **daugh**ter!

6D.1
a Would you like a crisp?
b Help yourself!
c Would you like another one?
d How much do you want?
e Do you take sugar?
f Try this. It's delicious!

6D.2
self!
yourself!
Help yourself!
sugar?
take sugar?
Do you take sugar?
another?
like another?
Would you like another?
crisp?
like a crisp?
Would you like a crisp?
delicious!
it's delicious!
Try this. It's delicious!
want?
do you want?
How much do you want?

6D.3
Iris Hello Sue. Would you like a cup of tea?
Sue Oh, yes please!
I Oh dear, I haven't got many tea bags. Have you got any?
S Yes. How many do you need?
I Two. No, nine or ten … some for later! … This is your milk. Is that OK? I haven't got any.
S OK. Help yourself!
I Oh, there isn't much … Oops, there isn't any for you, sorry! … How much sugar do you want? I don't take sugar in tea. Do you?
S Well, ehm …
I No, of course you don't. It's bad for you … I'd like a biscuit. Have you got any?
S Yes, I've got a lot of biscuits, but they're …
I Oh great. Thanks! … These biscuits are delicious! Where do you buy them?
S The pet shop. Would you like another one?
I They're dog biscuits!? Yuk!

6D.4
a **cup** of **tea**
some **bread** and **ham**
a **lot** of **cake**
with **cream** or **jam**

6D.5
A How are you this morning?
B I'm fine, thanks.
A What would you like to drink? Tea? Coffee?
B I'd love a cup of coffee, please.
A Coffee, OK … Here you are. Help yourself to milk and sugar.
B Thanks.
A What would you like for breakfast?
B Have you got any yogurt and fruit?
A We've got yogurt, but we haven't got much fruit I'm afraid, just apples. But we've got a lot of orange juice …
B OK, yogurt and an apple, please. No orange juice.
A Oh, OK. And would you like some eggs and sausages?
B Ooooh, yes please.
A One egg or two?
B Ehm, just one, please.
A One egg. OK.

6E.1
1 tea or coffee
2 an apple or a banana
3 coffee with sugar
4 soup with bread
5 potatoes or rice
4 a hamburger with chips
6 chicken or fish
8 pizza or pasta
9 soup or salad
10 potato with butter

7

7A.1
1 go sailing
2 ride a bike
3 go for a run
4 go fishing
5 go for a swim
6 read the newspaper
7 go roller-skating
8 play cards
9 play the guitar
10 play table tennis
11 play basketball

7A.2
Jim In my free time? Oh, let's see, ehm …, well I, ehm … in summer, I often go to the park … I sometimes go for a run and, ehm … yeah, and roller-skating, I sometimes go roller-skating, ehm … or sometimes I just sit and read the newspapers and … and feed the ducks or whatever, watch the people go by. What else? Basketball. I often play basketball and, ehm … I go for a swim. Oh yeah, and I ride my bike, and, ehm … that's all … that's what I do in my free time.

7B.1
This week's weather's warm, windy, and wet.

7B.2
This picture shows a street in a town in England. It's typical English weather. It's very wet. It's quite dark and there are lights in the windows. There are lots of people on the streets. The picture is by John Atkinson Grimshaw.

7B.3
This picture shows a very cold day in a park. It's snowy. There are trees and a small lake. There's ice on the lake. There's a boy on the ice. The picture's by Peter Doig. Which picture's this?

This picture shows fields in France. There are trees and some blue mountains. The weather's windy and cloudy. The picture's by Vincent Van Gogh. Which picture's this?

This picture shows some people – they're by a river. There's a small brown dog. There are boats on the river. The weather's warm and sunny – it's summer. The picture's by Georges-Pierre Seurat. Which picture's this?

7B.4

Conversation 1

A What shall we do?
B I don't know. What's the weather like?
A It's cold and wet.
B How about going to the shops?
A I haven't got any money.
B OK, how about a game of cards?
A Yes, all right.

Conversation 2

A What shall we do?
B I don't know. What's the weather like?
A It's warm and sunny.
B Let's go out.
A OK. Where shall we go?
B How about going for a swim?
A Yes, all right.

7C.1

I can **play** the guitar
Ride a **bike**, drive a **car**
I can **climb** up a **wall**
I can **run**, kick a **ball**
I can **jump**, I can **ski**
I can **climb** up a **tree**
I'm the **star** of the **gym**
But I **caaaan't swim**!

I can **skate**, I can **cook**
I can **read** a long **book**
I can **sit**, I can **stand**
I can **walk** on my **hands**
I can **write**, I can **draw**
I can **do** a lot **more**
I'm the **star** of the **gym**
But I **caaaan't swim**!

7C.2

I can swim.
I can't swim.
I can't swim.
I can swim.
I can swim.
I can't swim.

7C.3

Jim Can you do that, in picture 1?
Ana Oh, yes. I can do it easily. No problem. Look. But number 2, that's difficult. I can't do that. Can you?
J Ehm … yes, I can, but it's difficult. I can do it very slowly. Can you do that, in picture 3?
A Yes, I can, but not very well.

7D.1

Harry You're here for a haircut, I see! Me too. I hate having my hair over my eyes and ears! Would you like a magazine? There's one about fishing here … do you like fishing? No, you don't like fishing – you like meeting friends and dancing, right? Young people today haven't got hobbies. They just like talking on their mobile phones. I haven't got a mobile phone, but I've got lots of hobbies. I enjoy taking photos. I like listening to the radio. And I *love* watching Formula 1 on TV. What about you? Do you like Formula 1?
Secretary The vet can see your dog now, Mrs Blanche. Please go in.
H Vet? Isn't this the hairdresser's?

7D.2

1 I hate having my hair over my eyes.
2 You don't like fishing.
3 You like meeting friends.
4 I enjoy taking photos.
5 I love watching Formula 1 on TV.

7D.3

hair, hair, air
eight, hate, eight
ear, here, ear
hi, eye, hi

7D.4

A Have you got any hobbies, Jessica?
B Ehm, yeah, I like, ehm … taking photographs. I've got a digital camera, and it's really good, and I can, like, put the pictures on my computer, and, ehm … I enjoy going on the Internet, you know … and computer games … I love playing computer games and things, yeah.
A And what about sports? Do you do any sports?
B Well, I don't really like sports, and at school we can choose running or swimming, but I hate running and I hate swimming, so it's horrible and, ehm, yeah … but I like playing football …
A Football?
B Yeah, it's cool.

8

8A.1

1 go for a run
2 go for a coffee
3 go to the park
4 go for a walk
5 go for a sandwich
6 go to the pool
7 go to the shops
8 go to the gym
9 go to the cinema
10 go for a drink

8A.2

Pablo Hi Jim!
Jim Hello. Where are you going?
P We're going to the park. Would you like to come?
J Sorry, I can't. I haven't got time. See you later. Have fun!

Jim Hi Ana. What are you reading?
Ana It's a book by Dan Brown.
J Are you enjoying it?
A Yes, it's very good.
J I'm going for a walk. Would you like to come?
A Yes, sure. I'd love to.

8A.3

going for a walk … going 4 a walk
going to the park … going 2 the park

8A.4

going for a walk
going 4 a walk
going for a walk

going 2 the park
going to the park
going to the park

8A.5

I'm **go**ing for a **walk** – would you **like** to **come**?
Yes, sure! I'd **love** to!
I'm **go**ing to the **shops** – would you **like** to **come**?
Yes, sure! I'd **love** to!

We're **go**ing to the **park** – would you **like** to **come**?
Sorry, I can't. I haven't got **time**.
We're **go**ing for a **run** – would you **like** to **come**?
Sorry, I can't. Have fun!

8B.1

What shall I wear?
Jeans or trousers?
A dress or a skirt?
A coat or a sweater?
A jacket and a shirt?
A hat or a cap?
A tie and a suit?
Shorts and a T-shirt?
Shoes or boots?

8B.2

There's a bird on the board.
There's a board on the bird.
Don't wear shirts to walk.
Don't wear shorts to work.
I hate Earl's four coats.
I hate all fur coats.

8B.3

There's a board on the bird.
There's a bird on the board.
Don't wear shirts to walk.
Don't wear shorts to work.
I hate all fur coats.
I hate Earl's four coats.

8B.4

A I'm going to a wedding. What shall I wear?
B Wear a suit and tie. Have you got a suit?
A No, I haven't.
B Hmm … Have you got a jacket?
A Yes, I've got a jacket for work.
B OK, so wear a jacket and trousers.

8C.1

Moscow Madness

She's **smil**ing, she's **laugh**ing
She's **danc**ing in the **street**
She's **hav**ing **fun** out in the **sun**
In the **Mos**cow **sum**mer **heat**
One man's **play**ing the **sax**ophone
Another man's **play**ing the gui**tar**
Everybody's **watch**ing her
She's **feel**ing like a **star**
She's **danc**ing with a **sail**or
What's he doing **here**?
Call it **Mos**cow **mad**ness
It's that **time** of **year**

8C.2

thing
think
thin
think
thin
thing

8C.3

It's National Navy Day in Russia, and here in Moscow, people are celebrating and having fun. It's a sunny day. There are two musicians. One man's playing the saxophone and the other's playing

the guitar. A sailor's dancing with a girl. The girl's friends are laughing and the other people are watching the celebrations.

8C.4

It's National Navy Day in Russia, and here in St Petersburg, people are celebrating and having fun. It's a sunny day. There are three musicians playing guitars. Three girls are dancing. There are lots of people watching and laughing, and some of them are taking photographs.

8D.1

A spy with a secret … a tape … a murder … The Conversation … a Francis Ford Coppola movie, with Gene Hackman and Harrison Ford … coming soon to a cinema near you!

8D.2

Every evening, Harry arrives home. He opens the door and goes to the kitchen. He has a drink and then he has a shower. Then he listens to a jazz tape, and sometimes he plays the saxophone. The phone never rings – Harry hasn't got any friends and nobody knows his phone number. But today is different …

8D.3

Sound effects

8D.4

I'm listening to **you**, but **you** aren't listening to **me**.
We're listening to **them**, but **they** aren't listening to **us**.
He's listening to **her**, but **she** isn't listening to **him**.

9

9A.1

airport
bus
bus station
departure gate
plane
platform
taxi
train
train station
underground station

9A.2

You can walk there in an hour
Or take the underground
There's a bus every five minutes
And the ticket's just a pound
When you get to the station
Find the platform, take the train
When you get to the airport
Find the gate and take the plane

9A.3

Ana's in West Street, Glasgow …

Ana Excuse me, how can I get to Buchanan Street, please?
Man Sorry?
A How do you say this, please?
M Oh – Buchanan Street!
A Buchanan Street. How can I get to Buchanan Street?

M Well, it's three stops on the underground. The station's just over there, look. Take the Inner Circle line.
A The Inner Circle line? OK, thanks.

9A.4
Excuse me, how can I get to the station, please?
Excuse me, how can I get to the station, please?

9A.5
Excuse me, how can I get to the station, please?
Excuse me, how can I get to the station, please?

9B.1
at the corner
between
Go across the bridge
Go out of the door
Go past the bank
Go straight on
Go to the end of the street
next to
opposite
Turn left at the corner
Turn right at the lights

9B.2
Tourist 1
T1 Excuse me, is there a bank near here?
R Yes – there's a bank opposite the hotel. Just go out of the door and go straight across the road.
T1 OK. Thanks.

Tourist 2
T2 Excuse me, where's the museum, please?
R It's in East Street. Go out of the hotel and turn left. Turn right at the lights. Go across the bridge and straight on. The museum's on the left, opposite the castle.
T2 Opposite the castle? Thanks.

9B.3
Tourist 3
T3 Excuse me, where's the post office?
R It's next door to the hotel. Go out of the door and turn right and it's on the right. It's opposite the tourist information office.
T3 OK. Thanks.

Tourist 4
T4 Excuse me, where can I buy postcards?
R There's a souvenir shop just across the street, between the bank and the tourist information office.
T4 A gift shop?
R Yes. Or there's a bookshop on the corner. Go out of the hotel and turn left. Walk across the street and there's the bookshop, on the corner.
T4 OK. Thanks.

Tourist 5
T5 Ehm … hi. Is there a good restaurant near here?
R Yes. There's one in River Street. Go out of the hotel and turn left. Turn right at the lights and go straight across the bridge. The restaurant is there on the corner.
T5 OK. Thanks.

Tourist 6
T6 Where's the art gallery, please?
R Go out of the hotel and turn left. Go straight on past the lights and the art gallery is on the left, after the police station.
T6 OK. Thanks.

Tourist 7
T7 Excuse me, is there a supermarket near here?
R Yes. It's in West Street. Go out of the hotel and turn left. Turn left at the corner and it's on the left, after the shoe shop.
T7 In West Street, you say?
R Yes.
T7 Oh, OK. Thanks.

9B.4
left at the corner
out of the door
right at the lights
straight across
walk across
bank opposite
post office
tourist information

9B.5
Stop at the end of the street.
Turn left at the lights and walk across the street.
Walk across the bridge and stop opposite the castle.

9C.1
a crowded beach
cheap but dirty restaurants
a comfortable room with a sea view
exciting nightlife
friendly people
a noisy building site
a quiet pool
wet weather

9C.2
1 uncomfortable … comfortable
2 expensive … cheap
3 unfriendly … friendly
4 clean … dirty
5 boring … exciting
6 noisy … quiet
7 dry … wet

9C.3
A Hi Ben. How was your holiday?
B It was great. Really nice. I was in Sardinia …
A Oh, really. So what was the weather like?
B Perfect. It was warm and sunny.
A Where did you stay? A hotel?
B Yeah, a small hotel. Nice and quiet, with a beautiful garden and a lovely view of the beach and the countryside.
A Was the beach nice?
B Yeah, beautiful, yeah. And it wasn't crowded.

A What was the food like?
B Well, I love Italian food, so it was great.
A And the nightlife?
B There wasn't any nightlife in this place, but that's fine for me. I don't really want that on holiday, you know. I want peace and quiet. So, yeah …
A Hmm, sounds great.

9C.4
The beach is crowded.
The beach was crowded.

The rooms were noisy.
The rooms are noisy.

The people were friendly.
The people are friendly.

The place is nice.
The place was nice.

9D.1
Sound effects

9D.2
Nightmare Hotel
I **walked** up the **hill**
To the **Night**mare Hotel
I **stopped** at the **door**
But I **couldn't** see the **bell**
I **knocked** and I **waited**
In the **cold** and windy **night**
I **looked** in the **win**dow
But there **wasn't** any **light**
That's when I **noticed**
The **door** was open **wide**
Then it started **rain**ing
So I **walked** **inside**
The **door** closed be**hind** me
I **asked**, 'Who's **there**?'
That's when I **noticed**
The **rats** on the **stairs**
I **turned** round to **leave**
But I **couldn't** see the **door**
That's when I **noticed**
The **bo**dy on the **floor**
Then the body **moved**
The **wo**man wasn't **dead**
She **told** me her **story**
This is **what** she **said**:
I **also** walked **up**
To the **Night**mare Hotel …

9D.3
I stop at the door.
I stopped at the door.

I knocked and I waited.
I knock and I wait.

I look in the window.
I looked in the window.

I walked inside.
I walk inside.

I turned round.
I turn round.

The body moves.
The body moved.

9D.4
Steve stopped.
Walter waited.
Nick knocked.
Stacy started.
Wendy ended.
Luke looked.

9D.5
I visited my aunt the other day. She lives in a new house, and all the houses in her street are the same, and ehm, so anyway, I stopped the car and I walked to the house, and ehm … I, ehm … I knocked on the door and waited … and waited … and waited, well so finally I pushed the door, and it wasn't closed, so I opened it and walked inside and, and I noticed everything was different – it was the wrong house! I walked into a complete stranger's house! Oh no! Ooops!

9E.1
Man A city … what's your favourite city, Avril?
Avril Ehm, Rio, I think. Yeah, Rio de Janeiro, Brazil.
M OK, and a postcard view? Give me a typical postcard view of Rio.
A Oh, there are a lot of them, but let's see … ehm …Sugar Loaf mountain, I think.
M Uh huh. What's the perfect weather to be in Rio?
A Well, I like it hot. Hot and sunny.
M And where's a good place to stay?
A Oh, ehm … the Copacabana Palace Hotel.
M OK, and finally, give me three things to visit in Rio de Janeiro.
A The beach, of course. But there's a forest too – a beautiful forest. And you can visit the famous football stadium.

10

10A.1
What did you **think**?
What does he **drink**?
Who did she **know**?
Where did you **go**?
What do they **eat**?
Who did he **meet**?

10A.2
What do you **think**?
What does he **drink**?
Who does she **know**?
Where do you **go**?
What do they **eat**?
Who does he **meet**?

What did you **think**?
What did he **drink**?
Who did she **know**?
Where did you **go**?
What did they **eat**?
Who did he **meet**?

10A.3
Jim Hi Ana. Did you have a good weekend?
Ana Oh, hi Jim. Yes, I went to the theatre on Saturday.
J Oh really? What did you see?
A 'An Inspector Calls'. It was very good. What did you do?
J Not a lot. I went to Blake's on Friday. Do you know Blake's?
A Yes. I was there last Wednesday night.

J Oh yeah? OK, well, I can't stop. My class started three minutes ago. See you!

A OK, bye Jim. Have a good class!

10B.1

A Job Interview

Interviewer Come in and sit down.

Robin Banks Thank you.

I And you are Mr Banks?

R Yes. Robin Banks.

I Now, some questions about your career, Mr Banks. When did you leave school?

R Ehm, let's see ... I left school in ... 1995.

I And what did you do after that?

R I was with the police for a while.

I Oh, you joined the police?

R No. I took a police car and drove it into a wall.

I Oh, I see ... And what did you do after that?

R I went to Oxford.

I What, Oxford University?

R No, Oxford bus station.

I Were you a bus driver?

R No. I took mobile phones out of people's bags. Then I sold them in the market. I worked there for six months.

I Oh! And what did you do after that?

R A job in a bank.

I Ah, very good! You got a job in a bank. Were you there for a long time?

R No, only 15 minutes. Then the police arrived.

I Hmmm, I see. Well, thank you for coming to the interview, Mr Banks. Goodbye.

R It's for you.

10B.2

She rode horses.
She wrote 'horses'.

I can't write very well.
I can't ride very well.

I sent a lot of emails.
I send a lot of emails.

There's a 'd' in 'lived'.
There's a 't' in 'lift'.

10C.1

Jackie **want**ed **mon**ey
She **didn't want** a **job**
She **didn't want** to **work**
So she **didn**'t **marry Bob**

10C.2

A Did Lisa buy a bottle of poison?

B Yes, she bought a bottle of poison, yes.

A OK, ehm, so where did she put it? Where did she put the poison?

B In Jackie's toothpaste. She put it in Jackie's toothpaste.

A OK, but Jackie didn't die, so ehm ... did, ehm... did Jackie use the toothpaste?

B No, she didn't.

A Did Ernie use it?

B No, he didn't.

A OK, so Jackie didn't use the toothpaste, ehm ... she knew

about the poison ... did she see Lisa with the poison?

B Yes, she saw Lisa put the poison in the toothpaste, but ehm, she didn't say anything, and Lisa didn't know.

A Oh, I see. So ... so what did Jackie do?

B What did Jackie do? Well, Lisa went home, she ehm ... she went to her flat, and Jackie phoned her.

A Uh huh. What did she say on the phone?

B She said, she said, 'Your father's dead! There was poison in his toothpaste!'

A But Ernie didn't use the toothpaste.

B No, that's right. Nobody used the toothpaste.

A OK, I see. What did Lisa do?

B She thought, 'Oh no – I killed my father!', and then she, ehm ... she drank some poison and ... she died.

A Oh, so *Lisa* died – she killed herself!

B Yes.

10D.1

The price of peas
The prize of peas
The prize of peace
The price of peace

10D.2

Start
1990
1909
1945
1999
1995
2001
2004
2003
1830
1918
1916
1980
1981
end

10D.3

OK, first one, number one ... He was born in, ehm ... in 1929. He left school, ehm ... secondary school, when he was 15, and went to a university in Atlanta, Georgia ... that's in the United States. He got his degree, his, ehm ... university degree, in 1948 ...

10D.4

OK, first one, number one ... He was born in, ehm ... in 1929. He left school, ehm ... secondary school, when he was 15, and went to a university in Atlanta, Georgia ... that's in the United States. He got his degree, his, ehm ... university degree, in 1948 ... and then seven years later he finished his, ehm ... his doctorate in Boston. He married Coretta Scott, and they had four children. He worked in a church in Georgia. At that time, black people couldn't sit with white people on the, ehm ... buses, and ehm ... he didn't

like this and he worked to stop it, and he won – because in 19 ..., 1956, the law changed and then black people could sit anywhere on the bus. To the end of his life, he worked for black people. He won the Nobel Peace Prize in 1964. He was only 35, 35 years old. A lot of people didn't like him because, ehm ... of his work, and somebody killed him in 1968. That was in Memphis, in Tennessee. His parents gave him the name Michael, but later he changed it to Martin. The first letters of his name are MLK, M-L-K ... Martin ...

OK, now number two ... She was born in 1867 in Warsaw, Poland. In 1891, 1891, she went to university in Paris to study, ehm ... to study sciences, and then after that, she lived there in Paris. She became an, ehm ... a scientist, and she married another scientist – his name was Pierre. They won the Nobel Prize together in 1903. She was the first woman to get the prize, to get the Nobel Prize. But her husband, he died in 1906. She won a Nobel Prize again, for a second time, in 1911. She worked with radium, radium, that's a dangerous chemical. She became sick, she became ill, and she died in 1934. Her name was Maria Sklodowska, her name was Maria Sklodowska, but she, ehm ... she changed her name to Marie. Her husband's surname was Curie. So her name was Marie ...

And number three ... She was born in 1910 in Skopje – that's in Macedonia. Her, ehm ... her father was a farmer from Albania. She went to school, and she was at school, and when she was 12, she decided her career ... she decided she wanted to work for poor people, to help poor people. When she was 18, she left home and, ehm ... she went to work in Calcutta. Calcutta, India. She worked as a teacher in a school from 1929 to 1948. Then she left the school and went out into the streets of Calcutta, went out to help the very poor people of the city. A lot of other people went there to work with her. She won a lot of prizes. In 1979, she won the Nobel Peace Prize. She died in 1997. Her name was Agnes Gonxha Bojaxhiu, sorry, I can't pronounce that ... but most people know her by a different name. The first letters of this name are MT.

11

11A.1

Jim Hi Ana. Planning a holiday?

Ana Hi Jim. Yes, I want a weekend in the country, but the hotels are too expensive.

J Oh. You could stay in a self-catering place.

A Yeah, I know, but they're usually for one week minimum. And I hate cooking!

J I see. Well, why don't you stay at a campsite?

A The weather isn't warm enough – it's too cold.

J Right. You could stay in a bed and breakfast. Here's one, look ... 'Freshnest Farm'.

A The breakfast's too early. I don't get up before ten at the weekend!

J Ana, can I make a suggestion? Why don't you just stay at home?!

A Ha ha ha! Good idea!

11A.2

You could stay in a self-catering place.
Why don't you stay at a campsite?
You could stay in a bed and breakfast.
Why don't you just stay at home?

11A.3

attractive
beautiful
comfortable
delicious
excellent
expensive
fantastic
friendly
modern
peaceful
ugly

11A.4

friendly, modern, peaceful, ugly
attractive, delicious, expensive, fantastic
beautiful, comfortable, excellent

11B.1

1 There's a shelf in the bathroom.
2 There's a sofa in the living room.
3 There's a table in the kitchen.
4 There's a toilet, a shower, and a washbasin in the bathroom.
5 There's a window in the living room.
6 There's a chair in the bedroom.
7 There's a cupboard and a cooker in the kitchen.
8 There's a bath in the bathroom.

11B.2

1 bed
2 chair
3 cooker
4 cupboard
5 hall
6 shelf
7 shower
8 sink
9 sofa
10 table
11 toilet
12 washbasin

11B.3

Estate Agent We have to go up a few stairs, I'm afraid. The lift doesn't work. It's good to get a little exercise!

Woman That's too much exercise for me!

EA Come in.

W The hall isn't very big.

EA This isn't a hall. It's the living room and dining room. Look – there's a table, a chair, a sofa, and a TV.

W There aren't enough windows in this place.

EA You don't want too much light in the TV room.

W What's that shelf?

EA It isn't a shelf. It's the bedroom.

W Ooh! Too many spiders! And there isn't enough space for a double bed.

EA Don't worry. One of you can sleep on the sofa. This is the kitchen. There's a cooker. I'm afraid there isn't enough space for a fridge, but the cupboard's very cold.

W There aren't enough plates and cups.

EA You don't want too many things to wash up! This is the bathroom. There isn't enough space for a bath, but there's a washbasin and a shower. The toilet's always clean! What do you think?

W There isn't enough space for a mouse in this place.

EA Yes, there is – look!

W Yuk!!!

11C.1

Envy

A bigger flat
A warmer bed
A fatter cat
And fresher bread
Sweeter cakes
And greener grass
Bigger steaks
And business class
Expensive wine
A better view
The first in line
Is always you

A smaller flat
A colder bed
A thinner cat
Older bread
Harder chairs
And smaller plates
Higher stairs
And longer waits
Cheaper wine
A worse TV
The last in line
Is always me

11D.1

1 **Ana** I think the most comfortable sofa's the Comfort Zone.

Pablo Yes, me too. And I think the ugliest sofa's the Elegance.

A Oh. I quite like that one. I think the ugliest is the Standard.

P Which one do you think's the most attractive?

A Most attractive? Ehm ... I think the Picasso.

P A ... Yes, me too.

2 **Pablo** OK, what about the chairs?

Ana I think the Avant Garde's the most attractive.

P For me, the Van Gogh's the most attractive, and it's the cheapest. But the Director is the most comfortable.

A Yes. I agree.

3 **Ana** Tables ... hmm, for me, the Milano is the most attractive. I like modern furniture.

Pablo Yes, it's quite nice. But I think the Country Kitchen is the most attractive. And it's the strongest.

A Yes, it's the strongest. And the Favourite is the ugliest.

P Yes, I agree.

4 **Ana** Which desk do you think is the most useful?

Pablo Well, not the Victoria. It isn't big enough. Not enough space for a computer. I think the most useful is the Century.

A Yes, I agree. And the ugliest is the Work Station.

P Yes. And the most attractive?

A Well, for me, the most attractive's the Century.

P I think the most attractive's the Victoria.

5 **Pablo** OK, and the colours. Which colour is the warmest, do you think?

Ana I think red's the warmest.

P Yes, me too. And the coldest colour's blue.

A Green's quite cold too, but ehm ... blue's the coldest, I agree. Green's the most relaxing.

P Yes. And yellow's the most exciting. Or red. What do you think?

A Yellow, I guess.

11D.2

best, west, west
wet, vet, wet
best, vest, best
Ben, Ben, pen
vest, west, vest

11E.1

A polite young guest
From Budapest
Said to the host
'Your cooking's the best.'
'Look', said the host,
'It's only toast.'
'I know', said the guest,
'But it's better than most.'

12

12A.1

Start
first thing tomorrow morning
mid-morning tomorrow
late tomorrow morning
early tomorrow afternoon
mid-afternoon tomorrow
late tomorrow afternoon
early tomorrow evening
tomorrow night
the day after tomorrow
next week
end

12A.2

R Can I help you?

J Yes, I'd like to make an appointment with Ms Steel, please.

R Yes, of course. How about the day after tomorrow?

J Yes, that's fine.

R Morning or afternoon?

J The morning's better for me.

R How about mid-morning, say 11.30?

J Could it be a bit earlier, say 10.30?

R Is 10.45 OK?

J Yes, that's fine.

R OK, 10.45 the day after tomorrow. Name please?

12A.3

This after**noon**?
This after**noon**.
To**mor**row **morn**ing?
To**mor**row **morn**ing.
The **day** after to**mor**row?
The **day** after to**mor**row.

12A.4

This afternoon.
This afternoon?
This afternoon?

Tomorrow morning?
Tomorrow morning.
Tomorrow morning?

The day after tomorrow.
The day after tomorrow.
The day after tomorrow?

12A.5

Conversation 1

A Can I help you?

B Yes, I need some new glasses. These glasses aren't strong enough.

A So you want an eye test?

B Yes.

A OK, so let's see – would you like an appointment for tomorrow?

B Yes, tomorrow's fine. Could it be in the afternoon?

A Yes – is four o'clock all right?

B Four o'clock? Yes, that's great.

A OK then. What's your name, please?

Conversation 2

A Can I help you?

B Yes, I'd like an appointment with Doctor Bennett, please.

A OK. How about Friday?

B Could it be sooner – Thursday, for example?

A I'm sorry, there's no room on Thursday.

B OK, Friday then. What time?

A Half past ten in the morning?

B Half past ten? Yes, that's fine.

A OK. What's your name, please?

12B.1

1 head
2 neck
3 heart
4 stomach
5 arm
6 hand
7 leg
8 foot
9 back
10 well
11 ill, sick

12B.2

Put your hand on your heart.
Put your hand on your hat.

I've got a pen in my hand.
I've got a pain in my hand.

I can't fill my stomach.
I can't feel my stomach.

I see the doctor's note, there.
I see the doctor's not there.

There's no fun in the office.
There's no phone in the office.

12B.3

I **don't** feel **well**
I **think** it's **flu**
I **feel** really **ill**
What shall I **do**?
Don't go to **work**
Stay **home** instead
Phone in **sick**
And **stay** in **bed**

12B.4

A I don't feel well.

B Why? What's wrong?

A I've got a headache and back pains. I think it's flu.

B Flu? You look fine to me.

A I'm not. I feel really ill.

B OK. Don't go to work. Phone in sick.

A Can you phone for me?

B Oh, all right ... How do you feel now?

A Much better, thanks. Let's go out!

12B.5

Man Oh no – we haven't got any milk. Could you go to the shop and get some?

Woman I'm not dressed. Why don't you go?

M I don't feel well.

W You look fine to me ...

M I've got a really bad headache.

W Hmm ...

M Oh, go on ...

W Oh, all right then.

M And ... could you phone work for me?

12C.1

Holly You don't look very well. Are you OK?

Justin Yeah, I'm fine. I'm just acting ill for Mr Minnit. I'm taking Friday off sick so I'm preparing him for the phone call!

H Oh, I see! Ha ha, very good.

H So what are you doing on Friday?

J 'Officially', I'm seeing the doctor.

H And what are you doing really?

J I'm going to Paris for the weekend with Debbie.

H Oooh, very nice! How are you getting there?

J On the train.

H And where are you staying?

J We booked a cheap hotel on the Internet. What's wrong with your mouth?

H Nothing. I'm taking Friday morning off too.

J What for?

H 'Officially', I'm going to the dentist's.

J And really?

H I've got an appointment at the hairdresser's ... Quick, Mr Minnit's coming! Oh, hello Mr Minnit!

J Hello Bister Biddit! Achooo!

Boss You two look terrible! Never mind. Friday's a holiday, so you've got a long weekend to rest.

J/H What!!

12C.2

Where are you **go**ing this **eve**ning?
What are you **do**ing to**night**?
Who are you **meet**ing?
When are you **eat**ing?
Who are you **see**ing to**night**?

12C.3

J Let's go out for a drink one evening.

H Yes, good idea.

J What are you doing tonight?

H I'm having dinner with Dave tonight. How about tomorrow?

J Tomorrow's good. Oh no, wait a moment – that's no good. I'm meeting Debbie tomorrow.

H OK, What are you doing on Wednesday evening?

J Nothing. Let's meet on Wednesday.

H OK, fine. See you on Wednesday, then.

12D.1

Good Intentions
I'm going to **quit**, I'm not **jok**ing
I'm **go**ing to quit **smok**ing
I **quit**, that's **it**!
Yes, I'm **go**ing to get **fit**
No **stay**ing out **late**
And I'm **go**ing to lose **weight**
Less **su**gar in my **tea**
Fat-**free**, that's **me**!
Good, good, good
Good intentions!
I'm **go**ing to join a **gym**
I'm going to **run**, I'm going to **swim**
Less **stress**, less **mess**
I'm going to **learn** to play **chess**
I'm going to **drink** green **tea**
Watch **less** T**V**
Fat-**free**, stress-**free**
Smoke-**free**, that's **me**!
Good, good, good
Good intentions!

12D.2

A normal ... I'm going to have a good time.

B fast ... I'm gonna have a good time.

A normal ... What do you want to do?

B fast ... What do you wanna do?

12D.3

I'm going to buy a car.
I'm gonna buy a computer.
I'm gonna quit smoking.
I'm going to do more exercise.
I wanna go home.
I don't want to get up.
I didn't wanna do it.
I want to see you.

OXFORD
UNIVERSITY PRESS

Great Clarendon Street, Oxford OX2 6DP

Oxford University Press is a department of the University of Oxford.
It furthers the University's objective of excellence in research, scholarship,
and education by publishing worldwide in

Oxford   New York

Auckland Cape Town Dar es Salaam Hong Kong Karachi
Kuala Lumpur Madrid Melbourne Mexico City Nairobi
New Delhi Shanghai Taipei Toronto

With offices in

Argentina Austria Brazil Chile Czech Republic France Greece
Guatemala Hungary Italy Japan Poland Portugal Singapore
South Korea Switzerland Thailand Turkey Ukraine Vietnam

OXFORD and OXFORD ENGLISH are registered trade marks of
Oxford University Press in the UK and in certain other countries

© Oxford University Press 2007

The moral rights of the author have been asserted

Database right Oxford University Press (maker)

First published 2007
2013 2012 2011 2010
10 9 8 7 6 5 4

ISBN: 978 0 19 430478 8

Printed in Spain by Just Colour Graphic, S.L.

This book is printed on paper from certified and well-managed sources.

ACKNOWLEDGEMENTS

Illustrations by: Stephen Conlin p.88; Bob Dewar pp.72, 74; Mark Duffin pp.8,
26, 38, 56, 83, 86, 95, 110, 115, 116, 124, 127 (weather), 128, 129 (food), 130
(weather), 131, 132, 133 (food), 134 (weather), 135; Jon Fletcher pp.19, 31,
127, 137; Glyn Goodwin pp.27, 40, 98, 129 (Eric), 133 (Erica); Andy Hammond/
Illustration pp.61, 103, 107, 109, 114; Leo Hartas p.30; NAF!/Meiklejohn p.108;
Ben Kirchner/Heart pp.6, 60, 62, 66, 70; Jan McCafferty pp. 32, 33, 62; Frano
Petruso p.22; Gavin Reece pp.25, 46, 78, 79, 85, 129, 130, 133 (best friend), 134;
Neil Shrub/Collective Illustration p.92.

*The Publishers and Authors would also like to thank the following for permission to
reproduce photographs*: AKG-Images pp.68bl (Erich Lessing), 68t (Erich Lessing);
Alamy pp.10(12) (David J. Green), 10(15) (Jeff Greenberg), 20(1) (Frank Chmura/
ImageState), 20(2) (Aflo Foto Agency), 20(3) (Doug Houghton), 20(4) (National
Motor Museum/Motoring Picture Library), 20(5) (Juniors Bildarchiv), 20(6)
(Norma Joseph), 20(7) (National Motor Museum/Motoring Picture Library),
20(8) (Atsushi Tsunoda/IMAGINA Photography), 18(6), 50 (shop assistant/Kim
Karples), 126 (life/Arcaid), 126 (students/John Powel Photographer); Allstar
Picture Agency, 24r (Pictures Colour Library), 26(10) (Pictor International/
ImageState), 26(12) (Dominic Burke), 26(4) (Andre Jenny), 26(8) (Alan King),
26(9) (Anthony Harrison), 28br (Paul Springett/Up The Resolution (uptheres)),
36e (Rob Walls), 36f (Robert Slade/Manor Photography), 36h (Swerve), 44
(Derek Brown), 48(A2) (Paul Wayne Wilson/PhotoStockFile), 52A (Andersen-
Ross/Blend Images), 52B (Luc Porus/STOCK IMAGE/PIXLAND), 52C (Benno de
Wilde/Imageshop), 52D (ColorBlind Images/Blend Images), 52E (Claire Dubois/
STOCK IMAGE/PIXLAND), 52F (Dynamic Graphics Group/Creatas), 52G
(Dynamic Graphics Group/Creatas), 52H (Ingram Publishing), 70(12) (Pictor
International/ImageState), 86c (David Robertson), 86tl (C. Bowman/Robert
Harding Picture Library Ltd), 106bc (Aflo Foto Agency), 106bl (thislife pictures),
106br (Peter Cook/VIEW Pictures Ltd), 106tl (Mel Stuart/Westend61), 116d
(Mednet/PHOTOTAKE Inc.), 116h (Jeff Greenberg); Bridgeman Art Library p.68c
(Leeds Museums and Galleries (City Art Gallery)); Collections p.26(3) (Sam
Walsh); Colorsport p.48(O3); Corbis UK Ltd. pp.10(16) (Howard Pyle/Zefa), 10(4)
(Steve Raymer), 10(6) (Lew Robertson), 10(7) (Danny Lehman), 18(1)
(Bettmann), 18(13) (Jeff Christensen/Reuters), 18(4) (Bettmann), 18(5) (John
Springer Collection), 18(8)(Bettmann), 18cr (Robert Landau), 18 (9) (Lisa
O'Connor/Zuma), 18l (Lynn Goldsmith), 20a (Elke Van De Velde/Zefa), 20g
(Steve Prezant), 20h (Warren Morgan), 20j (Peter Beck), 20k (Bill Varie), 20l
(Helen King), 20m (Chuck Savage), 20n (©Lwa-Dann Tardif), 28(1) (Tibor
Bogn·R), 28(10) (Liu Liqun), 28(13) (Sergio Pitamitz/Zefa), 28(14) (Ladislav
Janicek/Zefa), 28(15) (Fridmàr Damm/Zefa), 28(16) (John Henley), 28(2) (Bob
Krist), 28(3) (Viktor Korotayev/Reuters), 28(4)(Jose Fuste Raga), 28(5) (Tibor
Bognar), 28(6) (Manfred Mehlig/Zefa), 28(8) (Thierry Tronnel), 34l (Lew
Robertson), 36b (Reuters), 40A (Ted Horowitz), 40B(Dennis Galante), 40D
(Fabio Cardoso/Zefa), 40F (Virgo/Zefa), 48(A3) (Jon Feingersh/Zefa), 48(I5) (H.g.
Rossi/Zefa), 48(I6) (Pat Doyle), 66tr (Rufus F. Folkks), 76(2) (Awilli/Zefa), 76(5)
(David Raymer), 76(6) (Fabio Cardoso/Zefa), 76(7) (Mika/Zefa), 76(9) (Chuck
Savage), 80 (David Turnley), 84br; 86bl (Macduff Everton), 90a (G. Baden/Zefa),
90b (Kelly-Mooney Photography), 90e (Paul Souders), 90g (Barry Lewis), 90h
(Dave G. Houser/Post-Houserstock), 94c (Laura Doss), 99t (Jlp/Sylvia Torres),
100bc (Matthias Kulka/Zefa), 100bl (H. Armstrong Roberts), 100br (Michael
Boys), 100tc (Hulton-Deutsch Collection), 100tr (Hulton-Deutsch Collection),
102(1903) (Bettmann), 102(1921) (Bettmann), 102(1962)
(Bettmann), 102 (1964) (Bettmann), 102(1971) (Bettmann),102(1979) (Reuters),
102(1986) (Wyman Ira Sygma), 102(1987) (Brian Snyder/Reuters), 102(1991)
(Emmanuel Dunand/Epa/Epa), 102(1993) (Str/Epa), 102(1993) (Katy Winn),
102tl (Bettmann), 104 (Bettmann), 114t (Christine Schneider/Zefa), 116a (Tim
Garcha/Zefa), 116b (Jim Craigmyle), 116e (Ausloeser/Zefa), 116f (Helen King),
116g (Steve Crise), 118(10) (Rcww, Inc.), 118bl (Jon Feingersh), 118br (Anthony
Redpath), 118cr (David Raymer), 122A (Jim Craigmyle), 122C (Jlp/Jose Luis
Pelaez/Zefa), 122G (Michael A. Keller/Zefa); Empics pp.18(10) (Associated
Press), 18(7) (DPA-FROM PA), 18r (Associated Press), 48(I4); Getty Images
pp.10(1) (Workbookstock), 10(17), 34r, 35t (The Image Bank), 48(O2) (Andreas
Rentz/Bongarts), 48(U6) (Andreas Rentz/Bongarts), 50 (newsagent/Andrew
Hetherington/Stone), 50 (greengrocers/Ghislain & Marie David de Lossy/Riser),
54D; 54E; 64; 66tl (STR/AFP), 76(1); 76(10); 76(3); 76(4) (Photographer's Choice),
76(8); 84bl; 84tl; 84tr; 88; 90c; 94b (Taxi), 94t (Taxi), 99c; 100bcr (General
Photographic Agency), 114bl; 114br; 116c; 118(11) (Stone), 118cl (Stone), 122B
(Stone), 122F (Getty Images/Photographer's Choice), 122K (Getty Images), 126
(couple on plane/Hans Neleman/Riser); Hemera Technologies pp.20c, 40G,
48(A4), 48(A6), 48(I3), 48(U1), 48(U2), 54B, 54C, 54F, 54G, 70(8), 112b, 112e,
112f, 112h, 112i, 112j, 112k, 112n, 112o, 112p; Ikea p.112l; iStockphoto
pp.10(10) (Holger Bischoff), 36a, 36g (Yuen Kuan Liew), 36k (Maurice van der
Velden), 48(A1) (Maureen Perez), 48(E3) (Cristian Lupu), 48(E5) (Sang Nguyen),
48(E6) (Stan Rohrer), 48(I2) (Michel de Nijs), 48(O4), 48(O5) (Cristian Lupu),
48(U4), 54H (Daniel Berman), 112a (Mark McNally); Kobal Collection pp.82(1)
(Paramount), 82(2) (Paramount), 82(3) (Paramount), 82(4) (Paramount), 82t
(Paramount); Lebrecht Music and Arts p.18(11) (Interfoto); Linographic pp.20b,
20d, 112g; Oxford University Press pp.20e, 20f, 24l, 26(6) (Mark Harrison), 27,
28(12), 28(7), 28(9), 35b, 35c, 45b, 48(A5), 48(E1), 48(E2), 48(I1), 48(O1), 48(O6),
54I, 70(10), 70(11), 90f, 99b, 106tc, 112, 112c, 112d, 112m, 114bc, 118(1),
118(9), 126A, 126B, 126C, 126D, 126E, 126F, 126G, 126H, 128(1), 128(2), 128(3),
128(4), 128(5), 128(6), 132(1), 132(2), 132(3), 132(4), 132(5), 132(6) PunchStock
pp12 (couple/Blend Images), 12 (shaking hands/Digital Vision), 50
(delicatessen/Photographer's Choice), 50 (female shop assistant/Digital
Vision), 126 (shaking hands/Photodisc), 126 (subway/Stockbyte); Photolibrary
Group pp.10(19) (Index Stock Imagery), 15 (Index Stock Imagery), 20o (Index
Stock Imagery), 100tl (Ibid); Redferns Music Picture Library p.18(2) (David
Redfern); Rex Features pp.18(12) (Patrick Rideaux), 18(14) (Jeremy Craine),
18(3) (Dave Allocca), 18cl (Atilla Kiss), 26(5) (Jonathan Player), 28(11) (The
Travel Library), 36c (Philippe Hays), 40E (Sonny Meddle), 48(U5) (Mike
Thomas), 66bl (Ralph Merlino), 66br (OLYCOM SPA), 102(1992) (Franceschi/
Percossi); Superstock Ltd pp.20i (Martin Black), 36d, 36i (Bartomeu Amengual),
48(E4) (Esseuve), 48(U3), 100bcl; Victoria Miro Gallery p.68br (Courtesy of
Peter Doig); Zooid Pictures pp.26(11), 26(13), 26(2), 26(7), 54A, 70(1),
70(3), 70(4), 70(9), 90d, 106tr (Dan Sinclair), 122D, 122E, 122H, 122I, 122J

Commissioned photography by: Gareth Boden pp.6, 7, 14, 16, 36 ('Good news,
bad news'), 40 (man walking into a door), 42, 45 (Justin & Mr Minnit), 56
(food and drink, Jim & Waitress), 58 (Jim & Waitress), 70 (Jim & Ana), 77, 86
(Ana in Glasgow), 96 (Jim & Ana), 98, 110 (Frank & Ricky), 115, 116 (Jim at the
dentist's), 120; Mark Mason pp.58 (the Greasy Spoon Café), 59 & 96 (handbag
& contents).

With thanks to the following for providing locations: British Study Centre, Oxford;
Six TV Studios, Oxford; St Clare's, Oxford.

*The Publishers and Authors would particularly like to thank the following readers and
teachers for their help with the initial research and piloting*: Sandra Maria Andrin,
Maggie Baigent, Jo Cooke, Ana Deptula, Jon Fitch, Anne Fowles, Rachel
Godfrey, Paolo Jacomelli, Amanda Jeffries, Maria Carmen Lasheras, Colin
Lockhart, Alejandra Macchia, Fiona McLelland, Marisa Perazzo, Caroline
Rodrigues, Graham Rumbelow, Enda Scott, Joanna Sosnowska, Meriel Steele,
Carol Tabor, Michael Terry, Gustavo Viana, Louise Williams.

Recordings directed by: Leon Chambers

Technical presentation by: Gerry O'Riordan

Words and music in songs by: Mark Hancock (except music for 'Greasy Spoon'
by Phil Chambon)

Musical arrangements by: Phil Chambon

Vocals in songs by: Jo Servi and Jude Sim